being dead
otherwise

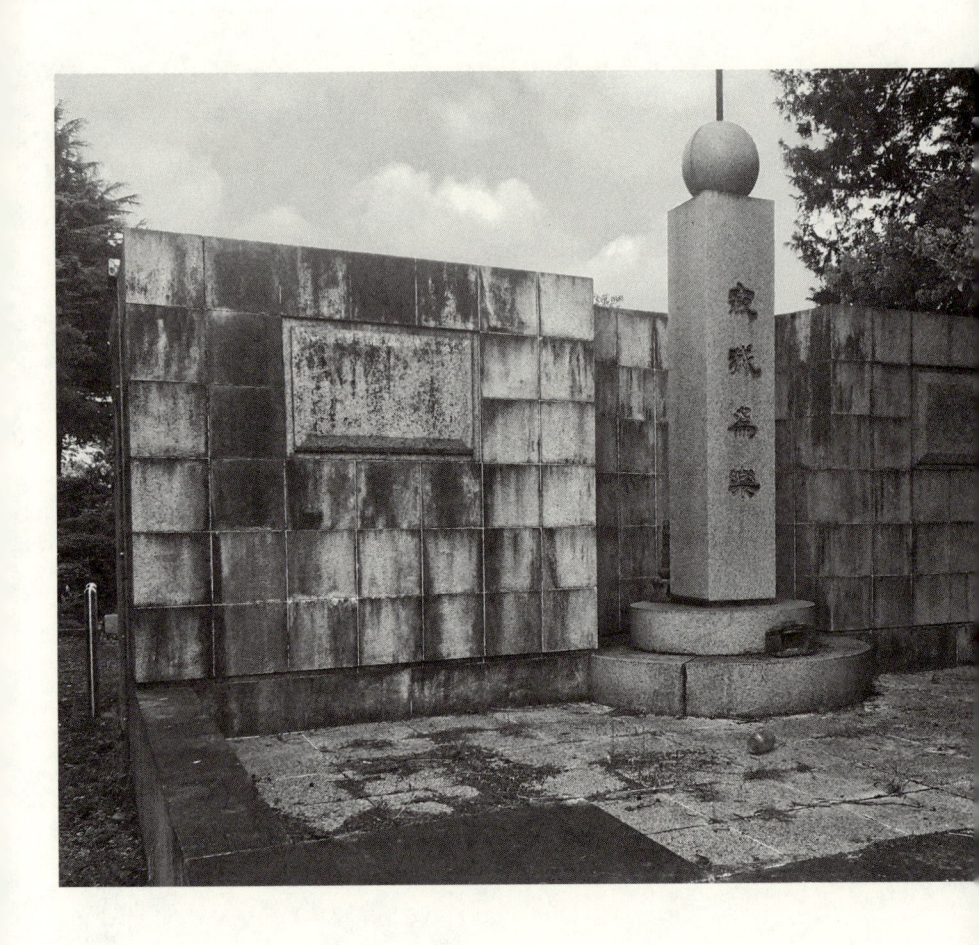

A stone marker for disconnected dead at
Tama Reian Cemetery, Koganei, Tokyo

being dead
otherwise

anne allison

duke university press   durham and london   2023

© 2023 DUKE UNIVERSITY PRESS
All rights reserved
Printed in the United States of America on
acid-free paper ∞
Project Editor: Lisa Lawley
Designed by Matthew Tauch
Typeset in Alegreya Regular and Degular
by Westchester Publishing Services

Library of Congress Cataloging-in-Publication Data
Names: Allison, Anne, [date] author.
Title: Being dead otherwise / Anne Allison.
Description: Durham : Duke University Press, 2023. | Includes bibliographical references and index.
Identifiers: LCCN 2022040878 (print)
LCCN 2022040879 (ebook)
ISBN 9781478019848 (paperback)
ISBN 9781478017141 (hardcover)
ISBN 9781478024415 (ebook)
Subjects: LCSH: Death—Social aspects—Japan. | Death care industry—Japan. | Funeral rites and ceremonies—Japan. | Japan—Social life and customs—21st century. | BISAC: SOCIAL SCIENCE / Anthropology / Cultural & Social | SOCIAL SCIENCE / Death & Dying
Classification: LCC GT3284.A2 A45 2023 (print) |
LCC GT3284.A2 (ebook) | DDC 393—dc23/eng/20221207
LC record available at https://lccn.loc.gov/2022040878
LC ebook record available at https://lccn.loc.gov/2022040879

Cover art: Kojima Miyu, *Miniature Model of a Garbage House in Tokyo*, 2018. Photo by Naoko Kawamura. Courtesy Asahi Shimbun/Getty Images.

To Yoshiko   For all you have taught me, shared with me, and accompanied me in

Contents

ix   PRELUDE
xi   ACKNOWLEDGMENTS

1   introduction

histories

25   1   Ambiguous Bones: Dead in the Past
47   2   The Popular Industry of Death: From Godzilla to the Ending Business

preparations

73   3   Caring (Differently) for the Dead
99   4   Preparedness: A Biopolitics of Making Life Out of Death

departures

123   5   The Smell of Lonely Death and the Work of Cleaning It Up
149   6   De-parting: The Handling of Remaindered Remains

machines

173	7	Automated Graves: The Precarity and Prosthetics of Caring for the Dead
191		Epilogue
197		NOTES
215		BIBLIOGRAPHY
231		INDEX

prelude

In a stream of new enterprises catering to death, this one washes and pulverizes human remains. Called a "bone business" (*hone-ya-san*), the company is small and sits quietly in a residential neighborhood in Tokyo. But things are active inside. Boxes of cremains from all over the country stand high in the main room. Posted straight from the crematorium or dug up from ancestral graves and destined for reburial in an urban cemetery, the ashes have traveled here to be further compacted. Whether to be scattered in the sea (*sankotsu*) or interred in a high-rise columbarium, bone fragments are sent to be ground into fine powder (*funkotsu*). This is a delicate process, the owner tells me, displaying the mortar and pestle he uses in the final step.

The body, in death, reformulated for changing times, reflecting a landscape where the dead don't necessarily wind up where they used to: in a family or ancestral plot in the ground, attached to a Buddhist temple passed down for generations, and tended fastidiously by patrilineal kin. This was once sanctioned by law in a genealogical principle that sutured the nation-state to the continuity of the imperial system incarnated by the emperor. But alongside reforms in the postwar "democratic" constitution adopted in 1947, the grave went from being a place to memorialize ancestors to a place for an individual's eternal rest. Since then, a number of factors have contributed to dismantling this family-based mortuary system even further: urbanization and sped-up lifestyles, an aging population with low birth rates, decreasing rates of marriage and cohabitation, the rise of Japanese citizens living and dying alone, and a shift away from long-term employment to more irregular jobs. For many today, relying on family members to bury the dead in graves in the countryside and to tend to them after that is no longer realistic.

But to be untended at death provokes the specter of disconnected souls (*muenbotoke*) who wander the earth, deprived as they are of a "home." As attested to by the endless stories these days of abandoned graves in the countryside and city dwellers whose remains go unclaimed after dying alone, their bodies discovered long after the fact (a phenomenon called lonely or solitary death), this is a real possibility. And it generates unease around death. But this, in turn, is being met by a wave of creative, commercial, and civic interest in what is a new politics of the dead: forging ways of handling the deceased less reliant on the ancestral grave, familial caregiving, or management by someone else.

We die alone and in a specific moment in time, biologically at least. But what happens to the dead after that—as material remains and as a presence maintained through memory, mourning, ritual, care—depends on others. How this relationship is undergoing radical change in the context of twenty-first century Japan is the subject of this book. Between the dead and their relationality with others.

Being dead otherwise. Recomposing decomposition in terms of how, where, and with whom one winds up after death.

acknowledgments

This book has been both hard and wondrous for me. About death(s) that pain the soul. But about trappings of life that accompany or embroider the dead as well. The voice of the priest greeting ancestors in the homes of his parishioners during Obon, the care of the cleanup workers gently removing the belongings of those who have died alone in their homes, the craft of the bone crusher lovingly completing the last step of his job with a mortar and pestle. I have been fortunate, in the long years conducting this research, to have had so many working in the intimate work of deathcare in Japan open their jobsites to me. I am grateful for their generosity as I am to that of all the Japanese who shared with me their ways of thinking about, dealing with, and managing (or not managing) ending plans. This is such personal terrain, embedded as it is in the (be)longings we have with others, including material (and nonmaterial) things. This project has been deeply enriched by all those who have been so willing and open in speaking about these matters with me. This includes dear friends (and my dearest Japanese friend, Yoshiko Kuga), close colleagues, my great partner and sons, a loving sister, the best editor ever (Ken Wissoker), smart students, all those who have encouraged this project with invitations to write or present on it, and an energetic core of fellow "death gals"—researchers as compelled as I am by this scholarly topic. I have learned so much from you all. And though "I" may not be overtly present in all the writing and stories that follow, to me, this is the most personal of all my scholarly endeavors. The journey I have taken here is, truly, my own journey in threading the edges of life and loss that I am still embarked on. It is also my response to what some have called the need to go beyond what they lamentingly see as the turn to the "suffering slot" in anthropology. This book is about death. But it is not about turning away from life—life can surge in and around biological ends. Rather, I see something like hope approaching, if not quite arriving, in the turn toward new ways of "being dead otherwise." This is what I aim to bring to the page here.

Thank you all: Mori Kenji, Inoue Haruyo, Kobayashi Tsuyoshi, Katsuno Shūbin, Nishimura Shūyō, Yoshida Taichi, Kojima Miyu, Matsubara Junko, Kai Koji, Kamada Akira, Kitami Takayuki, Hamashima Akio, Hida Kazuo, Takano Kokyo, Katsuya Yasuo (and to the memory of his mother, my "Japanese mother," Katsuya Etsuko), Kondō Yōko, Kuga Yoshiko, Kimura Shuhei, Yoshimi Shunya, Hirota Ryūhei, Ogawa Eiji, Ogawa Ryōkei, Nemoto Ittetsu, Takuma Manabu, Takuma Fumiko, Kuse Keiko, Nishimura Keiko, Nakamura Fuyubi, Shikimura Yoshiko, Eguchi Anna, Aoyama Tōru, Iwasaki Miyuki, Dōhi Masato, Uriu Daisuke, Takenouchi Hiroko, Hamashima Akio, Kiyotaka Miwa, Hida Kazuo, Nawa Katsuo, Honda Takao, Kone Hideto, Kamada Akira, Yue Eric Tojimbara, Nozawa Shunsuke, Mark Rowe, Hank Glassman, Matt Marr, Michael Berman, Jui-an Rae Chou, Chris Nelson, Danny Hoffman, Brian Goldstone, Peter Kussin, Mariske Westendorp, Danielle House, Matthew Engelke, Mona Oraby, Margaret Gibson, Larissa Hjorth, Achille Mbembe, Sara Nuttel, Ghassan Hage, Gavin Whitelaw, Orin Starn, Aaron Hames, Jason Karlin, Kyle Cleveland, Jason Danely, Patrick Galbraith, Sam Holden, Grant Ohtsuki, Simon Partner, Harris Solomon, Bruce Lawrence, Miriam Cooke, Nancy Armstrong, Leonard Tennenhouse, Harry Harootunian, Michelle Longino, Ranji Khanna, Michael Hardt, Kathi Weeks, Nicole Barnes, Jake Silver, Jieun Cho, Ruth Toulson, Hannah Gould, Tamara Kohn, Sally Raudon, Gertrude Fraser, Louise Meintjes, China Scherz, Emily Wang, Julia Morales Fontanilla, Gabriella Lukacs, Rebecca Stein, (in fond memory of) Diane Nelson, Jocelyn Chua, Leo Ching, Richard Jaffe, Ken Wissoker, Ralph Litzinger, Ryan Kendall, Kathy Rudy, Jocelyn Olcott, Chiyoko Lord, Hiroyuki Hino, Chikako Ozawa-Silva, Yohko Tsuji, Amade M'charek, Terry Vance, Amy Rotunno, Tom Allison, Adam Platzer, David Platzer.[1]

All of the photos in the book were taken by me. Tony Kim did all of the photo editing of the images and composed the collages. I thank him for the artistry of his work.

And my special thanks, always and forever, to Charlie.

introduction

The wake, held at nightfall, surges with mourners. A smaller but sizable crowd gathers the next morning for the upscale funeral in a hall filled with white chrysanthemums and designer photos of the deceased distributed throughout. Filing past the open coffin and lighting incense to the spirit of the deceased at the Buddhist altar, mourners gather outside for the casket to be loaded onto the hearse. Close relatives and friends now accompany the body to the crematorium, where, after final goodbyes and a short respite in a room with cool drinks, they reconvene an hour later in the furnace room. There they greet what has emerged: bone fragments and ash strewn across a gurney still radiating heat. Observing the cremains, the mourners approach the cart where, maneuvering a set of chopsticks, they join in moving a fragment from one tray to another. "Picking the bones" (*kotsuage*), a ritual of intimacy and respect, involves touching, seeing, and being with a loved one as they transition into something else. After this comes a communal meal shared between mourners, priests, and the deceased, whose ashes are now in an urn.

Or, another scenario: after the mandatory twenty-four-hour after-death waiting period, the corpse is taken directly from the hospital to the crematorium instead of to a funeral hall, where the bereaved would otherwise assemble for the wake the night before and the leave-taking (*kokubetsushiki*/ 告別式) the next morning. At the crematorium only immediate family convene. The ceremony there, quite barebones, is officiated by a staff member or Buddhist priest for a much lower price—as little as three thousand dollars versus up to ten times that amount for a fuller affair. At the crematorium the family is unlikely to engage in bone-picking or to hold on to the cremains for the traditional forty-nine days of Buddhist mourning during which the spirit is in transit from this world to the next. Instead, the urn will be deposited immediately: buried in the ground in a cemetery or placed inside an ossuary or in a high-rise locker or automatic-delivery-style columbarium—options becoming popular these days for their convenience and low cost. Such a "direct ceremony" (*chokusō*) takes place—hospital to crematorium to burial ground—all in one shot.

Or, consider this possibility: the deceased, a bachelor without children or close relatives, makes his own burial arrangements ahead of time. His death in a long-term-care facility triggers the stages of his prepaid plan. First the body goes to a holding room, then to a crematorium, and finally to a collective burial spot under cherry trees, to be interred as commingled ashes. Having chosen one of the different options in the burial grounds operated by the nonprofit organization he joined a number of years ago, the deceased will be memorialized by a collective ceremony held annually for all members who have died that year and before. As done in life, members often attend these rituals as well as the regularly held get-togethers for the future deceased to get to know one another while still alive. After cremation, ashes go into the earth alongside not family but "grave friends" (*haka tomo*)—the ties of affiliation that have been formed by virtue of membership in this alternative burial association. As advertised by the promotional brochure, interment in these burial grounds does not depend on having family or a successor. But "no one is lonely" by virtue of being interred alongside others as well as among the host of cherry trees.

Or, another prospect: three weeks after death, the body is discovered because of the smell of its decomposition and the buzz of flies outside the door. The landlord calls in the police, who find the corpse among clutter and garbage strewn inside. Estranged from family and friends, living on welfare since losing his job years ago, the deceased has died a "lonely death" (*kodokushi*). The only relation the local municipality can track down is a sister who refuses to claim the remains, saying the siblings have been disconnected for years, so the municipality will bear the responsibility and cost for handling the corpse. The body is sent to the local crematorium, then the ashes are interred in a designated Buddhist temple where there is a special plot and shrine for the disconnected (*muenbo*). Meanwhile, the landlord shoulders the expense of commissioning a special cleanup service to repair and restore the apartment to an inhabitable state. It is a massive job to remove the detritus of the lonely death, the numbers of which are rapidly rising these days—as are those of special cleaners who give witness to the life expired there.

....

As can be seen by this range of possible outcomes—the first becoming less and less common, the others rising in frequency—there are different ways of dying and being buried in Japan today. And as the example of those who end up in graves for the disconnected attests, this is a matter that demands some kind of social response. Even though (or particularly because) a corpse represents the not-ness of a life once there and now gone. That, rather than discarding them, the living have chosen to keep some portion of these remains as tribute to the dead in their midst, has been customary practice since at least Neolithic times, twenty thousand years ago. Differentiating us from animals, this is an act that philosophers have long taken to be constitutive of humanity: holding onto a remnant of those now departed in honor and recognition of the place they once held in the community. For Hegel, making houses for the dead signaled the onset of both memory and symbol-making, uniquely human capacities that extend us beyond biological survival and the temporal here and now. The ability to imagine an otherwise is harbored here. Whereas "houses for the living are mere shelter, structures for preserving life; a tomb is the work of the symbol-making architect" (Hegel, quoted in Laqueur 2015, 90). And to treat a dead body "as if it were ordinary organic matter" (4) is to deny its very humanity—what Thomas Laqueur in his cultural history of mortal remains calls a universal cultural logic.

In his anthropological study of death, Robert Hertz (1960) outlined the three main elements involved in mortuary practice: the corpse, the living survivors, and the deceased on their passage to somewhere or something else. The status of the dead is at once liminal and precarious, and caring for the dead depends on those still living who embark upon doing so at the site of the corpse. This entails a relationship between the living and the dead conducted around the material remnants of the deceased—a substance that, in the process of decomposition, indexes the present absence of a life once here and now gone. As Hertz pointed out for the Dayak of Borneo, the liminality of the corpse troubled the order of things, indicating a spirit in transition from this world to the next. But once the flesh had sufficiently dissolved, leaving bones neatly white and discrete, the dead were reburied closer to the living, who took solace in the belief that the departed had now arrived at their final destination (somewhere else). Hertz proposed that ritualizing the dead is a mechanism that reconstitutes, by reconfirming, the ongoing life of the community. Though a member has physically departed, those left behind are reminded of the ties they share that enable livelihood to continue. By honoring, but differentiating, the dead, a symbolics is enacted to a social/human enterprise that traverses the spectrum of existence and transcends any biological or temporal part. And by making a space for them to dwell among the living in a home all their own, the deceased are accorded the recognition that they (still) matter in this constellation, now stretching as it does to another plane.

Inherently social, the Hertzian model of a "good death" depends on others who attend to the material remains and spiritual aftermath of the dead, giving the departed the aura of belonging to those who remain behind. In the absence of this care, the deceased become something other than honored dead. These are the ungrievable, in Judith Butler's term, with lives that fail to matter; something less than human, as Antigone believed when sacrificing her own life to bury her brother in defiance of the king. As recorded by anthropologists from Robert Desjarlais (2016) observing diasporic Tibetan Buddhists to Scott Stonington (2020) studying northern Thai villagers and Sarah Wagner (2019) talking to Americans dealing with MIAs from the Vietnam War, a "bad death" is lonely and cold; unwitnessed, untidy, unadorned. This happens when someone dies far from home, estranged from family and friends; in sudden or painful circumstances; or has remains that go untreated, unrecovered, unnamed (Walter 2017). The opposite is being given a place of sorts among and by the living: remains that are tended to and a reminder of the deceased beyond the earthly existence of an individual. Entailing ritual care, this is not only social but constitutive of a sociality that many see as the essence of humanity itself—taking care of life beyond its existential or instrumental utility.

....

What happens when the dead can no longer be assured of such places among the living? And when the institutions governing the biopolitics of life-making become ever less resourceful in managing, or ensuring, those in the making of death? And when none of this is the exception—due to circumstances like war, being marginalized in life, or falling on hard times—but is becoming generalized, even normalized, for a community at large?

Being Dead Otherwise contemplates this necrosociological condition through the lens of Japan at the start of the twenty-first century. As the familial model that once handled mortuary arrangements is coming undone, the ranks of those bereft of the social others who once cared for the dead are on the rise. Signs of this appear daily in the news: abandoned urns on the trains, corpses of the lonely dead going undiscovered for months, the carcasses of ancestral tombs standing empty in rural cemeteries, unclaimed remains interred in tombs for the disconnected. More palpable still is a sense of urgency and unease around the need to prepare one's ending arrangements ahead of time, or to "close" ancestral graves and move the contents somewhere else to avoid the fate of winding up as "disconnected souls." New disposal methods with different (or no) provisions for mortuary care abound these days in what is a booming "ending industry" catering to a population less and less likely to have a predesignated grave or care providers to tend to the dead once there.

If the dead once relied upon the connections of others to avoid becoming a disconnected soul, how is the sociality and governance of mortality today changing away from family, intimate relations, and sometimes human mortuary care altogether? In such new age trends as outsourcing grievability to a company or interring ashes in an automated crypt, do we see a desire to innovate on ritual grieving or a willingness to let it go? What does it say—about a nation-state, a people, an individual once alive and now dead—when the management of grievability is in question? Do any of these social units really need grievability, in other words? What happens without it, or when grievability gets performed by a robot or by and for the self?

Being Dead Otherwise interrogates the interpersonal entanglements of death, considering Japan as a case study of possible futures in the weaning, transforming, and redesigning of others in the management of the dead.

....

Twenty-first century Japan is undergoing radical, rapid flux in attitudes and practices regarding death. Having "no place to go" (*ikiba ga nai*) rather than a grave already reserved is a possibility for an increasing number of the population. And the shards of family tombs that, no longer tended to, now stand abandoned constitute as much as 40 percent of the edifices in some rural cemeteries (Kotani 2018). This reflects a spatial problem in a land-poor country, particularly in cities, where plots in desirable cemeteries are exceedingly scarce and exorbitantly priced. But the scarcity at hand has more to do with relationality: the lack of others to be buried alongside or to care for one's remains and spirit once there. When family lines die out or kin stop maintaining graves or move far away, ancestral plots become "empty" (*akihaka*), and the contents are soon removed to be reburied in tombs for the disconnected. But the to-be-deceased face more challenges still. With the country's high aging and low birthrate demographics, death rates exceeding birth rates every year, and increased "singlification" of households and lifestyles, the still dominant familial model of death making leaves many in a quandary at the end. This is true particularly, but not only, for those without spouses, successors, or the financial wherewithal to enter a family grave. Without finding an alternative, a final resting place with some kind of ritualized care over time, these dead will wind up as disconnected souls (*muenbotoke*)—an unpleasant prospect that raises the specter of hungry, wandering ghosts.

Such a situation is hardly the way it used to be in Japan. People once lived in close proximity to the dead. Caring for the ancestors in graves that were usually in nearby domestic shrines where offerings, including food, were given daily was part of everyday routine. This continued, by custom and religious practice, for thirty-three years, until the dead were thought to have transitioned into ancestors. By that point, others were likely to have died and be on their way (to the "other world"), too, stitching the dead into the fabric of life and premising care on a principle of continuous regeneration. A temporality of "eternity" depended on exchanges of ritual—serving the ancestors and then being served by one's own descendants and becoming an ancestor as well—that were wedded, in turn, to a very specific rubric of and for social reproduction: a national-patriarchal structuring of belonging that dictated (and delimited) relationality through the patrilineal familial system (*ie*). The Meiji Constitution stipulated that all citizens be entered in the Family Registry in terms of patrilineal identification: family name (birth name for men, married name for women), order and position in family (hierarchized by gender and age), dates (of birth, marriage, and death), addresses, employment, and property.[1] The law also designated the grave (*ohaka*) as the material and symbolic seat of the patrilineal *ie* system, which became the ideological bulwark of the imperial nation-state throughout its militaristic buildup to establish, then lead, an

East Asian empire that ended disastrously. That architecture, grounded in a sociopolitical order at once close-knit and abstract, culminated—and also started—in the sacredness of the ancestral grave. Passed down from generation to generation and often, though not necessarily, located in a cemetery at a Buddhist temple to which the family was attached as parishioners (as all Japanese were once mandated to be), the grave was both owned and maintained by the patrilineage, with all the hierarchies and norms embedded therein.

With Japan's defeat in the Pacific War and its subsequent American occupation, the *ie* system was officially dismantled. In the "democratic" constitution of 1947, which decoupled religion from the state and remade citizenship around the individual versus the status of being subjects of the emperor, the grave shifted status as well. From the place where ancestors are accorded respect, it became the place where the individual eternally lives. A host of changes were triggered in the process of rebuilding the country and reorienting national priorities from militarism to economic (post)industrialization: urban migration, a shift away from agriculture to wage-based employment, households becoming more centered on the nuclear versus extended family, and an ethos of hard work and productivity implanted within the "social factory" of the family and consumerism. The 1950s were a period of hunger, a friend in his seventies whose family moved from Shikoku to Tokyo recalled. But by the 1960s, Japan's future—its period of high economic growth and rise to being a global superpower with the second largest economy in the world—was already on the horizon. But what this took, and demanded, of citizen-workers and mother-taskmasters was an incredible intimacy of hard work. Exacting and extracting performativity from everyone meant fortifying the individual self: honing the skills, discipline, and record needed to do well by the aspirational measures of a "good life" (graduation from a reputable university, employment in a prestigious company, marriage to a suitable spouse, and children primed to reproduce all of the above). Quite a different orientation from the duty and affection accorded the ancestors. That, gravitating around the grave likely to be hours away from the cities where a majority of Japanese currently reside, becomes increasingly hard to keep up.

....

In the early years of the new millennium, I was finishing up a project on Japanese techno-toys and waves of media-mix character franchises: Power Rangers, Sailor Moon, Tamagotchi, and Pokémon.

The postwar period was effectively and affectively over by then. The Japanese dream of hard work marked by steady marriage, lifelong employment, and the private ownership of "my home" and "my car" crashed in 1991 along with the bubble economy—the speculative real estate and stock market—launching an economic decline that has lingered ever since. Kids, whether grade-schoolers, teenagers, or young adults—were said to be feeling the shift from an era of clear futures to one where even high achievers couldn't be sure of what they would attain. The 1990s was the "lost decade" in which companies folded, longtime employees got sacked, and those coming of working age often failed to secure the kind of long-lasting ("regular") job they had been brought up to believe was both theirs and all that mattered. As this "lost generation" segued into another (and another), Japan's era of exponential growth and inflated speculation downshifted into one more of postgrowth, symptomized by domestic concerns over Japan's aging population, declining rates of both marriage and childbirth, and predictions of a labor shortage in the future (without any signs of a national willingness to open up its borders to foreign migrants). A mood of hopelessness swept the country, punctuated by the sarin gas attacks on Tokyo subways in 1995, the Hanshin earthquake in Kobe the same year, and reports of troubling social problems linked to loneliness, isolation, depression, and despair (such as a peak of 33,000 suicides in 1998, a rise in school refusal and youth social withdrawal, and an awareness of adults living and dying alone that volunteers brought to attention during the Hanshin earthquake).

One term for describing the times was "emptiness," as in horizons of expectation getting emptied out. But as a number of the designers of the toys I interviewed in the early 2000s said of their products, they saw the youth they were targeting as encumbered by something else. Not bereft of the hopes they ought to see realized, but deprived of something more capacious, and soulful, in the way of hoping itself. Tajiri Satoshi, the designer of the original Pokémon Game Boy game, for example, felt that youth, even before the crash of the bubble economy, were being so excessively programmed to industriously perform that their capacity to enjoy and sense the world (as well as others and also themselves) was severely constrained. It was to introduce them to another way of being that he created the imaginary universe of pocket monsters, modeled after the natural world of insects that he had grown up enchanted by (Allison 2007). As religious scholar Nakazawa Shinichi argued in the book he wrote about Pokémon, the playscape recrafts something from Japan's traditional past: an animist worldview in which humans can forge meaningful connections to gods, ghosts, and monsters, which are as viable as any life-form. For a lonely child anxious about their performance on a test, playing and bonding with a Pokémon can be healing: repairing what has been taken from and lost by children in the course of (post)industrialization (Nakazawa 1997).

I developed the notion of "techno-animism" through the ethnography I did with users, designers, and parents of children who play with such digital products as Tamagotchi. Techno-animism is the lifeform generated between, and beyond, the binarism of human and machine (Allison 2007). As the inventor of the Tamagotchi intended, what the user invests in the way of energy, labor, and care (birthing and raising the virtual pet) is key to both the game play and the connection that is formed. This makes for a relationship at once continuous, contingent, and everyday (slipping into the Tamagotchi's death when a player's attentiveness lets up), not simply an object that the user manipulates and owns. Part of the fabric of what Philippe Descola and others consider to be the ontology of animism—a fluidity and interdependence between physically heterogenous entities—the vitality offered by these techno-toys was frequently reported on as the affective attachment provided to kids (Descola 2005, 328). Said to be "soothing" (*iyashi* in times of anxiety, uncertainty, and loneliness, adults turned to digital companions as well. Tamagotchi was a huge hit with women in their twenties and fifties.

As I became aware when finishing my book on Japanese toys and their global trendiness, a sense of precariousness was gripping the country in the new millennium. While rooted in jobs, this extended much wider and deeper into the everyday. Activist Amamiya Karin, who used the word "precariat" to refer to young Japanese, called it the "pain of life" (*ikizurasa*) (Allison 2013). Once primed to expect and aim for long-term relationships that equated with security—in the workplace, marriage, and a home filled with material acquisitions and children—Japanese adults now found themselves in a different temporal order, one marked more by irregularity and flexibility than by permanence and continuity. Almost 40 percent of workers (and over half of all women workers) are irregularly employed today, thirty years after the bursting of the bubble economy, meaning they lack the security, status, and perks of steady employment. Fewer adults marry or have children these days, citing economic insecurity as the prime reason why.

The phrase I kept encountering in my study of precarity, used to refer not only to jobs but to the unease and unsettlement experienced more generally, was *ibasho ga nai*, meaning the absence of a place where one feels comfortable and at home. Alongside this were the tropes of the moment, much cited by scholars and commentators trying to grasp the sense of these post-bubble times: hopelessness and futurelessness which referenced something at once temporal, spatial, and socio-existential. As labor historian Genda Yūji (2013) described, it was the loss not merely of job but of purpose and belonging that troubled so many un(der)employed who consequently became disconnected from others, isolated, and withdrawn (solitary nonemployed persons, or SNEP). Lacking hope, seeing no future, unstitched from hominess made with someone(s) else. Even the college students I interviewed at a high-ranking university struggled to answer the question about futurity: few were sure what theirs would be, and only one in twenty thought Japan's future might promise something better, if different, from the past. But the sense of uncertainty triggered anxieties not only about how to make a living that was sustainable into the future but also about something quite different involving temporality and sustainability. What became the subject for the current book, like all my research projects, came to me in the field.

As I returned every summer for further fieldwork in Tokyo, I was struck by how often I heard the phrase "no place to go" (*ikiba ga nai*) in reference to mortuary planning. Starting around 2015, this was a topic that came up surprisingly often when talking with acquaintances and friends. Frequently this involved aging parents and pressing decisions to be made about burials in the not-so-distant future. But many people, I found, were also contemplating their own circumstances, and not only those middle-aged or older but also younger adults in their twenties and thirties. This matter obviously generated anxiety: worry over how (best) to manage multiple considerations and also how not to burden others after one has died (Long 2001).

Consider, for example, a childless couple where the husband is a second son (thus not eligible to enter his family grave due to the rule of primogeniture). The two want to be buried together but don't know where that will be. Meanwhile, they would like to relocate the woman's mother, aging and sick in faraway Shikoku, to their home in Tokyo. But, as the mother is currently the sole caregiver to her husband's ancestral grave and leaving would mean abandoning his spirit and those of the ancestors, she has refused. Where the mother will be buried in the end, and what will become of the father's (and his ancestors') ashes when their caregiver is gone, are worries that keep this woman up at night.

Or the middle-aged single woman who tends to her parents' family grave, where she assumes her sister, likely to predecease her, wants to be buried. But, as neither has a successor, she imagines that should she enter the grave as well, no one will be there to manage it nor to pay ritual visits. The thought of the grave falling into disarray disturbs her deeply, as does the thought of no one visiting her own grave—or paying respects to her parents—in the future.

Or the aging couple with children and grandchildren whom they don't want to bother with the upkeep of a grave or visitations to it. As they have not yet purchased a plot and cannot enter that of his family's grave (he's also a second son), they are seeking a simple arrangement for just the two of them. It must also be affordable as the man lost his private business in 2008 and is still working at a part-time job. Though they are concerned, their attitude is pragmatic.

For all these folks, it was managing not only the whereabouts of the dead but also the wherewithal of tending to them (in the way of Buddhist memorials, *kuyō*) that presented a problem. For home, even as a final resting place, depends on connections with others. Without that, where one is housed (as in tombs for the disconnected, *muenbo*) cannot be considered homey at all. A problem—what some have dubbed an "unrelational society" (*muen shakai*), pointing to a degeneration of Japan's collective sense of relationality and outcome of its hypercapitalist, hypermodernist trajectory—of not honoring the spirits of the dead and not maintaining the spirituality of Japan(ese) more broadly. This is an emptiness somewhat different from the loss of aspirational hopes (for middle-class abundance, high economic growth, long-lasting jobs, and "my homes") so mourned in the lost decades that have stretched to the current moment. This one materializes instead in abandoned ancestral graves in the countryside, the rising numbers of lonely deaths in the cities, and the barrage of media and commercial messages advertising all sorts of mortuary services to help a population increasingly "without anyone else to depend upon." What it traffics in is a currency of care rather than that of jobs, careers, lifestyles, or goods—care one needs (but doesn't have) from someone else and care that is now being sold, transacted, and reimagined in the new marketplace of endingness (*shūkatsu*) that has blossomed in the twenty-first century.

As with techno-toys like Pokémon and Tamagotchi, one sees that the promise that such necroscapes offer their users is a vitality of connectedness to heal and soothe the anxieties of being stranded and alone in a temporality lasting for eternity. In the energy circulating around the preparedness and planning given to it, death is productive: of a marketplace, of an array of new-style workers and jobs, and also of practices and activities that allow otherwise anxious to-be-deceased to take "anticipatory action," to use Ben Anderson's (2010) term, to ward off the possibility of a bad death. This efflorescence of interest around endingness also displaces concern elsewhere in the national landscape about futurity, sustainability, and the country's failure to socially reproduce. Devolving upon death, something lifelike animates ending planning these days: what I call necro-animism. Interrogating what precisely this entails, who benefits and who doesn't, and how both governance and care of the dead gets increasingly enwrapped in new sorts of human, nonhuman, and technological arrangements, I question how this both rehearses and reframes the sociology of death.

The activity around death these days both stems from and reconfigures the dire issue facing so many: having no final resting place nor caregivers to provide for one there. A problem of space and social capital, it is also one of temporality: of, to rephrase two Japanese scholars among many, "no future" for the dead. As religious scholar Mori Kenji (2014) has put it, Japan is facing a crisis in its failure to handle the dead. The dead are no longer cared for, and the living no longer care to care for the dead, a problem he calls the absence or refusal of others. Without intimates to join or to be cared by after death, the grave is either not an option or becomes a dumping ground in a collectivized, anonymized mass plot, more a wastebin than cipher of or for ongoing relationality. Something dies here, beyond the mortality of the deceased—the very soul of Japan, Mori believes, in a future that will be haunted by its loss.

While Mori fears that the death of death in a Hertzian sense (ritualizing the dead and according them an ongoing place among the living) is underway in Japan, the religious scholar Shimada Hiroshi actively encourages it. Advocating the abolishment of mortuary customs as anachronistic in hypermodern, hyperurban Japan, *0 (zero) sō: assari shinu* (Zero funeral: dying throughout), published in 2014, was a bestseller. Who needs a funeral or a grave, he ponders, in times so focused on the present and the individual as these? But Shimada's thinking also rests on the unjust nature of the current system, which still relies on having either patrilineal kin or the financial means (or both) to carry things out. The socially or financially precarious are far more at risk of abandonment at the end. And these ranks of disconnected dead are rising—unkind to them and egregious on the part of the country as a whole. Mori Kenji (2014), too, acknowledges that what has been the customary system, dependent on what he calls the "modern Japanese family," is riddled with both biases and gaps. Yet he sees nothing adequately replacing it—not even the new hybrid Buddhist-commercial operations that offer "eternal memorial" to substitute for the familial others that the dead are increasingly unlikely to have. Grievability requires something more authentic or reliable than this, he believes: an eternity of care assured by the bonds of duty and blood rather than the marketplace. Or, for people lacking the former, the state should step in: make the promise of a secure grave among the living—the marker of dignity for the dead—a constitutional right of all citizens.

Both Shimada and Mori Kenji see Japan as having no future for the dead and as a place that has no place for its dead on the horizon. But, for both of them, such a scenario rests in the investments in and failures of a very specific social model: the patriarchal, patrilineal form of belonging and caring for others. This model, one should point out, is not only increasingly outdated but was always already delimited in who and what it actually embraced. Queer theorist Lee Edelman has pointed out that political orders grounded in the reproductive futurism of capitalistic nation-states geared to expansion, extraction, and continuous growth invariably return to a notion of the heteronormative family built on the image of the child (2004, 2). This relegates those without such patriarchal, patrilineal ties to "no future," as does a death-making system in which ancestors' care and the path to becoming an ancestor oneself depend on a narrow genealogical template with the burdens and hierarchies this envelops. As long ago as the 1930s (at a time of natural disasters and economic unrest) this system failed to protect as much as 30 percent of the dead, who were consequently relegated to plots for the disconnected (Bernstein 2006). A plan to design public graves that would alleviate this problem and accord everyone the same dignified fate (in keeping with Marxist politics) was proposed in 1932 under the name "eternal tomb" (*fumetsu no funbo*) (Bernstein 2006). Though never built, it was based on the awareness not only that those without families are at risk but that the family model itself produces the precarity of possible abandonment in death. For when death making is premised on this, those with lines that die out, or whose family members are unable or unwilling to manage the task, or who are subordinated or marginalized by the system itself are left stranded.

Recognizing that there is a crisis of care worldwide, one spurred by overreliance on kin relations, which almost everywhere means overreliance on women and those least (otherwise) valued, the feminist members of the Care Collective released a care manifesto arguing for a new standard of care that would "promiscuously" treat everyone and leave no one behind.

"We have surveyed care at the scale of kinship because, within the current arrangements, it is all too often inadequate, unreliable and unjust. If care is to become the basis of a better society and world, we need to change our contemporary hierarchies of care in the direction of radical egalitarianism. All forms of care between all categories of human and non-human should be valued, recognized and resourced equally, according to their needs or ongoing sustainability. This is what we call an ethics of promiscuous care" (2020, 40). Promiscuity of care, in the sense of discriminating against no one (for lacking successors or relatives) and providing a service incorporating different elements, parts, and beings (rather than the standard family grave), is what Japan's new business in endingness promises. Filling in the gaps of a system no longer available or adequate for an increasing fraction of the population, the market offers replacements and alternatives for the kin once counted on to carry out the job. In doing so, an attempt is made to offer a modicum of security with a place to go and care to replace the ancestral grave and the family members tasked with tending to it. The desire is to avoid a "no future" of abandonment. As one alternative burial site advertises, "no one buried here is ever alone;" the dead and to-be-deceased belong to the community of the site as well as to the groves of cherry blossoms within which everyone finds their resting place. Rites are performed that, establishing their own temporality through actions with material objects in a set space (Willerslev, Christensen, and Meinert 2013), acknowledge and accompany the dead. In this case, it is an annual memorial service for all those already interred to which the to-be-deceased are invited as well. Even more popular is the service of Buddhist prayers (*kuyō*) conducted by the resident priest at facilities connected to a Buddhist temple. This, too, has a built-in temporality; it is usually done for thirty-three years, though it is called "eternal" in reference to the ongoing eternity that is the promise of the genealogy-based ancestral grave.

The care being sought to relieve one's anxieties about being stuck and placeless after death is conjured by new imaginaries and new forms of imagined communities today. No longer is the nation-state taming the fear of death by generating belief in the collective continuity of the nation, as sociologist Zygmunt Bauman (1992) has written about the handling of mortality during modernity with a timeline still hued to progressive betterment in the future. Today, when confidence in the future has broken down, a constellation of crises (nuclear, climatic, economic) brews uncertainty, and fragmentation and montage have replaced the linearity of grand narrative, something different has emerged. In the temporality of postmodernity, when a sense of collective futures or fates has become vaguer and far less tied to the authority of the nation-state, immortality is invoked through different means. Pursued through new medical breakthroughs, marketing fashions to ward off the effects of aging, exercise regimes, or migratory pursuits embarked on to enhance one's life prospects (albeit somewhere else, far from family and home), immortality is "regularly conferred and destroyed, through media, culture and emergency rehearsals, rather than assumed to follow the linear life-death-immortality trajectory as it did during the era of modernity" (Heath-Kelly 2018, 32). And, as in the case of mortuary management in Japan today, it means not putting one's hopes for final resting plans in the hands of others, to whom—as fellow ancestors—one is assumed to belong as in a collective continuity of patrilineage and nation-state. Rather, it is bringing the temporality of mortality into the here and now, where, through anticipatory planning, one winds up handling things for oneself ahead of time. An imagined sociality of quite a different order. Borrowing from Bauman and writing from a perspective of critical security studies, Charlotte Heath-Kelly proposes that the Euro-American governments she has studied adopt a similar anticipatory strategy of bringing the future into the present in their handling of possible futures that are uncertain but would be calamitous, such as terrorist attacks. Through reenactments, rehearsals, and precautions, governments engage rather than disarm mortality by the security policies and strategies they implement. And, by promoting resilience, governments ask the populace to embrace the possibility of danger lurking in the crevices of an everyday, where the future and the world are so unclear. By doing so, Heath-Kelly suggests, "Life is now used to defeat death, as it were" (2018, 33).

In Japan, too, the playing out of worst-case scenarios repeats often in what can be a surprisingly raw realism: stories and images of rooms where the corpses of the lonely dead have been discovered and the piles of stuff once hoarded are now decomposing along with the flesh. Whether in the news, photo exhibits, or materials used to promote one or another service in the ending business, I have seen such footage often, as I am sure many Japanese have as well. This not only unsettles viewers but also incentivizes them to follow what has become a mantra of these necro-animistic times: "prepare ahead of time." This renders the future actionable by what can be an entire regimen of activity in the here and now: plans made for everything from cleaning one's residence to arranging one's will, inheritance, and interment. What geographer Anderson calls a "presence of the future" takes place in workshops, information sessions, and also—a popular trend—keeping "ending note" journals of plans, thoughts, and desires regarding one's personal (*jibunrashii*) endingness. All of this anticipatory action is taken to tame, and mitigate against, the possibility of a no future as disconnected or abandoned dead. Bringing death into the present where one can "put one's affairs in order while still living" (*seizen seiri*).

When the catastrophic future being imagined is the next terrorist attack, this raises an issue of security that is handled by state governments in a governance of the future, calling on "actionism" of a very particular sort (Aradau and Munster 2012, 98). The case is different in Japan when the catastrophic deaths being imagined are due to the ebbing of the very familial (marital and parental) ties that the government still clings to, endorses, and attempts to get young people into by a series of policies that never seem to work. Still wedded to an ideology of reproductive futurism, failing though it is (as seen by the decline of childbirth, marriage, and the overall population of Japan since 2006), and without the legal and constitutional imbrications it once had in what was a national genealogical system (*kokka*), the nation-state no longer plays a major role in the governance of death making. This leaves the care of managing remains and ritualizing or grieving for spirits to promiscuous others. Examining this work, of the making of death in the face of the unmaking of family, is the focus of *Being Dead Otherwise*.

....

In the book I explore the choreography of death in the face of its de- and recomposition: when the retreat of the social hands once responsible for it leave more and more people susceptible to dying and being dead alone. In doing so, I attempt to make an intervention into the premise of what constitutes a good death—being accompanied into and beyond death by the living—by questioning the lines along which relations between self and other, living and dead, might align in other directions. For not only in Japan is the sociological grammar of caregiving the dead getting challenged on any number of fronts. The Japanese situation may remain unusual in the form and degree to which disconnected death is likely to occur at home rather than far away, as is the risk for so many global migrants today. Yet Japan provides a critical case study into what happens when postmortem care by intimate others becomes unrealizable, abandoned, or innovated upon in what can be radical ways. These include outsourcing death work to a robot, taking on the job of managing it by oneself ahead of time, and raising the possibility of abandoning the custom—of marking and memorializing the deaths of humans—altogether.

Using contemporary Japan as my lens, I follow three thematic lines of inquiry into the precarity and possibilities of death making that speak globally and temporally to current times. These are (1) the work done by workers handling the remains of disconnected dead (stranded dead), (2) the work done by individuals when assuming the role of intimate others in managing their own mortuary arrangements (self-death making), and (3) the work done by forms of mortuary arrangement non-dependent on intimate others or, sometimes, on humans altogether (necro-animism). My emphasis throughout is on the work itself that drives death making, and on the effects and affects of death making in the absence of intimate others.

1. *Stranded dead* are the deceased who are unacknowledged and unmourned by intimate others at death: a social and existential state that is also referred to, in Japan and elsewhere, as "lonely death."[2] Following the Hertzian point that the dead leave a wound in the fabric of the social that compels a ritual response—memorializing the ending of (a singular) life and the ongoingness of life in the living left behind—I ask: What kind of wound is incurred in the case of a stranded death, and what happens to it? Constituting an "ambiguous loss" (Boss 2000), this death-form may be intentional, as for those "disappeared" by the Argentinian military (Rosenblatt 2015) or as the threat of such a death is used as a deterrent to migration by the US government—or due to personal circumstances or the lack of intimate relations, as is the case with lonely death in Japan.[3] I am interested here in the response given to such deceased by those handling their remains who may constitute the only, or last, humans to touch them. Paying attention to the touch of this materiality itself (Ingold 2007), is there a certain vitality residing in the remains of those unidentified and unmourned, as forensic scientist Clea Koff (2004) has said of something still stirring in the bones when she pieces together such human fragments? This can make the response, when done with care, akin to the "adornment of washing, arranging, and tending of remains done by kin when mourning" (Davis 2017, 239, referring to the work of Seremetakis 1991). In the "practical work" of forensic scientists trying to identify the bodies of drowned migrants in the Mediterranean Sea, the "tinkering" they do engages body parts at the level of the persons to which they once belonged. Imparting "relationality" of a sort (M'charek and Casartelli 2019, 738–39).

The work, in this case of cleaning up the remains of stranded dead, is what led one Japanese worker to make miniaturized dioramas of the death scenes she finds at the start of a job. As described in chapter 6, Kojima Miyu does not exactly intend these to be memorials to the dead. But her miniatures are crafted to both linger with and acknowledge the life now passed of "dead unrecognized by anyone else."[4] A touching of, but beyond, the materiality of beings who die unknown, unidentified, and unmourned—a state that, given the precarity and uncertainty of the times, is on the rise globally, with massive migrations, climatic disasters, and food and housing insecurity of so many. Drawing on, and in dialogue with, the writings of other scholars working on (the workers who work on) abandoned or unidentified dead, I contemplate this condition of the stranded dead throughout the book.[5] What kind of disturbance does this leave behind, in whom and in what, and (how) does the touch of attending to the material remains of stranded dead constitute a form of death work by other means or hands—as I argue that it does, or might?

2. In what a recent anthology of Japanese scholars (Suzuki and Mori 2018) calls Japan's new "era of family-less dead" (イエ亡き時代の死者), the risk of a disconnected death is well understood by a public once used to relying on kin for mortuary preparations. But what could be a crisis, and is for some, has also fueled ways of producing structures of care to replace familial ones. In the booming ending industry that has emerged over the last twenty years, the individual, acting as a consumer, is increasingly taking up the role of organizing, arranging, and paying for mortuary care ahead of time (while still alive). I call this *self-death making*. And it has some salutary effects. For example, as feminists (and others) in Japan have noted, shifting responsibility for death work away from family can free people from a system long tied to the duties, hierarchies, and labor of a patriarchal sociopolitical order that has been burdensome and exclusionary to women and to a number of men (Ueno 2015; Yamada 2014; Inoue 2012). The obligation borne by the family (and, disproportionately, by women) to shoulder so much in the way of care (of children, elderly, diseased, incarcerated) extends to the United States and many other countries far beyond Japan, as feminists working on care ethics such as political theorist Kathi Weeks (forthcoming) have pointed out. Demanded here is a "more capacious notion of care" (Care Collective 2020, 41) that would mean attending to the needs of one another in ways that decenter, and find alternatives to, what has been—in the United States, Japan, and just about everywhere else—an exclusive reliance on the family.[6] For Weeks, this would mean not simply better families but a society that depends far less, if at all, on the family to be the life support of its citizens. In calling for the "abolition" of family, she

joins the Care Collective in seeking to broaden and diversify care provision/providers by a notion of "promiscuous care" (Care Collective 2020, 40).

As seen in Japan, one alternative to family-brokered deathcare is assigning or allowing individuals to take this activity on themselves. While tethered to the neoliberalism of "self-responsibility" (and the financial resources this requires), the new culture of attending to ending preparations opens up a zone—temporal, social, aesthetic—in which the individual makes the "craft of dying" (Lofland 1978) an activity carried out by, but also for, the self. Afternoons spent designing one's own coffin, making a scrapbook of one's memories, deciding between burial options, and updating one's daily "ending notes" can generate "creativity" around loss and an energized "yielding" to the becoming-of-death (Danely 2014, 58–59, 122). I have also heard this called "self-care" when the orchestration of death work is directed not to the ancestors but to oneself, as discussed in chapters 4 and 5. Considering the implications of this rearticulation of deathcare away from familial others and onto or by the self—for Japan/ese but also beyond—is what I see as one of the major contributions of this book.

3. Rituals have long been central to death making in Japan and everywhere else. Largely shaped by Buddhism, mortuary rites (a large part of the religion in Japan) are somewhat mechanical in nature and today can be facilitated by a range of substitutes, prostheses, or actual machines (Rambelli 2018; Duteil-Ogawa 2015).[7] *Necro-animism* is what I call Japan's wave of new-style craft and activities of endingness in which mortuary arrangements are being carried out by a range of actors and means, blurring the borders of self and other, human and nonhuman, person and thing. With a tradition of folk Shintō along with other folkloric and Buddhist trends, a highly modernized everydayness is infused with animism in postindustrial Japan. Following those who treat animacy as less a property of nature or life than as a "dynamic transformative potential of an entire field of relations" (Ingold 2006, 10; also Descola 2013, xix), I agree with John Clammer, who, speaking of new religions in Japan, sees animism as less worship of nature per se than a pursuit, at once pragmatic and possibly political, of getting things done in an "experiential, active and everyday relationship to creatures and things in nature" (2004, 87).[8] The getting done of death making today is carried out in the shadow of precarity; the rituals of the grave and of kin caregiving the dead are becoming remnants of the past. But, rather than abandon death work altogether or resign oneself to the fate of becoming an abandoned dead, the turn, for many, is to something(s) else that harbors spirituality or hope. It may be robotic priests, automated graves (as dealt

with in chapter 8), or the mixing of cremains into wearable pendants. As the director of the company that started memorial diamonds in Japan has said, he was motivated to create a "beautiful trace of himself" that would both last over time and alleviate the need for his wife and children to visit him in an ancestral grave. The deceased ontologically shifting into something blending object, person, relationality, life, and death (Duteil-Ogawa 2015, 233).

This is my final provocation in the book: considering new ways and manners of tending the dead that go beyond the availability, or ontological form, of human/intimate others. While resorting to robots or automation may seem like the endpoint of death making for humans, I suggest something else. I see the willingness and desire to uphold the treatment of the dead and spirits as mattering to those still alive. This is a refusal to accept the death of death in a Hertzian sense by continuing to make a place among the living, within life, for the dead.

....

Following this introduction, the book is arranged in three sets of paired chapters and concludes with a final standalone chapter and short epilogue.

HISTORIES

Given the inherent ambiguity of being dead—the absence of someone once present whose corpse is a material reminder of the immateriality that the deceased is now becoming—the work of death making is complex and ambiguous itself. Contours of how this has been handled across Japanese history are traced in chapter 1, "Ambiguous Bones: Dead in the Past"—more a history of the present than an exhaustive historical account. Returning to the present, I lay out the topography of mortuary trends in Japan today in chapter 2, "The Popular Industry of Death: From Godzilla to the Ending Business," by considering how the threat of dying alone is driving a new industry and marketplace in endingness. New alternatives to the family grave are rolled out in what is now an annual convention for those in the cemetery and funeral industry. Called ENDEX (Ending Exhibit), this is held in Tokyo Bay—the site from which Gojira was stirred into action on the cinematic screen in the early years following the war. Another figure, from a different era, turning danger into a source of popularity.

PREPARATIONS

As the old relations of death making fall apart, new socialities and subjectivities are emerging around care and self-care for the dead. In chapter 3, "Caring (Differently) for the Dead," I consider the social politics of the familial model: what it presumes, whom it includes and excludes, and how the sociality of ancestors is both ritualized and rehearsed at key moments such as Obon. Starting and ending with two different versions of an Obon ceremony (to honor the dead), the chapter tracks alternative burial arrangements when care work for the dead is disarticulated from the family and rearticulated by either the self or nonfamilial others. The stress placed on anticipatory action in the present—on planning and preparing for one's ending plans—is taken up in chapter 4, "Preparedness: A Biopolitics of Making Life Out of Death." The activity around self–death making can be both pleasurable and intense, which I explore through various activities and practices that call upon the responsible individual to micromanage their ending while still alive so as to avoid the distasteful prospect of becoming a disconnected spirit once dead. The role played by lonely death—a phenomenon used to incite a moralism and politics around ending-actionism in the present—is addressed as well.

DEPARTURES

This pair of chapters shifts the temporality of death away from anticipatory planning to dealing with the material remains after the fact. Staying with the focus on death making, chapter 5, "The Smell of Lonely Death and the Work of Cleaning It Up," looks at one of the newest genres of companies that has arisen in the last two decades under the umbrella of the ending market (*shūkatsu*). Selling the services of ordering, cleaning up, and disposing of the belongings left behind by the deceased, these companies are also commissioned when a lonely death has been discovered after the body has been decomposing for what may have been a long time. Encountering both the smell (of what I call an unsocial death) and the rot from hoarding—as the press often reports about these cases—cleanup workers are the ones who deal with the mess of deaths and dead like this. As is argued, this work is not only manual cleanup but also affective labor, caring for the living by removing such unseemly matter but also caring for the dead by according them what may be their last, and only, form of memorial. Chapter 6, "Departing: The Handling of Remaindered Remains," considers what happens to the handling of remains and to the lines by which the materiality is regulated and distinguished in the face of shifting necro-sociology in Japan today. Through the lens of four different situations—bone-picking by intimate others, unclaimed remains in a municipal city hall, the ashes (as well as "leftover ashes") that come out of crematoria, and a bone-crushing business—I look at the trend toward downsizing and dematerializing remains. But, as I note throughout, there is considerable resistance to getting rid of remains or memorial rituals altogether. What precisely is this that lingers, or haunts, this land where lonely death, abandoned graves, and unclaimed remains are all rising (some say precipitously) at the same time?

MACHINES

In the seventh and final chapter, "Automated Graves: The Precarity and Prosthetics of Caring for the Dead," I consider the possible trajectory of moving the grievablity of human dead to a nonhuman register: that of machines carrying it out in the face of a care-deficit of intimate others. Looking at a new-style urban columbarium that deploys an automated delivery system to move remains from a warehouse (where they usually reside) to a handful of graves (for visitation, but only if someone actually visits), I explore the space-time compression afforded these places that, compacting thousands within a relatively small space, are at once affordable, convenient, and aesthetically pleasing. Users include those without family members but also families who move the contents of ancestral graves in the countryside to this cheaper, easier-to-manage site in the city. In both cases, as with all those interred there, all deceased are given memorial (*kuyō*) by the resident Buddhist priest and have the premises, including the signature graves, attended to with utter diligence and care. No one falls into abandonment, in other words, even if their remains sit forever in the warehouse. The structural logic of such a grave park rests on what I argue is a prosthetics of sociality: just-in-time grievability that stretches, rather than gives up, the human commitment to find a place for the dead among the living. The implications of such alternatives for those who might otherwise become disconnected dead, and for a Japan that, losing its old system of care, may be becoming a place that has no place for its dead (as a number of Japanese scholars and practitioners have already argued), are profound.

histories

In Japan, almost all religions are based on the assumption that once a person dies, their soul wanders about lost. This is why we perform various funerary practices, rituals, and rites related to the "soul" such as using just a single stick of incense (producing a single trail of smoke the soul follows) and having funerary tablets (where they can "reside") and performing services to send good merit (in case they need it).

Shakyamuni told his followers to let the laymen dispose of his corpse. Shinran also said, "After my eyes have closed for the last time, place my body in the Kamo river and let the fish feed on it." He regarded his corpse as little more than an empty shell. Let me put it this way: if a person can treat his own corpse like an empty shell, that person is an enlightened one.

Shinmon Aoki, *Coffinman* (2002)

ambiguous bones
dead in the past

In his cultural history of mortal remains in Western Europe, Thomas Laqueur examines the "work" the living do for the dead. This is inherently ambiguous terrain, involving "lifeless matter from which a human had fled." And yet, as he asserts, "the dead body matters, everywhere and across time, as well as in particular times and particular places" (Laqueur 2015, 1). As when ordered to toss the body of the ancient Greek philosopher Diogenes over the walls to be devoured by beasts, his followers chose to bury him instead.

The very state of death itself is existentially, ontologically precarious; the sociologist-philosopher Zygmunt Bauman has called it absolute otherness (1992, 2). We can see and be with others as they encounter it, but we won't experience it ourselves until after the fact. This makes death unknowable by the measures of life on earth. Death, at the limits of human mortality, with a certainty seared by the uncertainty of precisely when and how it will take place, evinces something else—menacing or promising. Making sense of this is the work of culture, according to Bauman: culture imbues the juncture of death with meanings, stories, cosmologies, and rituals that are shared by (and go beyond) individuals, helping to ease the precariousness of it all.

Still, the process is riddled with ambiguity as the notness of lives now departed abuts against the presence they once had. Matter out of place is what Mary Douglas (1966) called things that have slipped from the categories they once held—a slipping that can register as pollution and dirt, making things utterly profane unless work is done to reorder them as sacred. These residues shift from one social/material/spiritual plane to dangle rather than dissolve into thin air (Hetherington 2004). "Forgotten but not gone" is how a newly minted professor emeritus characterized his situation when, though he was given recognition upon his retirement, the department continued on just fine without him (Roach 1996, 2). As Joseph Roach, a well-known scholar of performance, has said about what he calls the three-sided relationship of memory, performance, and substitution, as mortals die, something arises to both mark and recover the loss. This may be enacted through ritual performativity (mourning, burial, lamentation), but things can also slip in the dance to rejuggle the composition of things when rituals go unperformed or the dead refuse to leave, perhaps angry about being improperly grieved. Even when all seemingly goes well, unease can linger in what Freud and so many others have understood to be the ambiguous loss of death. Throughout it all, what is retained and what is not, for whom and for how long, is the work of mortuary care performed by the living. As Roach comments about his professor friend, "As he was fading away, my retiring colleague stumbled over the paradox of collective perpetuation: memory is a process that depends crucially on forgetting" (1996, 2).

In this chapter I take up the idiom of work: the work done with, for, and on the dead by the living in terms of both their material remains and their afterlife. As the dead can't tend to their own corpses, the matter must be handled by others and is one that bears the ambiguity of the death process and also the precarity of dependence on the "social network of hands" (Butler 2009, 14) of other humans. Embedded in existential and social liminality, the corpse also succumbs very quickly to decay, making for a materiality with a "dangerous potential" (Hallam, Hockey, and Howarth 1999, 125) that tends to spur fastidiousness in how corpses are treated, no matter where and how that is done. Meanwhile, around (and beyond) this physicality are the ties between the living and dead as well as the future trajectories of both. As Robert Desjarlais describes this process for Tibetan Buddhists from the Yolmo region, while the living and dead are attached to one another, they have now embarked on separate trajectories and need to start detaching: the dead from this world and the living from the dead. This work involves "technologies of cessation and transformation," which he has lyrically termed the "making of the unmaking" and has also called "poiesis" (2016, 9).

How the making of the unmaking of death has been variously handled, altered, and performed across Japanese history is what I look at here. I am particularly interested in the contours of ambiguity. For this is a topography ambiguous still. There are signs that the necessity or ethics of respecting the dead is fading: the rise of unclaimed remains, lonely death, and trends in minimizing or even foregoing the rituals of funeral and burial altogether. But these exist alongside a surge in protecting or refurbishing mortuary care, as in projects to build collective graves for aging laborers (most of whom are unemployed and subsisting on welfare) in the Tokyo neighborhood of Sanya or in the burgeoning "ending market" in which anticipatory arrangements are made by the individual herself. To help make sense of what is emerging today, I take a brief look at historical patterns of how this troubling border between the presence and absence of the dead and the materiality or immateriality of their remains has been conceptualized and handled by the living in the past. My aim here is quite basic, and I trace the history through a few patterns of how human remains have been treated and mapped onto various political, social, and cosmological worlding(s) of the deceased. I am more interested in the present, where remnants of the past still mingle, than in the past per se. Following Foucault, I see this as a "history of the present" (1979, 31) in which it is the sociological care for the dead and treatment of corporeal remains that I pay particular attention to.

MATTER OF THE DEAD

The earliest record is sketchy. Archaeological remains include urns from the Jōmon Age (Neolithic, 7000–250 BCE), cist and pottery graves from the Yayoi Age (Bronze Age and Iron Age, 250 BCE to the third century CE), and huge burial grounds for emperors and tombs shaped like keyholes for coffins crafted from hollowed-out logs from the Kofun period (protohistoric, second through sixth centuries CE) (Kidder 2007). These seem to have been limited to those with status. For commoners, there is less evidence that any burial rituals were practiced. Their bodies may have been left out in the open for the wind to decompose them; one of the earliest recorded methods of corpse disposal in Japan has been called both "wind burial" and "abandonment of the corpse" (*shitai iki*/死体遺棄). Because they were thought to harbor danger for the living, corpses were kept distant from human habitation even when they started getting buried in the earth (Tanaka, quoted in Mori Kenji 2014, 70).

The association of dead flesh with pollution goes far back in Japanese history. This is linked to Japan's indigenous religion, or what Japan's great folklore scholar Yanagita Kunio calls its "native" culture (as opposed to "foreign" influences such as Buddhism or Confucianism, both of which have greatly shaped Japanese practices and attitudes regarding the dead since before the seventh century). In Shintō, which is organized around an animistic panoply of gods (*kami*) and a set of origin myths, the land of the dead figures in the very origins of Japan. According to the *Kojiki*, the book of Japan's "ancient matters" and oldest extant chronicle, dating from the eighth century, the sister-brother pair Izanami and Izanagi created the islands of Japan. But when Izanami died giving birth to fire, she was consigned to the land of the dead. Izanagi sought to follow her there. Izanami agreed, on the condition that her brother refrain from looking at her. But, unable to resist, Izanagi lit a flame. Disgusted by what he saw—Izanami's body overridden by maggots—he fled the land of the dead and pushed a boulder in front of the opening. Enraged, Izanami sent minions after him and joined in the pursuit. Failing to catch him or force her way out, she threatened to kill 100 humans. But her brother responded by promising to birth 150 people, thereby ensuring that the force of life would triumph over that of death. Back on earth, Izanagi attended to his own well-being by performing rituals of ablution in the river to purify himself from his contact with the dead.

In practice, the pollution associated with dead corpses has manifested in an array of customary behavior including a "double-grave system" much along the lines reported by Robert Hertz ([1907] 1960) for the Dayak of Borneo. There, to shield the living from decomposing flesh, bodies were first buried at a distance then reburied closer to human residence after the corpses had transformed into clean bones. A similar custom (*ryōbosei*) was once practiced in parts of Japan.[1] The corpse, buried remotely in the mountains, went unvisited and unmarked while a second grave, closer to home and without remains, became the site for ritual and visitation. While, in this case, the material remains were kept, though separated from where the immaterial spirit was to be tended to, Yanagita (who spent years in rural Japan in the early 1900s researching local traditions) wrote that the practice of preserving corpses, or keeping markers of any kind to the dead, was not commonly practiced until the mid-1800s except by some in the upper class. This was not a sign of neglect as much as of the desire to protect both the living and the spirit of the deceased from being polluted. As Yanagita put it, the impulse was to "hasten the purification of the soul of the newly dead from pollution which it bore so that communication between this world and the other world could be established soon" (Yanagita 1975, 131). And it was as purified spirits that the living hoped the dead would return to visit with them during what became the ritualized season (Obon) for inviting the deceased back to earth for two days every summer. Since, by the beginning of the twentieth century, spirits were thought to reside closer to where bodies had been buried, this meant fetching them at the grave for the visit back home.

As can be seen from the above, not only death but the physicality of dead flesh is polluting in Shintō cosmology. To ward off *kegare* (impurity, uncleanness), practitioners adopt stringent rituals of purification and take precautions to avoid contact with death in the first place. These include delimiting those who work with the dead: leather workers, butchers, and morticians.[2] Still, death poses a problem to Shintō that the introduction of Buddhism in the sixth and seventh centuries helped to resolve by taking over the rituals and practices associated with death. In what has evolved as a syncretic blending of Buddhism and Shintō (seen in how Japanese still practice Shintō for births, Buddhism for deaths, and marriage in Christian church settings), ancestor worship has been part of the mix. Ancestor worship predates everything, according to Yanagita (1975), as the ancestral spirits (*ujigami*) that, emerging alongside territory-based clan units (*uji*), were venerated as gods. As clans enlarged into small states and were fought over and pulled together by powerful leaders (e.g., the Yamato clan by the mid–fifth century), localized gods evolved into a more centralized system under the edifice of an emperor bearing the status of "manifest god" since the seventh century. Tracing its descent from sun goddess Amaterasu, the originating goddess of the Japanese people, the imperial line was taken to be direct and unbroken since the first legendary emperor, Jinmu, inherited the gift of the three sacred treasures in 660 BCE.

Shintō, which became the state religion during Japan's period of modern nation-building and militaristic ambition to rule an East Asian empire that imploded with the country's defeat in the Second World War, has been the node around which power struggles have been conducted under the rubric of the sacred. The postwar constitutional changes overseen by the occupying forces in 1946 desacralized the emperor and institutionalized separation of religion and the state; but even today, Shintō represents something deeply cultural as well as ancestral: lines of inheritance to land, gods, and the past that many still consider natively, essentially, or indisputably "Japan/ese." In fact, "Japaneseness" has incorporated ideas and concepts coming from elsewhere at least since the seventh century. Yet throughout this, as argued particularly by those studying and invested in Japan's native culture, local customs were never totally wiped out or made unrecognizable by assimilation into other beliefs (Harootunian 1988).[3] Rather, they persisted in carrying out everyday life, a big part of which was managing what is beyond the here and now: gods, ancestors, and the dead. This perpetuates the problem of how to juggle avoiding the pollution of death and venerating the ancestors that the deceased are thought to eventually become.

ORDERLY TRANSFORMATION

At death, a body must be managed and the spirit of the deceased ritually attended to. It has long been the custom in Japan for this work to fall primarily, if not exclusively, to the household. At one time this meant that those who had had contact with the body were confined to mourning huts for a certain period of time and excluded from participating in ceremonies, Shintō festivals, and other social activities for even longer (Yanagita 1975). In addition to caring for the body, the household had another duty: to oversee the ritual ceremonies needed to help the spirit of the dead (*shiryō*/ 死霊) move from the polluting and dangerous corpse to become a purified ancestral spirit (*shorei*/諸霊). A gradual process that culminates, after thirty-three to fifty years, in the loss of the spirit's individual identity and its mergence with the generalized ancestral spirits. A becoming that rests on an "orderly transformation" dictated by ritual and upheld by the work of household and kin (Smith 1974).

This is the domain of ancestor worship (*sosensaishi*) where, as noted by Herman Ooms, "household members alone, through their observance of the rites, prevent the ancestors from becoming wandering spirits" (*muenbotoke*) (Ooms 1967, 257–58). But the relationship is more one of continuity than of "absolute otherness," as the living will become ancestors themselves (Yanagita 1975). Meanwhile, a tie of mutuality is forged over time: the living visit the dead and the dead look out for the living. That such an attitude still persists I was reminded of recently when a friend, anxious about her sister starting chemotherapy, told me that she had visited her parents' grave. "Perhaps they will help us," she wrote me by email. Another related the monthly visits made to his father's ancestral grave, where he goes to pay respects and to communicate, recounting what he has been up to and occasionally seeking advice.

But another case of the intimacy between living and dead skews the relationship in a different direction. In the tale of the mountain of abandoned grandmothers (*obasuteyama*), the elderly are taken to die on the mountaintop once they can no longer work to produce the food they consume. The inspiration for a famous Noh play in the fifteenth century and retold in endless folkloric renditions ever since (as collected and studied by Yanagita), it also speaks to the present, as captured in Imamura Shōhei's achingly poignant film *The Ballad of Narayama*, released during the peak of Japan's bubble economy in 1983. In the movie, which earned critical acclaim and the Cannes Film Festival's Palme d'Or award, it is the caring love of the son, tasked with carrying his mother to her death on top of the mountain, that forms the crux of the narrative tension. Struggling to fulfill what his mother herself calls his duty—the dereliction of which would dishonor the family (as his father had done, in other ways)—the son eventually complies, transporting her on his back as a mother would carry her child. As he approaches the place to leave her, strewn as it is with the bones of other "abandoned" elderly, the son chokes with emotion. But the mother insists that he detach. Doing so, he is reassured when snow falls during his descent from the mountain: a sign that his mother is already transitioning into a god. As argued by Jason Danely in his book on aging and loss in contemporary Japan, it is this cycling into a spiritual afterlife that structurally resolves the ambivalence posed by the *obasuteyama* legend between caring for and abandoning the elderly (2014, 13). The degree to which this story still captures the modern imagination speaks of a residue lingering in the cultural tissue of Japaneseness: of interpersonal ties involving both sacrifice and belonging that exceed the life or death of any single person.[4] And the ending here, which is also a beginning (when the son returns home, his wife is pregnant), inscribes the entire cycle in sacredness—of a mother becoming an ancestor to feed the lives of those left behind.

Buddhism has played a critical role in the necro-topography of transforming polluted corpses into pure objects of reverence in Japan ever since gaining a stronghold by the eighth century. Having entered from the Korean Peninsula and overcoming resistance by being adopted by the powerful Soga clan, Buddhism was involved in rituals treating the dead from the outset. Buddhism incorporated and transformed ceremonial exchanges already existing in ancestor worship by easing the specter of pollution affixed to death under Shintō. By offering methods for acquiring merit for the dead and a cosmological worldview that yields rebirth in Pure Land or other heavenly realms (after transition through six forms of existence along the way), death became associated with "becoming Buddha" (*jōbutsu*)—a word still used today for death.[5] Throughout the Heian and Kamakura periods (794–1333 CE), the hope of dying in a "beautiful, ritualized manner" became increasingly popular (Stone 2016, 1). Adherence to rituals—deathbed rites (*rinjū gyōgi*), tonsure into Buddhist priesthood even as one was dying, anticipatory mortuary ceremonies[6]—was thought to assure, and quicken, the passage to Pure Land (*ōjō*).

Practitioners also sought to ease the burdens of those Shintō deemed polluted, incorporating a scripture (*ketsubonkyō*) to cleanse women of the pollution of menstruation and childbirth, for example (Bernstein 2006, 28). And ritual procedures were put in place for the gradual separation of the spirit from the flesh (*bunri*). These included a forty-nine-day period of mourning, giving the dead a distinct name (what Laqueur [2015] calls *necronominalism*, in this case crafted by a Buddhist priest), and inscribing the *kaimyō* (posthumous name) onto a memorial tablet (*ihai*) that was made permanent after the forty-ninth day to reside alongside those of all the other ancestors on the Buddhist altar (*butsudan*) kept in the home (Smith 1974).[7] The memorial act of *kuyō*—bowing head, clasping hands, offering a sutra—was also introduced by Buddhism, to be done whenever visiting the dead. As Mori Kenji puts it, *kuyō* concretizes the abstraction of honoring the dead. *Kuyō* is a "concrete act of individually recognizing the dead that expresses their wish to pass over to the other world—a transition connected to happiness" (Mori Kenji 2014, 81).

Along with Buddhism came cremation. While there is earlier archaeological evidence of cremation, the first recorded instance is of a Buddhist priest, Dōshō, in 700 CE.[8] The practice spread by inculcating what historian Andrew Bernstein calls its "pedagogical function" (2006, 29). Demonstrating the Buddhist teaching of impermanence (*mujō*), it also signaled the transition from corporeal pollution to a spiritual state beyond. Because the Buddha himself was thought to have been cremated—and his "becoming Buddha" linked to it—cremation spread among the four methods of disposition sanctioned under Buddhism (earth, water, wind, and fire). By the Kamakura period (1192–1333), commoners were also practicing cremation, particularly in the centers of the Jōdo Shinshū sect (Niigata, Toyama, and Ishikawa) whose founder, Shinran, was cremated in 1262 and his remains interred at the head temple. In India, where Buddhism and Buddhist cremation originated, it is believed that the spirit of the dead immediately separates from the body, and the ashes of the dead are neither memorialized nor retained. Some in Japan believe this, too, including Shinran, as mentioned in this chapter's epigraph. But, due perhaps to the intermingling of other customary behavior, including the importance placed on ancestor worship, Buddhist practice in Japan has developed around the treatment, rather than elimination, of remains.[9] Even Shinran's remains, interred in a mausoleum, became the center of the temple he left behind.

But the inherent ambiguity here—of spirits, remains, and ancestors beholden to the caregiving of descendants—makes the handing of the physical remains as well as the trajectory of spirits potentially fraught. As religious scholar Mori Kenji has written, the disposal (*shori*) of cremains is the biggest problem with cremation (2014, 96). Once thrown into rivers or onto mountains like refuse, they started being buried in the earth by stones with the spread of Buddhism in the twelfth century. Over time, ashes were put into urns and placed in Buddhist temples or ancestral graves (*funbo*), or sometimes in residential graves above the ground (Mori Kenji 2014, 89–90). From the sixteenth century onward, commoners started performing *kuyō* (and other rituals), often at the grave, to ensure the transition of the departed into an ancestral spirit. Concern also developed about disconnected souls (*muenbotoke*), a category developed during the Muromachi period (1338–1573)—those who had died violent or unjust deaths, or who lacked descendants required to take care of them. Fearful that these could become hungry and angry ghosts (*gaki*) wreaking damage and spewing curses on the living, people started performing special festivals (*segaki*) to tend to them. Often done in coordination with what were, by the early 1400s, annual "ghost festivals" (*urabon*, now called Obon) to honor the dead, by the late 1500s *segaki* had become mass events staged in public to pacify dangerous spirits (Glassman 2012).

I went to one of these, held at Eifukuji Temple, Saitama Prefecture, in August 2017, where attendees followed a procession of priests from the temple and down the country road, blazing in the sun, to a small pond. Here, to the blowing of conch shells, the pounding of drums, and the chanting of sutras, a ceremony takes place at the time of Obon to do repentance and seek merit for all beings and things, including bad ones. The day I went, with my good friend Yoshiko, a parishioner showed us around. As he explained, the *segaki* is done for the disconnected. By moving to the "spirit home" and releasing the small fish (loaches) waiting in a basket, sending them down a bamboo chute to the pond, we were participating in a ritual to transmit acts of charity (*kudoku*) that would honor and release the spirits of all living things. For participating in this *kuyō*, this act of release (*hōjō*), the charge was ¥300 ($3). Once the squirming loaches reached the pond, they were thought to attract a dragon that would carry the souls of all beings on its back to paradise.

At another temple I visited the following summer, also during Obon, a Rinzai priest showed me and another friend how they tend to disconnected souls. After a tour of the temple, starting with the main hall and all the adjacent rooms, including the one buried deepest in the bowels of the place—a darkened room holding shelves of black lacquer funerary tablets for the ancestors—we were taken to the periphery. There, on the outside wall, sat a ceremonial altar lined with melons and treats for the *muenbotoke*. Opening the sliding doors, the priest pointed to a colorful flag lashed high on a flagpole outside. It attracts wandering spirits, he told us, and signals to them that the temple is a safe haven to rest for a bit.

The priest performs *kuyō* for both the ancestral and wandering spirits. A ritual technology, it goes beyond cremation to deal with what—or who—can linger within or outlast physical remains. An act of care for the dead, it is also intended as a protective mechanism to safeguard the living. Mori Kenji captures this ambiguity: "Because of the possibility that dead spirits can linger, and curse (*tatari*) [the living], memorial services of *kuyō* are done for generations, ritualizing them as ancestral spirits" (2014, 98).

GOVERNANCE OF AND THROUGH DEATH MANAGEMENT

If we think of death as the limit case of the social, and of the social as always getting undone by the deaths of its members (Hertz [1907] 1960; Durkheim [1917] 1947), it is reasonable to assume that periods of great social upheaval are particularly marked by changes in the management and regulation of the dead. This was certainly true in the Tokugawa era (1603–1868) when, having consolidated regional daimyo under his authority, the Tokugawa shogun established peace (after warfare had plagued the country for centuries) but also radical isolation; the policy of national seclusion (*sakoku*) lasted 250 years. Banning the Christianity that Portuguese and Spanish Catholic priests had introduced in the late fifteenth century, the shogun also forced Japanese believers to renounce their faith under a brutal regime of apostasy meant to eradicate this trace of foreignness in the country. At the same time, to enforce an administrative means by which to surveil and govern all residents of Japan, the government appropriated what Buddhism had begun to systemize: a standardized apparatus for ritually dealing with the dead. It became mandatory for all families to register at a local Buddhist temple. Doing so as a patrilineal unit, and being ordered to become parishioners at the temple that would continue with one's successors, Japanese were now enveloped within two systems of governance: one of corporate patrilineage and the other of parishioner membership at a temple (*danka seido*). The two systems became co-constitutive with a temporality of continuity that brought death into the fold of a biopolitics of making life.

While ancestor worship and Buddhism had been entangled for centuries, there had been much variability and leeway in the way of local practice(s) (Ooms 1967). That all changed when households were forced to establish formal ties with a local temple where they were registered by name and patrilineal unit and to which they were channeled for dealing with the ancestors according to Buddhist protocol. The system had sweeping implications for Buddhism, which became politically powerful and financially enriched during this period. In addition to providing an administrative structure for registering and supervising the population, it monopolized the service of handling the dead. As this had increasingly become a progressive process—a series of rituals starting with the funeral, cremation or burial, and then successive memorials on various anniversaries as well as during designated ceremonies such as Equinox and Obon—temples were extensively involved in the lives and deaths of their parishioners. The performance of such ancestral and mortuary rites came to constitute the basis of a temple's economy and the work it provided its parishioner clientele—a legacy that lingers in Buddhism's reputation as a "religion of death" that relies on financial contributions (*ofuse*) that many no longer feel willing or able to pay in what has become an increasing distaste, and distrust, of the religion's mercantilism.

Within Buddhism itself there has been criticism of how one-sidedly its religious attentions have been concentrated on death and, within that, on accommodating Japanese ancestral beliefs. Some have even said that, having strayed so far from its orthodox (Mahāyāna) roots, Buddhism died out in Japan by the early Tokugawa era. More accurate perhaps, as argued by Robert Smith (1974), would be to say that a Japanese form of Buddhism had emerged by the end of the seventeenth century. This consolidation and its increasing hold on the country also provoked a nativist critique that Buddhism distorted what had been the "Japanese" way of dealing with their dead and ancestors. Borrowing from Confucianism, political philosophers such as Kumazawa Banzan (1619–1691) and Kaibara Ekken (1630–1714) advocated for prioritizing filial piety, which would have demanded a different set of rituals (Harootunian 1988). Rather than sending the spirit to a place of purity far away, the focus, they believed, should be more on mourning parents in the place and time where the living resided. They opposed cremation as too summarily dispensing with a parent's corpse; it was seen as akin to "slicing them up with a sword" (Banzan, quoted in Bernstein 2006, 44–45). More appropriate would be for the offspring to "love the flesh of the parent" and to "treat them as if still living" even after death (Bernstein 2006, 45).

Other nativists went further. Rejecting anything tainted with the foreign altogether (such as Confucianism), Motoori Norinaga (1730–1801) embraced the bleak rendering of the afterworld (Yomi) in the Izanagi and Izanami myth as recorded in the *Kojiki*. Others (such as Hirata Atsutane) saw death as the endpoint of only the corpse and argued for an invisible realm of the spirit closer to Japan than that conjured by the Buddhist concept of Pure Land (Bernstein 2006, 50–51).[10] Whatever the specifics, it is significant that death and the treatment of the dead figured in political debates brewing in the eighteenth and nineteenth centuries over the future direction of the country's leadership (Harootunian 1988). As factions aligned and Admiral Perry forcibly entered the country in 1853 by sailing his American frigate into Tokyo Bay, demanding that Japan open up to foreign trade, a revolution brought down the Tokugawa shogunate. Done in the name of restoring imperial rule, the new government announced its double commitment to advancing the country and defending its traditional (East Asian) values. Nativism was brought to modernization: the name Meiji, meaning "enlightened rule," was given to the new era and the new emperor initiated by the Meiji Restoration of 1868.

The approach taken as Japan rapidly modernized was to be both forward leaning—acquiring the technology, industry, and knowledge befitting a modern nation—and "restorative" of its cultural past. Falling under the scrutiny assigned to governance, the management of death was marked by the ambivalences of the moment. On the one hand, the enshrinement of war dead in a Shintō shrine where their souls became the purview of the nation-state started in the very first year of the new era.[11] Yet on the other hand, the state officially abolished the legal statuses of *eta* and *hinin* (lower castes of "nonhumans" that included those dealing with corpses and the dead) in 1872 and, the following year, modified its regulations restricting the movement of people exposed to someone considered polluted (*kegare*). Now, by performing an act of purification, a Shintō priest could resume worship of the gods merely one day after attending a funeral. As noted by Bernstein, "In one stroke the council dispensed with the centuries-old belief that pollution dissipated slowly over time, replacing it with a ritual technology that could eliminate pollution literally overnight" (2006, 63). Implemented here was a time-space compression to speed up, but not remove, the process of ritual purification to the end of accommodating a modern lifestyle still fashioned as "Japanese."

The role of technology figured even more prominently in a controversy that erupted over cremation. Fueled by Shintō-inspired opposition to the practice and complaints about the offensive smell and unhygienic conditions of crematoria, in 1873 the government issued a ban on cremation within a designated red line in Tokyo. The backlash was immediate. Townspeople long accustomed to this practice struggled with the rising costs for full-body burials and diminishing land space in which to hold them. City planners recoiled at the prospect of abandoned bodies and disorderly treatment of the dead. By 1875 the ban was repealed and the Home Ministry issued new guidelines for building modern crematoria outside the red line, tastefully hidden by walls and hygienically designed with smokestacks to better disperse the smoke of burning flesh. By these adjustments, cremation was now touted as not only "civilized" but a better and more efficient method for handling dead ancestors: by compacting the remains, more could be fitted into a smaller space close to Tokyo, enabling more frequent visitation to the grave (*ohakamairi*) than cemeteries in the countryside could (Bernstein 2006).[12]

SACRED SUCCESSION: A MODERNITY OF FAMILY GRAVES AND DISCONNECTED DEAD

By being buried, ritualized, and treated as an ancestor-in-the-state-of-becoming, the deceased are promised a temporality of eternal memorialization. This eases the state of liminality entered upon death: still hovering close to earth, on the way to somewhere else but not there yet, tainted by the impurity of dead flesh. It is the work to be done by the living that moves the dead along.

In the Meiji period, this work became increasingly the purview of the patrilineal corporate unit (*ie*).[13] The Meiji Civil Code of 1898 mandated that all residents be registered in the family record (*koseki*) according to patrilineal name (of birth or, for women, marital family). This was also the designation by which they were to be buried in a grave and tended by (and be property of) the patrilineal line traced through the legal successor.

Registration of households was done directly by the state rather than the Buddhist temple—a state that fashioned citizenship on the genealogical model headed by the emperor as father of the nation and also head Shintō priest (the imperial family nation-state/*tennōsei kazoku kokka*/天皇制家族国家). This made wives and children subordinate to the husband/father in the household; due to the principle of primogeniture, all offspring were subordinated to the first son, who became the inheritor of the family line, the household property, and the ancestral grave (Ueno 2009). Forced out from the main house (*honke*), subsidiary brothers were to establish their own households (*bunke*) and build their own graves. Women faced different circumstances. Officially separated from their natal household upon marriage, they entered their husband's family at the lowest ranked position of outsider, moving up only over time and thanks to much labor in a graduated process much like that followed by a dead spirit. Then, after death, they were to be buried in the ancestral grave of their husband's family—unless, due to divorce or some other reason, the tie to their marital family was broken. In that case, because she had already changed her name but the law allowed only those with the same family name to be buried together, a woman was also excluded from her natal family's grave. Such was one state of the disconnected dead.

The sociological rubric for belonging narrowed during the Meiji period (1868–1912) with significant implications for the handling of the dead. In the village, the locale (*chiiki*) had once been actively involved in carrying out both the funerals and burials of its members. Most also had mutual aid associations (*gōjokai*) that would help pay ceremonial costs. And the work itself, such as digging the hole for earth burial (*anahori*), would have been conducted by neighbors (*kinrinsōshiki*) or the village association (*shūrakukyōdōtai*) to spare the immediate kin from having to do so themselves. An expression of the social thickness surrounding death were the processions (*sōretsu, nobeokuri*) entire villages would join when transporting the coffin or urn to the cemetery. By the Taishō period (1912–26), however, processions were largely banned for their obstruction of the business of modern life and replaced with a stationary altar (*saidan*) as the ritual vehicle to "socially display the dead" (Mori Kenji 2014, 105). Another time-space compression where technology collapsed the movement of both people and time. The altar, fitted as it was with a constellation of ritual objects rented or purchased by the family, reflected not only the diminishment of social hands but also the increased commercialization in care of the dead.[14] Professional ritual specialists, such as funeral companies (*sōgisha, sōsaigyō*), emerged, and the Tokyo Professional Union of Morticians and Goods (*Tōkyō Sōsaigu Eigyōkumiai*/東京葬祭具営業組合) formed in 1919. While money became ever more a factor, paid-for service providers also started performing ever more practices of ritual care. This commodification stretched in both directions as corpse washers and morticians not only earned a wage but also stood in for mourners by wearing the appropriate garb themselves. In this way, the affective work of tending to the dead became a service that families could commission as customers rather than receive from fellow villagers by virtue of belonging to the same locale.

In the face of a changing everydayness, the government still upheld a national ideology based on ancestor worship that, by drawing on past traditions, was meant to foster social stability for a modernizing nation. But this often butted against people's shifting lifestyles: moving to cities far from village and kin, pursuing jobs that would yield social mobility, raising families in an era of burgeoning consumerism. The topography of graveyards changed as well. Tama Cemetery was built in the suburb of Koganei in the wake of the Kantō earthquake of 1923, in which over 140,000 people died in Tokyo, and the urban landscape underwent major reconstruction (Seidensticker 1983).[15] It was a new "garden-style" (*teienteki*) cemetery, intended to offer city dwellers a reprieve from urban living as much as a place for visiting their dead.[16] Laid out on a grid and arrayed with lawns, trees, and flowerbeds, Tama Cemetery was to be a place for family picnicking, where visiting the grave became, literally, a stroll in the park. The cemetery was designed by the chief of Tokyo municipal parks Kiyoshi Inoshita, who also directed the planning for another cemetery in the northeastern suburbs, Yabashira. As with Tama Cemetery, this was to be called a spirit or soul garden (*reien*/霊園), a gentler term for cemetery than the older name, *bochi* (墓地—literally, "the place for graves") (Murakoshi 1981). As conceived by Inoshita, these spirit parks were to "retain sacredness perpetually" (Bernstein 2006, 125) though not by impinging on the constitutional separation of religion and state. Yet even with such new-style spiritual design, the social logic of usage adhered to ancestor worship.

As dictated by the Home Ministry, burial required documentation: first a death certificate issued by a doctor, then cremation and burial permits issued by the local municipality. Then, in public cemeteries like Tama Reien, a ritual successor (*saishishōkeisha*/祭祀承継者) was needed to guarantee maintenance of the grave and annual payment of fees (*kanrihi*). Upholding the principle of patrilineal succession, the model for burial followed normative lines: the "modern Japanese family" (*nihonkei kindai kazoku*) of family members buried together in an ancestral grave (*funbo*/墳墓) with the family name usually etched on one large gravestone. But only those related by blood or marriage were considered family now, unlike in the past when non-kin (such as an adopted son-in-law or those working for the family as help) could be folded in and given its name (Mori Kenji 2014, 120). This meant that the family grave was delimited to family members as defined by the patrilineal line of succession. Accordingly, the ritual successor should be the direct descendant: ideally, the first son. Given this, Inoshita's aim to make Tama Reian a place that "retains sacredness perpetually" retains the reference to ancestors whose line of succession over time is the temporality of sacred eternity—as is that of the emperor.

Just as the premise of the state was that every citizen had a family, so was the premise of cemeteries that the deceased had a successor to pay the fees and care for the grave. As dictated by Article 987 of the Meiji Civil Code, "ownership of the genealogical records of a house, of the utensils of house-worship, and of family tombs belongs to the special rights of succession to headship of house" (quoted in Bernstein 2006, 130). By such a principle of reckoning, those falling outside a family line or lacking a male successor to maintain it—divorced women, single men, married couples without male successors, those far away or estranged from their families, all offspring but the first son—were precarious at death and likely to fall into the ranks of the *muenbotoke* (Hara 1992). The implications of this are as puzzling as they are shocking: why would a state intent on reproducing itself do so with a genealogical principle that would seem to put so many at risk? The legacy of this is an issue I track throughout the book, considering how it plays against scholars, such as Émile Durkheim and Robert Hertz, who have argued that death making for any social body is done in ways that re-create and recraft the social.[17] As early as the 1930s the numbers of those disbelonged in death, by the Meiji system of calculating social membership, were on the rise. This included not only *muenbotoke* but also disconnected graves (*muenbo*): ancestral graves where, because the family moved or lacked a successor, annual fees stopped getting paid. Under these circumstances, cemeteries had the right to terminate usage and dig up the remains (after spending a designated amount of time doing due diligence to locate and inform the next of kin). In both cases, those who started out disconnected or became so by being displaced from their ancestral grave became the responsibility of the local municipality.[18]

As noted by Bernstein, the Meiji government's policies for handling the dead created an "official break between handling the souls and disposal of the bodies" (2006, 97). The former fell under the purview of religion, the latter of the state. This meant that the remains of those legally identified as disconnected entered a communal grave (*gōdōbo*/合同墓) in the municipality; their ashes would be intermixed, collectivized, and unnamed. More a matter of disposal than grievability, this site stands in public cemeteries as the "grave of the disconnected" (*muenbo*/無縁墓). By the 1940s, Tama Reian had become the gathering point for all *muenbotoke* in Tokyo's publicly administered cemeteries; in the high-end Aoyama cemetery, one-third of all graves were disconnected by this time (Bernstein 2006, 126). In his 1932 book *Fumetsu no funbo* (The eternal tomb), the Marxist Hosono Ungai considered this spread of abandoned graves to be the direct result of entrusting care of the dead to the family. Far better, he advocated, would be to allocate the disposal and grieving of the dead to local governments. To ensure that no one would bear the fate of the disconnected, Hosono proposed the building of huge communal tombs where everyone would be buried and mourned, and which would simultaneously serve the living as civic centers and gyms. A progressive idea that never took hold.[19]

DOLLS AND BOXES FOR THE DEAD: WARTIME AND BEYOND

Under the Meiji Constitution, Japanese were not citizens but subjects under the emperor. And under the Imperial Rescript of Education—the ideological map for the militaristic design meant to establish an East Asian empire (the East Asia Co-Prosperity League) under Japanese rule—all subjects were expected to sacrifice themselves for the emperor. As the Rescript, issued by Emperor Meiji in 1890, admonished "Should any emergency arise, offer yourselves courageously to the State." And indeed, from Japan's first incursion into Manchuria in 1931 until the Pacific War ended with the emperor's August 15, 1945, declaration that "the war did not turn in Japan's favor," Japanese subjects were expected to fight, and die, like 100 million shattered jewels (*ichioku gyokusai*).[20] They obeyed their emperor's mandate to "endur[e] the unendurable and [suffer] the unsufferable" and do whatever it took to fight the enemy and win for Japan its place at the top of the new East Asian empire.[21] The incredible brutality leashed to this end—across China, Korea, Indonesia, and elsewhere in Southeast Asia in the way of comfort women, conscripted labor, massacres, horrific death marches, and forced suicides in Okinawa so that Japanese soldiers could occupy the safety of caves during American airstrikes instead—is all too familiar by now. As is the fact that such atrocities rested on a mindset of seeing one's enemies as expendable, unworthy, and altogether nonhuman. Resting on a hierarchical principle of social order, everything became geared to winning the war by those deemed to be at the top. This meant that many Japanese were brutalized in the war effort as well; soldiers were persecuted by their superior officers in a military system notoriously cold-blooded.

In keeping with my aim in this chapter to briefly trace a history of the present in terms of the ambiguity between the living and mortal remains, I consider two examples of how Japanese dealt with their own dead during wartime—both the already dead and the to-be-dead.[22] The first involves "dolls" that were made and sent to soldiers in the field to accompany them in fighting and possibly into death; the second involves the boxes of ashes in which those who died away from home were to be transported back to their families for burial or memorial. Both were objects to accompany or contain the dead, intended to embed the dead in a relationality with others and to provide care in times when, due to violent or distant deaths, remains were often unretrievable and the deceased were at risk of disconnectedness. A time when the technology of substitutes became critical in the work of caring for the dead.

Starting as early as 1936 and continuing throughout the war, girls and women in Japan made small dolls (*imonningyō*) that they sent to military personnel stationed throughout the Japanese empire. Put into "comfort bags" (*imonbukuro*) to give solace and distraction to soldiers as they fought far from home, the dolls were originally designed as amulets and mascots.[23] They were fashioned from old scraps of kimono and shaped as female caregivers (*komori*), sometimes with a baby doll attached to the back. Their makers were female as well, and constructed them out of a personal relation (as sister, sweetheart, wife) but also as part of a civic campaign to support the troops by reaching out to an individual soldier. Often accompanied by a letter, the dolls could generate deeply affective connections. In her trenchant analysis, anthropologist Ellen Schattschneider (2005) has studied the achingly close ties sometimes formed. As with a soldier who, after receiving his own doll, became so attached that he carried his "younger sister" everywhere, dying with her bloodied by his wounds. A few days after the battle that killed him, a reporter encountered his unit and saw soldiers carrying the ashes of fallen comrades in boxes, including one with the doll in her now bloody dress. Writing the story up under the headline *Chizome no ningyō* ("Bloodstained doll"), he also reported that the unit had taken over the work of caring for the doll.

How to explain the striking dissonance of soldiers who cared so sentimentally for a handmade doll in the midst of launching horrific violence against the civilian populations they were sent to conquer? According to Schattschneider, these dolls mediated the ambivalence that foot soldiers were facing while far from home, fighting for the emperor in the killing fields of Japan's would-be empire, still alive but in the shadow of death. Drawing on anthropologist Yamaguchi Masao's concept of *mitate*, she argues that the dolls served as a form of sacrifice or gift between humans and gods: a stand-in for their bearer giving their own body (which many did as well) to the emperor-god. They also operated as amulets, long a tradition in Japan, meant to be worn on the body as protective shields that remove, by absorbing, bodily or external dangers. Amulets move with the person like a guardian spirit, engendering a relationship like what, in analyzing the bonds and care work formed with the virtual pet Tamagotchi, I elsewhere refer to as prosthetic sociality (Allison 2006). As Freud says of the uncanny, the dolls captured a slice of home in the very unhomeliest of places, evoking female domesticity in the homosocial space of the battlefield where soldiers on a mission of violence are cared for by girl-dolls (Schattschneider 2005).

But if the presence of *imonningyō* was meant to be protective, it was also about saving soldiers from dying all alone. The same was true of the sashes made with a thousand stitches from a thousand sets of hands (*senninbari hamaki*), sent to the battlefront to accompany unto (possible) death those fighting for the country far from home. They served as an inoculation against dying disconnected and leaving behind a wandering soul.

As the war proceeded, the *imonningyō* became ever more imbricated with death: they were sent to the corps of airmen scheduled to be suicide bombers (*tokkōtai*)—the kamikaze pilots. Several photographs of *tokkōtai* show them with mascot dolls dangling from their uniforms or strung from the cockpits of their planes. In the vehicles that were to be weapons, and on their bodies (weaponized as well), hung dolls animated with the vitality of the young female hands that crafted them. In Yasukuni Shrine, where the souls of these dead pilots are enshrined as heroic spirits, there is a small display of *imonningyō* alongside a number of *hanayome ningyō*—beautiful wife dolls that families of the deceased sent on their behalf, sometimes years after death (Takenaka 2015). Serving as substitutes (*migawari*) for the wives these young men never had, the dolls keep the dead soldiers socially, if virtually, connected to a genealogical principle of sacredness for which they gave their lives (Schattschneider 2005).[24]

A substitution of a different kind transpired in the boxes of remains returned from the war and from satellite communities of Japanese sent to populate the new empire. When the bodies could be cremated, the ashes were to be returned to families at home to perform the appropriate ceremonies and bury them in ancestral graves. When the dead was a fallen soldier, their comrades were to bring them home and return them personally to the family.[25] But, as the war went on, and more and more died in battle with fewer and fewer resources to cremate and gather the ashes, boxes came back with only parts of the dead—a finger, nail, lock of hair, or a substitution for the corpse such as a stone. If remains came home at all. And in the wholesale devastation the country faced upon defeat—when winning the war had been the only option, and losing it a shame no soldier should willingly bear by coming home alive—the state of the dead became yet more ambivalent. There were the veterans who did make it back, typically disabled and scarred, but rejected for failing the country rather than welcomed.[26] Some had already been declared dead, their funerals conducted and gravestones erected. Their reappearance made them the "living war dead"; dislodged from nation and home, many resorted to begging on the streets. But, as so eloquently recorded by historian John W. Dower in his book *Embracing Defeat* (1999), these dishonored vets were hardly the only "improper" people now in Japan. In a country where "there existed no strong tradition of responsibility towards strangers, or of unrequited philanthropy, or of tolerance or even genuine sympathy toward those who suffered misfortune" (Dower 1999, 61), a proliferation of misfits emerged—those insufficiently tied to others or place. Such as war widows, orphans, the "contaminated" victims of the Hiroshima and Nagasaki atomic bombs, Okinawans caught on Japan's mainland and now displaced there in camps, and the endless hordes of the homeless, hungry, diseased, and unemployed.[27]

Then there were the numbers of Japanese stranded overseas: 6.5 million in Asia, Siberia, and the Pacific, including 3.5 million soldiers and sailors. Although repatriation started right away, the tempo was uneven and slow; a year after the end of the war, more than 2 million had not yet returned. When bodies did come back, they sometimes did so as ashes, sometimes unidentified. There is a photo in Dower's book of a group of Japanese children returning orphaned, repatriated from Manchuria. All look scraggly and distraught; around one's neck is the familiar white pouch holding a box of ashes. But, as Dower notes, it is unclear whose remains they contained—when asked, the child reported losing her father, then mother, then sister. Only the family name appears on the box, so the ashes could be of any or all of them. The collective dead, as if joining the ancestors. Except would anyone be performing those rituals with so many of the family now gone?

Life remembered or forgotten in death?

CONCLUSION

The ambiguity of the dead and how delicate the work of making the unmaking of death by the living is what I have traced in this chapter through various iterations and contours in Japan's past. I have looked at how the physical remains and spiritual afterlives are tended to through rituals of memorialization, burial, and care, questioning the politics of such death work, the poetics of how it is carried out, and the precarity (for the dead but also the living) when memorialization isn't (or can't be) performed according to customary practice. The pain of the latter—of untended and untending spirits—was highlighted recently in the aftermath of the compound disaster (earthquake, tsunami, nuclear meltdown) of March 11, 2011. On top of 18,500 killed, half a million displaced from their homes, and the devastation as well as radiation of the landscape, there were bodies never found; such a build-up of the dead that proper management was impaired; and vast numbers of ancestral graves, memorial tablets (*ihai*), and temples utterly destroyed. As Richard Lloyd Parry has written in *The Ghosts of the Tsunami* (2017), "So many died, and all at once. At home, at work, at school—the wave came in and they were gone. The dead had no time to prepare themselves. The people left behind had no time to say goodbye" (107). As for the already dead, many of whom lost the descendants who had once cared for them, "At a stroke, thousands of spirits had passed from life to death; countless others were cut loose from their moorings in the afterlife" (110). In the morass of the ecosystem left behind, the ghosts of unhappy deceased—young children drowned far from parents, elderly stranded at death all alone, a dog left behind that starved to death, a soldier and suicide victim who had died violently years ago—started emerging. Their sightings were much reported on in the news. Parry recounts that one Buddhist priest asked to exorcise such ghosts from the living found them to be a highly unsettling presence. Disturbed and disturbing: spirits insufficiently laid to rest.

In the rest of the book, I turn to this issue of death work—the managing of physical remains and spiritual afterlives—in an era when the who, what, and how to do it are up for question. Haunting this query is the question of, when not an exceptional moment like the crisis of 3.11, what happens to the "ordinary" dead who simply die without others to tend to them?

hist connection to "death work"?
no setting of a standard death, so what is death "otherwise"?

Gojira was a brooding and dark film that drew on memories of Hiroshima and the firebombing of Tokyo in a visually arresting, emotional style. The story of a Jurassic survivor rendered huge and radioactive by U.S. hydrogen bomb testing in the South Pacific, *Gojira* traces the monster's attacks on Tokyo—rendering the city a smoldering, flattened wasteland, much as it had been in 1945—and the creature's ultimate destruction by a new super-weapon devised by a Japanese scientist.... As a number of commentators have observed, however, *Gojira* was, for all the scenes of Tokyo in flames, the images of irradiated infants, and its often funereal tone, a fundamentally optimistic film. For despite all of Godzilla's destructive fury, the monster is eventually defeated and the Japanese nation, even if wounded by this latest radioactive menace from across the seas, survives intact at the end.

William M. Tsutsui, "Oh No, There Goes Tokyo" (2020)

the popular industry of death
from godzilla to the
ending business

TRACKING TIME AT TOKYO BAY

Tokyo Bay hugs the city of Tokyo. Lying off the country's southeastern region of Kantō, it spans the coastlines of Tokyo, Kanagawa, and Chiba Prefectures and connects to the Pacific Ocean through the Uraga Channel. Representing a border with the rest of the world, it was here that Commodore Matthew Perry entered Japan with his squadron of four American ships in 1853 demanding the country break its two-and-a-half-century isolation. Initially rebuked, he returned with nine ships the following March, securing the Treaty of Kanagawa on March 31, 1854, which opened the ports of Hakodate and Shimoda to American trade and established a US consulate in the country. The geopolitics of Japan radically changed. With the shogunate government soon ousted and direct imperial rule officially restored, the nation underwent a period of rapid modernization. Technology was adopted under the imprimatur of retaining ties to a cultural past. From a sequestered island archipelago, the Empire of Japan entered the global arena. Fifty years after Perry forced his way into Tokyo Bay, Japan waged a victorious war against Russia (1904–5), becoming the first Asian power to defeat a European stronghold.

Forty years later, the endpoint of its militaristic ambitions to establish the Greater East Asian Co-Prosperity Sphere across Southeast and East Asia was staged in Tokyo Bay. Two weeks after Emperor Hirohito made his radio announcement to the nation, the Empire of Japan signed its official surrender signaling the end of hostilities in World War II. Aboard the USS *Missouri*, docked in Tokyo Bay on September 2, 1945, the signing of the Japanese Instrument of Surrender was completed in twenty-three minutes. Standing under two American flags, one from Perry's mission almost a century earlier, Douglas MacArthur, US army general and supreme commander of the Allied powers, officiated. Representatives of the Japanese government signed the documents, witnessed by representatives of eight other nations. With this began the Allied occupation of Japan—the first and only time the country had ever been occupied by a foreign power. Under his supreme command, MacArthur allowed the emperor to remain on the imperial throne. But as the iconic photo of him towering over a diminutive Hirohito showed the world, the moorings of this empire ruled by a sacred god were things of the past. Accepting a democratic constitution, sweeping social reforms, and economic policies reminiscent of the American New Deal of the 1930s, Japan embarked upon a period of radical shifts and rapid (post)industrial growth. In 1952 the Allied occupation officially ended. By the end of the 1960s Japan had become the second-largest economic power in the world.

Spectral imaginings of its place in the world, defeated in war but headed toward more promising futures: Japan's first blockbuster hit of the postwar era captured this in the tale of a monster set in Tokyo Bay. An ancient reptile, slumbering at the bottom of the bay, becomes a radioactive mutant from American nuclear testing nearby. Released in 1954 by Tōhō Studios at unprecedented cost and with stunning special effects, the story of *Gojira* appealed to a populace still recovering from war. Its plotline of a country getting pummeled into destruction was said to have been cathartic for Japanese. Yet charged with ambivalence, the beast conjured both admiration and fear. Evoking "the souls of Japanese soldiers who died in the Pacific Ocean during the war," its movements were purposely stylized to mimic the deathly air raids of US B-52s over Tokyo (Ifukube Akira, quoted in Igarashi 2000, 116). Replaying Japan's war experience as one of victimization, the film staged the country as a recipient, rather than as an aggressor, of violence: a whitewashing of historical facts. The story also ends in a victory of sorts when the country survives by the wits of a Japanese scientist who, inventing a deoxygenator machine, deploys it by jumping into Tokyo Bay and sacrificing his life. Performing grief, *Gojira* incubated something about/for Japan moving forward as well. A mutant whose architectonics of power and death embedded transformations, *Gojira* became a global hit (albeit under its American remake as *Godzilla*) and anticipated Japan's emergence following the war as an industrial superpower that deployed atomic power to refuel its economy. Nuclear power plants were built under its Atoms for Peace initiative (started in 1956), many in the Tōhoku region of northeastern Japan. Here, following the earthquake and tsunami on March 11, 2011, a nuclear meltdown occurred at the Daiichi nuclear power plant, provoking an atomic crisis of profound implications. With radiation seeping perilously, if invisibly, into the environment, Japan/ese were reminded of the atomic bombs that, dropped over Nagasaki and Hiroshima sixty-six years earlier, left such a horrific effect and also radically changed the course of the country.

The third millennium. A half century since *Gojira* first hit the screen, and a century since Japan embarked on its militaristic buildup to the Pacific War. The threats endangering its livelihood are configured less by the figures of external enemies today, whether marauding beasts or American B-52s. Rather, the country faces internal challenges brought on by implosions in the very directions it took to transform from an imperial to a postindustrial power following the war. That was when, achieving high economic growth by expanding productivity in manufacturing from automobiles to household electronics, it acquired global stature for its much-touted "economic miracle" in stages that went from recovery (1946–54) to high economic growth (1954–72) before steadying (1972–92) into low increase today (1992 to the present). Rather than fight to the death to win the war for the emperor, the populace was directed to work hard for the nation and itself in a productivity to be compensated by a burgeoning consumer culture. And indeed, in the urban migration that followed the war, when farmers left the land and headed to office or construction jobs in the cities, the ecology of everyday habitation radically changed. Family size immediately decreased, residences became anchored to the nuclear (rather than extended) household, and the focus of people's lives increasingly shifted to the capitalist logics of productivity and consumerism. The sociology of belonging shifted as well: more toward the nuclear family and the individual and calibrated to such measures as academic record, workplace, material income, and wealth. But, while the longue durée ties of patrilineal ancestry and land began to diminish, durable bonds (as in lifetime employment and marriage) still constituted the markers of both normativity and security, adding up to the well-being of having a good life.

This notion of the Japanese dream—ownership of one's own home, stable (heteronormative) marriage and family, permanent employment (at least for men)—has become elusive for ever more Japanese. The same is true of Japan's postwar dream to generate an ever-expanding economy with ongoing high industrial growth and exponential productivity. With the bursting of the bubble economy in the early 1990s triggering economic decline and a "lost generation" of youth entering the job market—which, alongside shifts to more flexible employment, has led to the new normal of an irregularly employed workforce—these horizons have been tamed. Coupled with a less booming economy are the high aging and low birthrate demographics (*shōshi kōreika*). As people live longer and reproduce less often, the population has literally declined since 2006. With fertility as well as marriage rates on the decline, and the number of postproductive citizens not only on the rise but increasingly living—and dying—on their own (one in three live in single-person households, including those over sixty-five years old and the "high" elderly over seventy-five), Japan faces a crisis in social reproduction. The fear of "no future" (Edelman 2004) lurks in the national imaginary, generating endless government policies intended to overturn it (by incentivizing childbirth or "work/home" balance for working mothers, for example), none of which have worked (Ogawa and Kingston 2015). And the most sensible option—liberalizing immigration by foreigners—remains unpopular with a populace still resistant to opening its borders to "non-Japanese" (Shirahase 2015). Meanwhile, the sense that everyday life and prospects for the future are riddled with uncertainty gives rise to feelings of uneasiness (*fuan, fuantei*). A precarity that reverberates in such national crises as the rise in suicide, the rise in lonely deaths, and the compound disaster in northeastern Japan (Allison 2013).

The year 2016. A new iteration of the Gojira story. Reflecting current dangers—of a postnuclear Japan where the declining birthrate threatens the viability of national futures—*Shin Gojira* (New Godzilla) came out following the 3.11 nuclear meltdown at the Daiichi nuclear power plants. Discovered to be endlessly mutating and empowered by nuclear fission, Gojira poses a danger to the entire planet. And because it sits in Tokyo Bay, the United Nations has come up with a plan, with international buy-in, to bomb the city in order to save the rest of the world. That is, unless Japan can figure out a way to disable the monster in time. Tokyo is doubly imperiled by the monster in its midst and the fact that it is now the target for possible elimination by the rest of the world—an image of dystopic futures. But, echoing the plotline of the original *Gojira*, Japanese scientists devise an ingenuous invention that saves the day: a component that coagulates Gojira's blood, freezing and disengaging him. This is the state he is in as the movie closes.

Hovering over the city, gigantically icicled, the monster becomes part of the landscape rather than submerging back into Tokyo Bay. This also suggests, as the scientists implied, that Gojira may have utility for their future. Its powers of endless mutation, indicating an evolutionary stage surpassing that of humans, holds possibilities for engineering the sustainability of the planet and human race. Not just a threat, then, Gojira also represents a potential: for life mutating into what could be a new kind of existence. Tellingly, it is a creature that reproduces asexually, providing a fantasy for a nation where what has historically reproduced the population—marriage, childbirth, a genealogical principle connecting ancestors, descendants, and the sacredness of gods, including the Japanese emperor and empire—are all on the decline. As the movie fades out, Gojira can be seen on Tokyo's horizon. Standing immobilized (for now) in a body that, having become less alien throughout the film, bears the traces of something humanoid comingling with those of the beast (Lamarre 2018).

A promissory note of/for the future?

NECRO-ANIMISM: AN ENDING MARKET THAT GIVES
LIFE TO DEATH

Sixty years after the original Gojira terrorized Japan, Tokyo Bay has become the site of something else, as tempered by the times and as creatively fashioned around death, futurity, and technology as the 1954 monster movie. This is ENDEX, a national convention for those in the "ending business" that takes place every August in the season of Obon, when dead spirits are invited back to earth to revisit family and home. Showcasing a kaleidoscope of services and goods, business is pitched to the lifestyles and needs of a consumer base experiencing an era of rising deaths, high aging/low childbirth demographics, and weakening parishioner and family systems (once the mainstays of mortuary management). Starting in 2016 to much media hype, the setting is Tokyo Big Site, the huge convention complex in Odaiba, the high-tech shopping and entertainment area constructed on the artificial island built from landfill in Tokyo Bay.

Developed in the 1990s from what was originally a port built in 1860, Odaiba houses concert halls, leisure arcades, a series of malls including the Edo-era Oedo-Onsen Monogatari, a giant Ferris wheel with enough electric voltage to light up the entire bay at night, and multiple museums, including a futuristic science museum (Miraikan, Museum of the Future) where visitors mingle with robots. One of Tokyo's top-listed tourist sites and a popular destination for families, dating couples, and teenagers alike, Odaiba lends Tokyo Bay a forward-looking New Age flavor—a far cry from the dwelling place of a prehistoric beast associated with darkness, ancient myth, and hostile aggression. Tokyo Disneyland is just a few kilometers away, nestled in the bay. The most profitable Disneyland in the world, built in 1983 at the height of the bubble economy, it is less a sign, Yoshimi Shunya (2000) has argued, of Japan's infatuation with American pop culture than of its wherewithal to sport its own iconic Disneyland that Japanese can visit without ever having to leave home.

The convention is popularly known as ENDEX, which stands for "ending exhibit" (*endingu sangyō*/エンヂィング産業). A trade show for those in the business of funerals, graves, and anything pertaining to either (such as gravestones, flower arrangements, crematoria, and Buddhist shrines), it eschews the standard word for death (*inakunaru*) in favor of the softer, cooler name given to the turn of the century trend in businesses catering to endings: *shūkatsu*. Using the characters for "end" (終) and "activity" (活), this roughly translates as "ending activity" and nods to another well-known activity: job-seeking, also called *shūkatsu* but with different characters (就活, standing for *shūshoku katsudō*), usually done by third-year college or high school students seeking jobs before they graduate. These activities and others that have become popular today, such as "marriage-seeking" (*konkatsu*, a form of speed dating to find possible marriage partners), are markets, putting those seeking a particular outcome in touch with those in a position to provide it.

The job market practice emerged in the context of postwar Japan, when the acquisition of long-term ("lifetime") employment at a reputable company with the guarantee of stable income, gradual promotion, and annual bonuses and perks became the sign of social adulthood (particularly for men, though true for women as well): the sine qua non of what enabled, and signified, one's place in Japan's middle class. In an era when heteronormative marriage was as mandatory an aspiration as a career, it represented the end goal of the years spent in education, abetted by cram schools and tutors to do as well as possible on entrance exams in order to have one's choice of high school, then college, and finally job placement. With so much riding on what was likely to be a job that would last for most if not all of one's working years, the practice developed of seeking employment well ahead of time, usually the year before graduation. A form of insurance, as it were. For, if such a job hasn't been secured within a year, or at most two, of graduation from either high school or college, one's prospects may well diminish thereafter—something those in the "lost generation" who came of working age after the bursting of the bubble well understood, when job market precarity froze them out of desirable employment, often forever (what activist Amamiya Karin [2004] coined the "precariat" of insecurely un- and underemployed).

Like the job market, the ending market is in the business of transacting an outcome at once desirable and marked by scarcity and need. Both matters involve temporality: securing something for the future. But what that is differs significantly. In the former, it is a long-term, regular job, so foundational to the postwar Japanese dream of being middle class; in the latter, it is the security of a final resting place and being given a modicum of care as the deceased. As has been much rehearsed already, these are the conditions surrounding endingness today: Japanese live longer (the mean life expectancy is eighty-seven for women and eighty-one for men), but they tend to do so in a state of immobility for years before death (the current "healthy" life span is seventy for men and seventy-three for women) and increasingly alone (26.5 percent of those over sixty-five now live alone) (Tsuji 2021). Meanwhile, care has become a pressing issue for the aging; despite a progressive care insurance bill enacted in 2000, the number of care facilities as well as workers to staff them are increasingly insufficient (Tsuji 2021)—which leads to the contingent issue, highly contested in Japan, of whether or not (or to what degree and under what conditions) to open up care jobs, and thus national borders, to foreign migrants (Shirahase 2015).

Following the end-of-life stage comes that of after death. The number of deaths has exceeded those of births in the country since 2006. Already at a historically unprecedented high (1,340,000 in 2017; 1,370,000 in 2018; 1,400,000 in 2019—contrasted to 920,000 births in 2016), deaths will continue to rise, predicted to peak in 2040 at around 1,700,000. The demographics of Japan as a "mass death society" (*kashi shakai*) are occurring at the same time that the social relations that once handled matters pertaining to the deceased have weakened nationwide. This means that how, by whom, and where the dead will be accommodated has become a nagging worry for the to-be-deceased in the early twenty-first century.

Organized for those in the business but attended by plenty of press and private citizens as well, ENDEX is called both a "life ending industry expo" and "Japan's funeral and cemetery show." Run by JETRO (Japan External Trade Organization), it attracted 20,224 visitors over three days in August 2019 and featured a total of 324 exhibitors promoting services, products, and companies to help manage the departures and remains of both humans and pets. The exhibition floor, buzzing with activity, sports everything from serenely beautiful granite gravestones, Japanese-style coffins, and upscale wooden *butsudan* (household shrines) to digital memorial devices, floral arrangements dotted with manga characters, and hearses and crematoria expressly for pets. In a panoply of designs ranging from traditional and Japanese-style to cosmopolitan and New Age (including capsules for cremains to be sent by rocket into the stratosphere), the convention stages apparatuses for handling and housing the dead crafted to appeal to the consumerist appetite for choice. The catchword *jibunrashii*—"do it your own way"—reverberates on almost every display, capitalizing on the individualism bred by the times, rendered positively here as the "freedom" (*jiyū*) to customize ending arrangements even if, or particularly, by and for oneself.

But exhibitors are equally attentive to the needs and challenges of those requiring mortuary services that fall increasingly to the individual: the speeded-up urban lifestyles; the economic downturn and desire for affordability; the curbing of parishioner status at temples (where priests would be already in place to perform memorials); the sociological shifts to fewer, farther away, or less available family members to manage mortuary arrangements; no grave for the deceased to enter; and neglected ancestral graves in the countryside to either abandon or move. Given all the uncertainty that ending arrangements can entail, particularly when the to-be-deceased may have no one else to handle (or not want to burden others with handling) them at the time of their death, there is considerable anxiety associated with them. This is what *shūkatsu* is intended to relieve by offering convenient, affordable options that provide mechanisms or personnel to stand in for the local priest and family members unavailable to perform the rituals as once expected.

Selected as one of the pressing buzzwords of the moment in 2010, *shūkatsu* refers to not only end-of-life preparations but the activity of putting these in place well ahead of time.[1] As defined by one of the many associations promoting themselves at ENDEX, "this is an abbreviated word for end-of-life activity which means activity for the ending of human life." The nonprofit, a national senior life support initiative, describes its purpose as helping seniors to prepare for death in order to live well until the end. Because, due to such factors as high aging, low birthrate, and the decline of marriage, "we need to strive to be self-sufficient and independent (*jikatsu jiristu-*/自活自立) in aging." This means being on top of a range of tasks—making a will, deciding on funeral and burial plans, allocating inheritance—and also anticipating possible end-of-life scenarios for which one should already have solutions in mind. As its promotional pamphlet lays out in detail, these may include becoming terminally ill, requiring a wheelchair, having a sudden accident, and getting dementia; in response to each, one must consider having a legal guardian, entering a long-term facility, acquiring home healthcare workers if remaining at home, and signing do-not-resuscitate orders.

As pointed out by another in the *shūkatsu* business who conducted one of the numerous seminars held during the three days of ENDEX that I attended in summer 2019, many negotiating aging today are doing so as *miyori ga nai*. A phrase also gaining currency these days, it translates to "having no one else to depend upon." The founder and president of Total Life Support, a consultancy firm with a cadre of specialists (social worker, priest, tax specialist, medical doctor) to assist with the matters of aging any time of day, Mikuni Hiroaki identifies as a middle-aged bachelor, socially single, and *miyori ga nai* himself. But there is nothing inherently dreary about this, he boomed out the day I heard him speak in a room packed with others in the business. The key is preparing well in advance. By "putting affairs in order while still alive" (*seizen seiri*), one can be relieved of the anxiety regarding death management and manage to "be lively" (*ikiiki-suru*) until then.[2]

Ordering activity, as I discovered over the course of fieldwork, can be considerable for the demographic of Japanese—aging, but in a period of postproductivity that can last thirty or more years before life's end—most inclined to engage in *shūkatsu*. It also constitutes a vital new business opportunity, inspiring innovations and inventions in mortuary arrangements and a diverse range of services, initiatives, and workers to feed this market of giving life to death practices on the brink of sociological decline.

I call this necro-animism. Animating the ordering and ritualizing of preparations for the dead in an age of shrinking sociality.

The marketing of end-of-life is not, itself, new in Japan. It goes back to, most recently, the turn of the twentieth century, when, in the flush of modernization and the building up of urban lifestyles and rhythms, more and more people became reliant on funeral companies (*sōgisha* or *sōsaigyō*) to take over work that once had been handled by village or workplace organizations alongside family and kin.³ Even before that, when the shogun dictated in 1603 that all citizens register with a Buddhist temple as a means of regulating and policing the populace, local temples became instrumental in overseeing the rituals and gravesites of the deceased—a "business of death" as empowering as it was enriching for Buddhism. Intertwined with this, in a governance of biopolitics extended into death, was a genealogical principle of patrilineage: families had to register with temples as patrilineal units, making them parishioners (*danka*) in a relationship of belonging (*danka seido*) that would pass down the familial line from generation to generation. This all made the treatment of the dead much more standardized and dictated by Buddhist ritual than had previously been the case in the heterogeneity of customary practice.

A temporality of continuity marked by the family grave converged around land, religion, polity, and kin. Erected in cemeteries attached to temples where generations of a patrilineage (*iedaidai*/家代々) were to be buried in what came also to be known as the ancestral grave (*bodaiji*), this symbol of familial succession is as grounded in space as temporalized to be eternal (*eikyū*). As religious scholar Ian Reader describes, the family grave serves as "receptacle for the spirits of the ancestors, a site for ritual offerings to the dead, and a symbol of family continuity and belonging" (Reader 1991, 96). But all of this takes work, which falls to living successors performing care for thirty-three years (the length of time conventionally thought to take the spirit of the deceased to become an ancestor, *senzo*, or god, *kami*). In the interim, the grave should be visited on significant anniversaries as well as on New Year's, Obon, and the two equinoxes; certain memorials performed, particularly on key dates; and a degree of upkeep maintained, including paying offerings to the temple or annual maintenance fees to the cemetery, keeping the grave tidy, and tending to the Buddhist shrine at home on a daily basis. By the time the soul of an individual has joined the collective ancestors, other family members are likely to have died, enjoining those still alive to care for them in an ongoing process of memorializing the familial dead at the ancestral grave.

The legal meaning of a grave changed radically after the war. Whereas once it was "the place to give memorial (*kuyō*) to ancestors" (*senzo wo kuyōsuru tokoro*), under the 1948 civil code it became "the place where one sleeps eternally after death" (*jibunga shigo ni eiminsuru tokoro*). Alongside various shifts prompted by the end of war—massive migration to the cities, the shift from an agricultural to a wage-earning workforce, smaller families increasingly organized into nuclear (not extended) family units, increased focus on productivity and consumption in an era of what Morris-Suzuki (1994) calls national capitalism—the sociological contours of everyday life loosened from the anchors of the patrilineage (*ie*) to those organized by the nuclear family and by the demands placed on the individual to work hard and materialistically consume. But even as more and more Japanese moved away from the countryside, leaving the ancestral grave behind, the succession model for burying the dead was not immediately replaced by the individualist graves now designated by the law. In practice, the former has lingered, in part because viable alternatives have been slow to emerge, in part because a successor is still required in order for a deceased to be buried in most (private, public, and religious) cemeteries even today. But the succession model (*keishō seido*) shows ever more signs of being crimped by the exigencies of post-postwar Japan; it has been so compromised that it is not only being abandoned but leaving abandoned the dead themselves. This can be seen, for example, in the increase in ancestral graves in the countryside getting "emptied" due to the dying out of family lines or simply the distance or disregard of living kin who have moved to cities. More than 40 percent of graves in some cemeteries have been emptied; 414 graves are empty of 450 graves total in one cemetery in the rural town of Hitoyoshi City in Kumamoto Prefecture (Kotani 2018).

In his debut film *Osōshiki* (*The Funeral*), released in 1984, acclaimed film director Itami Jūzō captured these tensions in the story of a mortuary practice in the process of becoming outdated. The parody follows a well-placed Tokyo couple faced with the responsibility of staging a respectable funeral for the woman's father in the countryside. Busy with high-pressure acting careers in the city, the couple wants to send the father off in traditional style nonetheless. Set at the height of the bubble economy, when real estate speculation was skyrocketing, consumer culture booming, and middle-class Japanese life as secure as it would ever be, mortuary arrangements are treated here as both a burden and opportunity for conspicuous consumption.

The couple models postwar ideals: married, with two children, driven by work, professionally ambitious, inhabiting both the rigors and riches of a productively consumerist lifestyle. That they are also self-absorbed adds humor to the plot, part of which involves their return to the woman's natal home to organize the funeral for her father, who died at sixty-nine from a heart attack. Clueless as to how to do this and out of sorts in the rural setting, they nevertheless embark upon the necessary steps—choosing a coffin, hiring priests, holding the wake, planning the burial—by relying on an instructional video that teaches them formal funeral etiquette. Bending to traditional roles for a man who had been difficult in life—a Japanese patriarch who had expected subservience from his family—the urbanites stumble and chafe as they proceed through the three days of mortuary arrangements. In the end, though, the results are surprisingly satisfying. The full-blown funeral with no expense spared winds up producing something in its execution. As the family is gathered, performing tradition in the village, there is a sense that this, after all, is how death should be handled. Although the movie is a comedy, the final affect is solemn and calm. The film did exceptionally well in both critical and popular reception. Hitting a nerve in what were the shifts and strains of the times—as expressed, here, around death.

The 1980s were a period when mortuary expenditures (funerals, gravestones, burials) skyrocketed, reflecting the affluence of the moment. But by the 1990s, this had radically changed. In the job insecurity and recession triggered by the collapse of the bubble economy in 1991, household finances became curbed and new lifestyle trends embraced minimalism.[4] This has been the direction in deathstyles as well. Shaped by financial concerns but also by the demographic and social shifts outlined above, the trend has been toward convenience, simplification, and economization. The catalogue accompanying the 2019 ENDEX convention summarizes data related to funerals, graves, and *butsudan* gathered from consumer surveys taken over the previous ten years. It reports an overall reduction in cost and simplification in the methods and types of mortuary arrangements. In 2011, 85 percent of new graves were family-style and in the ground (*ippanhaka*), averaging $16,770.[5] Only 41 percent were buried this way by 2018, and the cost for this kind of burial had also gone down (to an average of $14,130).[6]

Today, funeral halls or *saijō* (crematoria with funeral halls), where over 90 percent of funerals are held, provide at least three categories of service: general funerals (*ippansō*), the largest and most formal, with over one hundred guests; family funerals (*kazokusō*), limited to family members; and direct funerals (*chokosō*/直葬 or *jikisō*), in which the body goes directly to the crematorium with basically no service at all. Most funerals were formal, as in *Osōshiki*, through the end of the 1990s. But by 2017, the proportion had dropped to only slightly more than half (53 percent), with more than a third (38 percent) being the most streamlined of all (direct burial). By this time 50 percent were completed in under two hours, one in four had fewer than twenty attendees, and though the average spent on funerals came to $16,000 (down from $18,600 in 2013),[7] plenty of funeral halls were offering an array of options with competitive pricing. Two I visited—a recently renovated one in Ebina, on the edge of Tokyo, that has been family run since 1923, and a new-style one-stop operation in Shin Yokohama called Lastel (after "last hotel" for the provision they also have of holding corpses until they can be accommodated at crematoria, which now can have a long waiting list)—both offer a wide range of options. At the former, Fujimi Shikiten, there are four categories: direct service at the crematorium ($2,000–$5,000), single day service ($4,000–$11,000), family service ($4,600–$14,000), and general service ($6,000–$15,700), with the last two including the provision of a beautifully kept room where family members can spend the night with the corpse following the wake and before the funeral and cremation the next day. At Lastel, the spectrum ranges from $2,776 for a direct funeral, $5,360 for a family funeral, or $6,126 for a "living room family service" (that includes a night for the family to stay with the corpse), to $8,902 for the highest level of general funeral with over one hundred guests. In the competitive open marketplace that the ending business has now become, one sees advertisements for these services virtually everywhere—subway stops, billboards, community bulletin boards; even, in the case of Lastel, on a roster listing all its services by category and price posted on the wall outside the entrance. Serving up death management like a fast-food restaurant. To be chosen, as any commodity, by weighing quality against convenience and cost.

Even more striking in recent mortuary trends are the sociological shifts: deviations from the succession system (*keishō seido*) of being buried alongside and tended by patrilineal kin once instituted by the Meiji Civil Code and normatively practiced throughout the twentieth century (Kotani 2010). The story of transformation here involves a number of key players, among them an urban feminist sociologist and a rural Buddhist priest.

A young journalist at the time, Inoue Haruyo experienced the death of her mother in 1979 when the latter died suddenly at the age of sixty-two and had no grave to enter. Due to the principle of primogeniture, Inoue's father, as a second son, did not have access to the grave of his ancestral family (*honke*) and, while expected to purchase one for his own family (*bunke*), had not yet done so. The experience was terrible, Inoue recounted to me. Her mother had nowhere to go; it was as if she were homeless. For, due to changing her name when she married, the mother couldn't be buried in the plot of her own natal family. Temporarily interred, the body was eventually moved into a permanent grave when the family purchased one a year later. But the entire state of affairs made Inoue realize how "relationless" (*muen*) is the positionality of women within patrilineal systems. Expected to marry and thus inhabit the grave of their husband's family, they are prevented from doing so if either unmarried or divorced. Or, as with her mother, once she had married and changed her maiden name, she could no longer be buried in the grave of her natal family. Such precarity, as Inoue realized, also extends to a number of men: all but first sons who lack the time or the means to build their own family graves, all those estranged from their paternal families, and nonparishioners lacking the security of a long-standing relationship with a Buddhist temple (with a priest to perform services and a place reserved in the cemetery). But her concern was mainly for women.

Arguing against the constitutional mandate that women change their maiden names at marriage in her first book, written in 1980, Inoue later returned to school to study sociology and turned to reforming the grave system.[8] Influenced by feminist scholar Ueno Chizuko, a strong advocate for the robust lives of single Japanese (about which she has written a number of books), Inoue established an alternative burial association to assure "dignified departures" extricated from the succession principle in 1990. In 1996, Ending Center became an NPO with its own burial grounds within a Buddhist cemetery in Machida, at the outskirts of Tokyo (Inoue 2012).[9]

In 1989, Myōkōji, a Nichiren Buddhist temple in the countryside outside of Niigata City, in Niigata Prefecture, became the first officially sanctioned cemetery in the country to offer the choice of nonfamilial burial plots. Inspired by the fact that he lacked a male successor to take over his position, Ogawa Eiji, the head priest, designed and conceptualized a burial mound (given the name Annonbyō) open to anyone whether or not they were a parishioner of the temple (*danka*) or had a successor or family members.[10] He also wrote a controversial and much debated article on "How to avoid dying without a grave." Having read it and become inspired on her own trajectory, Inoue approached Ogawa in 1990 to co-run a body of scholars and practitioners, The Society to Think about Graves and Flexible Relations in the Twenty-First Century, to rethink the state of mortuary practice in Japan.

In the 1990s, the movement to open up and flexibilize grave membership continued. Various initiatives, organizations, and businesses were established that catered to alternative burial options of various kinds. These included Onna no Ishibumi, an association and burial ground for single women in Osaka aimed at aging women who, due to the shortage of men killed in the war, couldn't marry midcentury; Moyai no Kai, a nonprofit promoting ash scattering and other forms of disposal of dead remains; and Sōsō No Jiyū No Susume Kai—the Association Advocating Freedom of Send-offs—supporting a diversity of methods including a form of direct burial into the earth called tree burial (*jumokusō*).[11] As laid out more in the following chapter, diversification of belonging has become a strategy adopted by even so-called conventional establishments (such as Buddhist temples that once served only long-standing parishioners) as a means of staying afloat, or exploiting a new opportunity, in the death business. As I saw advertised on the signpost of a small Buddhist temple on the west side of Tokyo in summer 2019: "cherry blossom burials" open to nonparishioners, not reliant on a successor, with the service of eternal memorial (*eitaikuyō*) performed on-site. And as I learned when visiting Myōkōji for its thirty-year anniversary of Annonbyō at the time of Obon, revenues for the temple come from both the old-style parishioner system (where the living give annual offerings and the dead are buried in family plots) and the new-style membership system (where members pay a one-time fee to be buried in Annonbyō and are buried individually, but communally, as nonparishioners—even non-Buddhists). As one parishioner joked to me, "the temple wouldn't be here today without the members," reckoning that at least 60 percent of operating costs derive from the latter.

Released in 2008, *Okuribito* (*Departures*), another Japanese film on the theme of handling the dead, became a classic. Winning a plethora of awards both in Japan and internationally (including Japan's Academy Award for Best Picture, the US Academy Award for Best Foreign Film, and the Grand Prize at the Montreal World Film Festival), the story is set in the era of lost jobs and adjusted aspirations that followed Japan's high economic growth spurt. Fittingly, the lead character (Kobayashi Daigo, played by popular actor Motoki Masahiro) finds himself unemployed after the Tokyo-based orchestra where he has been playing cello goes bankrupt. Daigo sells his instrument, returns to his hometown in Yamagata to live more cheaply in the house left behind by his deceased mother, and answers a job advertisement for "assisting departures." Surprised that this is mortician's (*nōkanshi*) work instead of a travel agency, he resists the urge to leave when his new boss (played by Yamazaki Tsutomu, the famous actor who performed the role of the husband in *Osōshiki*) gives him wages the very first day. Anticipating his wife's disapproval of a profession still stigmatized, Daigo keeps what he is doing a secret from her. But he becomes adept at the trade, which, by a practice that occurs someplace in the countryside, entails washing, redressing, and cosmetically making up the body of the deceased in preparation for the afterlife. Done in front of family members scrutinizing his every move, Daigo performs with a delicate precision that earns him the gratitude and respect of his clients. Enveloped in an intimacy that renders the deceased beautiful, Daigo—abetted by soft close-ups and gentle musical score featuring cellos throughout—makes the work akin to art.

Daigo's wife, however, is repulsed when she learns of his job. Insisting that he quit, she moves out when he refuses to do so. Similarly, a former classmate, with whom Daigo had reconnected since moving back, stops talking to him upon discovering how he is employed. Yet, when his own mother dies and it is Daigo performing the service of tending to her body, which is done in front of the classmate as well as other family and friends (including Daigo's wife), they all are deeply moved by the manner in which he touches the dead.

Shinmon Aoki, the Buddhist mortician and author of the book on which the movie is based,[12] points to accepting the impermanence of existence as the crux of spirituality. Being present with the dead; gathering life from this encounter rather than turning away in either sadness or disgust. The mother had been the operator of the public bath and opposed her son's wish to sell it to a developer to rebuild into something far more modern and upscale. In her death, the attachments she had to tradition get honored and revered—most keenly by Daigo in the artistry he brings to dignifying her body in a custom remade by the stylishness of his craft. In this, he is something of a hybrid who, though a transplant from urban modernity, brings to his work a sensitivity befitting the past. A cyborg in Donna Haraway's sense: a tool (the worker plying his trade) and a myth (of the modern comingling with Japanese traditions in both beauty and style) that culminate in the portrayal of an emergent new/old profession(al) (Haraway 1991). *Okuribito* is a movie as much about death workers as death work: a profession that the film has done quite a bit to popularize as trendy and cool.

Just like *The Funeral*, *Departures* is a product of its times. Reflecting the socioeconomic strains twenty-five years after *The Funeral*, the focus in *Departures* is less the family unit than the worker who, having lost one job, finds another in the ending business, where servicing the dead has been elevated into something of both value and care. The story is a commentary of healing and hope around loss: remaking life through a business of death that is as much about Japan today as it is about any individual. Set in a reverse migration from the city to the countryside, where the evacuation of jobs has co-resided with the roots of ancestral tradition, the figure of the neotraditional death worker is a forerunner of new possibilities. Care for the dead in a "mass death society" (where deaths exceed births every year at a rate predicted to peak around 2040) at a time when the relations that once attended to this are wearing thin. Presented here as work that is also a practice, with Buddhist as well as animist implications[13]—introducing the viewing public to the ending business with its array of mortuary services and workers who no longer need to be derided for their association with death. And, in this, giving soul to the dead: a message of the movie for a country struggling to come up with new ways for not abandoning its ancestors.

ENDEX

The first time I attend ENDEX it is summer 2017, the fourth year of its operation. In the middle of August, the height of Tokyo humidity and heat, I take the monorail from downtown and am dislodged at a station perched high in the sky with glass walls on either side. Fitting for Odaiba, this island artificially built from landfill, with a sense of both spaciousness and play quite at odds with the frenzied density of the city just fifty minutes away. The structures here, while huge, are spread far apart, and the spaces in between sport interesting things: a towering Ferris wheel in the distance, a "life-size" Gundam robot sixty-five feet high, Odaiba's very own Statue of Liberty standing in the water. Joining the streams of commuters exiting from a host of stations in the vicinity, we all pour into a gargantuan plaza, many, like me, headed for Tokyo Big Site. The concrete is wide and open; the glare of the sun strong. But the walkways are threaded with sprinklers spraying walkers with a cool shower of mist. At the Big Site itself, huge buildings have been divided into geographical zones. I find my entrance— East Wing, first floor—and enter the doors into the convention center, another cavernous space. Grabbing coffee and making my way to ENDEX, at the entrance booth I meet a fellow anthropologist, Hannah Gould, who is finishing her fieldwork on the *butsudan* industry in Japan.¹⁴ Signing in and grabbing our free entry badges, we head onto the floor. Where things are lively right off the bat.

As advertised, this is "an exhibit for the services, equipment, and facilities pertaining to *shūkatsu* involving memorial (*kuyō*), burial, and funerals." Accordingly, the floor is divided into seven zones: gravestones and memorial stones, Buddhist altars and equipment for temples and shrines, burials and memorials, equipment and services for funerals and memorial ceremonies, bereavement for survivors, Shintō shrines and Buddhist temples, and pet funerals and memorials. Many booths are brightly decked out, with staff dispensing pamphlets and information, and some staging demos or enactments. Whether promoted by long-standing companies or new upstarts seeking to get into the trade, the goods and services represent a vast spectrum from classical and traditional to digital and new-style, with a sizable portion offering blended options—novel variants of the old. Like headstones for what would be traditional graves in the ground, but designed here out of luminescent art glass that shines iridescently no matter the season or time of day, offering the dead spirit a "fourth place" to sleep peacefully. This is called *hikaribo*—a shining grave that reconceptualizes the grave's place from one of giving respect to ancestors to something luminescent for the deceased herself. There are beautiful porcelain urns by Koransha, a reputable company in the business, designed in multiple colors and shapes including purple irises. And "respectful rice," small packets of organic rice to place inside butsudan as offerings to feed the spirit(s) of the deceased. "Handheld memorials" (*temoto kuyō*) to hold onto a few cremains for those choosing to scatter ashes (*sankotsu*) are a notable trend here as well. One of these, "pearl of life" (*inori no shinju*), grinds ashes into a pearl with a price tag of ¥250,000 yen ($2,400). Another alternative (then one year away from launching) goes in the opposite direction: sending cremains in rockets to outer space (*sankotsu uchū*). Designed by NTP (Nippon Trans Pacific Corporation), ten people had already signed up in 2017.

Reflecting a bounty of innovative design, the products and services are driven by the marketplace, which itself is driven by current conditions and trends. But of particular interest to me is how stalwart, if reconfigured, the continuity of some semblance of both ritual and sociality seems to be. As in Fenestra, a "digital memento" revamping the *butsudan*, designed by Uriu Daisuke, an engineer and anthropologist who wrote his dissertation on traditional death practices. In a technological device outfitted with a wirelessly connected mirror, photo frame, and electronic candle, the living can

2.1 *Hone Pods* (bone pods): cat- and dog-themed urns displayed at ENDEX, a national convention for those in the Ending Business.

access memories of the deceased, which, pulled onto the screen, give the affect/effect of interacting with the dead. And they can do so, as the company promoting Fenestra points out, with a highly compact, portable device extremely user-friendly for anyone (Uriu and Okude 2010). As Japan/ese face the ebbing of the traditional family grave and funeral system, it is better to come up with new forms of mortuary practice than to lose the means to mourn altogether, Uriu tells us when Hannah and I meet him for lunch our first day at ENDEX. This, too, would seem to be the gist of the reporting that, closely following the convention, tells the story of the handling of death getting animated in the face of a loss that, for some Japanese and for the country at large, is becoming harder to memorialize.

An air of excitement greets us in the morticians' contest (*nōkanshi kontesto*/納棺師コンテスト), one of several events, demonstrations, and seminars conducted over the course of the three-day convention to generate public interest. This one has triggered considerable buzz, as we can tell by all the press passes and cameras strategically placed throughout the room.

Staged by Okuribito Academy, a training school for morticians that materialized in the wake of *Okuribito* and whose founder trained the film's actors, the contest is a marriage of pop culture and business. Things are arranged as if for a fashion show: a big basket of flowers on the floor, a mic at the front where emcees will narrate the entire affair, two huge screens where the audience can watch the detail of action, and a stage neatly set with four pallets where the four contestants will compete in two rounds, fifteen minutes each, of preparing corpses for departure by re-dressing them from one set of clothes to another.

The two emcees, smartly attired, take up their positions and start promptly. Both teachers at Okuribito Academy, they begin by explaining the profession and rules of the contest, then introduce us to the three judges and four contestants (all women, though we later learn that men and women are equally represented in the profession today). Handiwork is important here, so we're told to look at the huge screens for better viewing. Each contestant stands in front of their corpse, played by living people doing their best to mimic the dead. As the clock starts, they set off: shifting the body from *yukata* to dress clothes of white shirt, dark pants or skirt, and suit jacket in the first instance and from *yukata* to funereal kimono in the second. To the cello strains of the *Okuribito* music score, the event is played for high drama as the contestants move quickly, massaging arms and legs; moving limbs into and out of sleeves, pantlegs, jacket, or kimono; adding socks and ties; and finally crossing the feet and wrapping the hands around Buddhist beads (*juzu*). As the emcees tell us, the trick is not to show any flesh in the process (as this would disrespect those before whom this would be done in real life), and to move efficiently but discretely, with "feeling" (*kimochi*). Assessing the correctness of what has been done, the judges climb on stage after each round and pull out sleeves, check on buttonholes, and lift up pant legs to look at the socks underneath. In the end, the winner, a woman in her thirties and a graduate of Okuribito Academy, has been selected for both the deftness of her movements and the polite feelings rendered in executing them. As she cries with emotion, the audience exhales in delight. At spectating a ritual reformulated here in a commodity form for popular dissemination.

A Japanese version of *American Idol*, performed not in song but in care given the dead, the mood here is at once lighthearted and earnest. Playfulness, as I discover in the course of fieldwork on *shūkatsu*, need not be at odds with the subject of death. Indeed, this is what a Buddhist priest who designed, and now carries out, memorial services for robotic

2.2 Demonstrating the work of a mortician at the booth run by Okuribito Academy at ENDEX.

dogs has said motivated him as well. Showing respect for the capacity of robots to evoke surprise, charm, and a sense of playfulness in their interactions with humans, Ōi Bungen, a priest at the rural Nichiren Temple in Chiba, agreed to give memorial services for AIBO robotic dogs now debilitated by old age (White and Katsuno 2021). Released by Sony Computer Science Laboratories in 1996, the AI dogs were highly popular and much loved by those who acquired them. But when Sony stopped producing them in 2006, users were left with aging machines. A former employee, Norimatsu Nobuyuki, set up a repair business to service them (called A-Fun) and sought an "interesting" priest who would perform *kuyō* on now-defunct AIBO to release their spirits in order for parts (called organs) to be harvested as replacements for other repairs (White and Katsuno 2021, 241).[15] Recognizing how deeply attached humans had become to their mechanical pets, Ōi drew on what he saw as a sense of life transcending the human-machine border by offering a ceremony, personally crafted to incorporate both the old and the new, that uniquely emphasized feelings (*jikkan*) in this memorializing of death. But playfulness is at heart of the religiosity proffered here. As Norimatsu explained to the two anthropologists studying the phenomenon, amusement is what drew consumers to

THE POPULAR INDUSTRY OF DEATH   67

their AIBO, and it is also what made AIBO part of the family.¹⁶ Amusement too, is what inspired his idea for an AIBO *kuyō*, as it did for the Buddhist priest who felt this best recognized the life within the robotic machine of the Buddha spirit transcending a divide between the human and artificial (White and Katsuno 2021, 241). A sense of delight that is also deadly serious.

This, too, is the mood at the morticians' contest. The audience is palpably amused but also riveted to the details of what is transpiring on the stage. We scrutinize what is being done to the corpses on their pallets, leaning into rather than away from what once would have been regarded with disgust. But it is less truth being sought—as in Rembrandt's famous painting of 1632, *The Anatomy Lesson of Dr. Nicolaes Tulp*, of a corpse being dissected by an early anatomist—as something else. The "politeness" and "feelings" of a death worker on display, (re)making this profession into something palatable, trendy, and cool. Not high-end fashionable; more the kind of affective labor that can be bought and sold these days in the marketplace of endingness. And packaged here with attributes (time, precision) that can be quantified for sale.

The contest over, I leave the room with the energy still simmering. Immediately outside is the booth set up by Okuribito Academy, staffed by a bevy of remarkably young, handsome men, all stylishly dressed. They could be celebrities (*tarento*), looking as they do like the lead actor of *Okuribito*. Working the crowd, they amiably reach out, inviting folks to take brochures for the training program to become morticians. In a trade that can take as little as three months to pick up, they are the ones who embody the new spirit of this profession—called *ikumen* in their promotional material, referring to a nonmacho type of man who can dispense care (by cooking, raising children, or, in this case, tending to the dead) with feminine sensitivity.

Things are hopping but my attention is drawn to the action down the hall. A crowd has already gathered for what my program announces is one of three demonstrations today introducing Pepper, SoftBank's humanoid robot, performing here as robotic Buddhist priest. Pepper itself is not new. Designed by SoftBank as what it calls the world's first social humanoid robot able to recognize faces and basic human emotions, Pepper has been on the market since 2015 (where it can be purchased for $8,800, or leased) and is a familiar presence in Japan. I had seen one just days before at the company's Harajuku main store and would encounter it again at Narita International Airport, where it directs visitors leaving the country through immigration. It is sold as a prosthetic stand-in for human workers and has been deployed in sushi restaurants, hotel lobbies, and pharmacies as a greeter. But Son Masayoshi, the CEO of SoftBank, whose investment oversaw the design and launching of Pepper, always primarily intended the robot to "stay close to, talk to, and entertain people" (quoted in Nishimura 2021). It was to address a labor shortage but also the social problem of communication in Japan that Son implemented its development in the first place, announcing that the "world's first robot with emotion" offered a solution to what he saw as the spreading problem of solitude among Japanese. With its qualities of "humanlike kindness and love," the hope was that Pepper would bring happiness to people, fomenting a form of connection through its stylized communication that would be both entertaining and warm.

Today, Pepper is communicating affectively and effectively. Dressed in proper robes, intoning sutras in its singsongy mechanical voice, the robot is charming and cute with a face that has large, manga-like eyes and a mouth that is more like a dot. The crowd is entranced, exclaiming—as those around me do in loud voices—that the performance resonates with a fidelity they find authentic (enough). Meanwhile, the (human) priest sitting behind the robot and ringing the bell is all but ignored, as Pepper performs under a banner reading "Do-It-Yourself Funeral (*jibun de sōgi*): Pepper." The promotional materials call this "an IT revolutionary solution," proposing that, for customers who otherwise lack access to a priest (because they aren't parishioners or don't want to pay the high cost of offerings at a temple that may be inconveniently located in the countryside), Pepper could become an affordable, flexible alternative. For, as the text continues, while the institutions that once enveloped mortuary processes—the parishioner system and family grave—are diminishing, the desire to maintain some iteration of Buddhist rituals remains strong. Here it is provided robotically in what could be thought of as a proxy for the social apparatuses now gone. A "survival," as early anthropologists termed practices that outlive the institutions or conditions that called them into being, yielding a structural lag or what Harry Harootunian (2009) calls uneven temporalities in the everydayness of practice. That is handled as well, as Keiko Nishimura notes in her doctoral dissertation on the subject, through the playfulness Pepper evokes. Play (*asobi*), as she points out, refers not only to the affect conjured up by interactions with the robot but also to something spatial—the space between linked parts that places restraints on, by allowing for a flexibility of, structure (Nishimura 2021, 32). This, like the morticians contest, the memorial service for AIBO, and almost all the businesses and products being promoted at ENDEX, engages in a playfulness that is opening up the work and care surrounding death in ever new—marketable, consumable, flexible—ways.

In the case of Pepper, the event at ENDEX 2017 was more a pilot staged in the realm of the possible. At the time, it had only appeared in a memorial service (*ireisatsu*) put on by Nissei Eco that spring. Still, it portended the future of extending into the transhuman the work of humanizing death—something also envisioned in a play following the compound disaster of 3.11 staged with a robot that walked along the coast giving memorial to the dead washed out to sea (Otsuki 2019). Even though there has been pushback by some Buddhist practitioners on the grounds that a machine can't subjectively experience the emotions needed to correctly perform these ritual sutras, robots have been deployed elsewhere to aid in spiritual affairs, including at a temple to explain matters of Buddhism to visitors. Filling in the gap of an emptying in death making both threatening and already happening across the country in the twenty-first century due to sociologies, economics, and trends in grave keeping.

CONCLUSION

Gojira configured a particular kind of threat posed to Japan/ese. In the form of an ancient beast triggered by nuclear testing done by Americans, it bolted out of Tokyo Bay on a path of destruction as a mutant with powers foreshadowing changes the country, too, would undergo. On the artificial landfill where ENDEX stages its convention for the ending business, a different kind of threat—more domestic, threaded around homes, graves, and the cusp of living and dying with(out) others—is invoking its own responses, some as technofuturist yet tethered to tradition as Gojira. One sees playfulness at work in such new innovations as Pepper and the morticians' contest, too, signaling an imagination tempered to contemporary times for dealing with the problem of "family-less dead."

preparations

Their significance is visibly decreasing. We can no longer speak of everlasting memory and the veneration of our forebears. On the contrary: the dead must now be cleared out of the way as quickly and comprehensively as possible.

W. G. Sebald, *Campo Santo* (2005)

The kanji for burial is made up of the kanji for death (死 *shi*) sandwiched between two characters for "grass" (草 *kusa*) at the top and bottom. We can extrapolate from this that at the time the kanji for burial 葬 was conceived, the practice of burying the dead was to abandon the corpse among the meadow grasses.

Shinmon Aoki, *Coffinman* (2002)

caring (differently) for the dead

Even Tokyo slows down during Obon, the season of greeting and revisiting the dead. It is August 2013, and I am traveling with a fellow professor at a local university to a cemetery at the edge of town. She has asked me to accompany her on the visit today, knowing that I am newly interested in matters of death. As she tells me of her grandmother's generation, these rituals were once stitched into the everyday.

People died at home, were buried close to rice fields, and their spirits communed with at household altars, where incense and offerings were replenished daily. But now that 85 percent of Japanese expire in a hospital, close to half have remains that wind up somewhere other than in a family grave, and the traditional *butsudan* is getting abandoned. Still, while contemporary Japanese are less tethered to the land and their ancestors buried there, paying homage this time of year to the dead remains salient nonetheless. As this plays out in households across the country and in the national imaginary itself, ritual gatherings of family around the dead reiterate a sense of belonging—to a place, to others, to a continuity beyond the here and now. An iconic expression of Japaneseness itself.

Japanese come together around traditional cultural practices at New Year (Oshōgatsu) as well. Rigorously cleaning the house and heading to Buddhist temples at midnight to purge the buildup of earthly sins by ringing the bell 108 times for the 108 earthly sins in Buddhist doctrine, people then head off to eat noodles for longevity and spend days visiting family and friends to share glutinous rice balls (mochi) and special foods. Obon, by contrast, celebrates the dead who, having departed to another world (*anoyo*), are welcomed back for two days at summer's end (mid-August) to the homes and relations they once inhabited. In customs whose traces still linger across the country, the dead are brought back through relations with the living—the kin who fetch them at the grave, show them the way with lanterns, and have them ride atop carefully crafted cucumber horses and eggplant cows. Then, two days later, the spirits are gently but insistently escorted away, sometimes by the glowing light of lotus boats floated out to sea. Rituals of repetition and return pulsate this time of year throughout the country, even in the cities, where collectivities (neighborhoods, work groups) thread through the streets, dancing to drums (*bon-odori*) and carrying portable shrines to energized crowds in a celebration that rehearses communality. An animation inspired by the dead.

The spirits, too, fold back into a vitalism continuing forward—but only if they have intimates to carry this out. "Practice of concern," anthropologist John Traphagan (2004) calls this moral apparatus of tending to the dead by acts of caregiving (*mitoru, mimamoru*)—visiting the grave, tending daily to the domestic altar, performing ceremonial rituals as at Obon—that he considers to be constitutive of what stands for religion in a country where most don't identify as religious at all. Sociality is what renders these practices sacred. Its absence makes for something bordering on the profane.

On this day, the temple is quiet. We are the only visitors to the cemetery, and Maia finds the grave she is seeking with ease. As she anticipated, the plot is unkempt—the telltale sign of neglect by family members who should be tending it: a wife and stepson, in this case. "Just as I suspected," she says under her breath as she greets the friend, a former colleague, buried there. Pressing hands together and bowing her head, she quickly sets to straightening things. Weeds are pulled, pebbles swept away, dead twigs tossed, and water—after I have fetched it from a faucet nearby—poured over the gravestone in a gesture of purification that recreates the flow of water from the mountaintop to the base (Danely 2014, 73). Meanwhile, she speaks softly, communicating with her friend. She mentions a recent retirement at work (*Should we replace him or make do without?*), how she's been doing this year

(*Apart from a bout of flu, pretty good*), and the visitor she has brought here today (*Anne-san has come here, too; aren't you pleased?*). The flowers she carries are put in stone vases on the grave and two bunches of incense kindled, then placed in the altar box underneath. Then she lights a cigarette, puffing briefly, telling me that this is fine because he liked to smoke, too. Bending to pull a few weeds, she sweeps the stones again in front of the grave and looks up and down the row of gravesites. Finally, exhaling purposefully, Maia brings her hands together and bows once again. I follow her lead and then we walk off.

The visit has been good, and Maia tells me she is happy she has come. But it is not her place to be tending the grave, as the priest keeps telling her. Yet those whose duty it is—the designated ritual successors (*moshu*)—are being remiss. And Maia bears her own guilt in not being more attentive to her friend when, due to cuts at the university that affected his research, he fell into a deep depression. He joined the ranks of those committing suicide in the wake of the economic decline. The number of suicides, which peaked in 1998 at 33,000, has remained troublingly high (about 30,000 per year) since then. Another sign, like the almost equal number (33,000) of those who die lonely deaths every year, of what some pronounce the dissolution of the social bonds (*muen shakai*/無縁社会) once at the heart of Japanese culture. The very culture ritualized in this season of Obon in these spaces of family burial grounds.

Leaving the cemetery, we see the plot assigned to the disconnected dead. In a corner of the graveyard labeled 無縁墓 (*muenbo*) the grass is overgrown and there are no offerings (or containers for them) of any kind. Most cemeteries have these plots, Maia tells me. "Just look for where things are a mess." Of course. Composed from the characters for lacking (*mu*/無), connection (*en*/縁), and grave (*haka*/*bo*/墓), *muenbo* is the collective plot for the untended (*muenbotoke*, "disconnected buddhas"). The likely fate for her own friend, Maia tells me that day, despite her efforts to tidy his grave and tend to his soul. As the priest tells her, it is up to the man's closest kin do the memorial rites and pay the temple's annual maintenance fees. Because they fail to do so, the deceased will soon become an abandoned soul, which means his remains will eventually be moved from the family grave, where he is marked by name (family name and posthumous Buddhist name, or *kaimyō*) on a mortuary tablet of his own, to the grave for the disconnected, where his ashes will commingle with others and his identity will become both collective and unknown.

Just as she couldn't keep her friend tethered to life, Maia can't save him from abandonment in death. And, as I will learn when interviewing the priest years later, such cases of unaffiliated dead (*muenbotoke*) have rapidly increased recently in Japan; his temple used to have one or two cases a year but now it is between ten and twenty. As he told me in 2018, "This year at Obon, I realized that our columbarium for the disconnected was totally full. These are the people without anyone to depend on (*miyori ga nai*). Or they might have families, but their families have refused to claim their remains or maintain their graves." While his temple still had 104 families of parishioners (*danka*), 10 percent of those lacked successors; even the successors who do exist may well not want to continue the practice of maintaining the grave, the priest continued. As he summed up, "While communing (*tsukiai*) with ancestors was once part of everyday life, today people prioritize their own lifestyles and tending to the grave may well be considered a nuisance they would prefer to avoid, both for themselves and for their children, should they have any." Communing, tending, caregiving, obligation: these are all tropes of the social. What does it mean when these turn into burdens or fail to extend to increasingly many who fall outside the net?

This is a dilemma my colleague faces as well, as she related on the slow train ride back to Tokyo. A single woman with no children and no siblings to provide successors or caregivers for the family grave after she is gone, she didn't know what arrangements should be made. For, without fees being paid, the grave would become abandoned, and all its remains (hers and those of all family members) would eventually be removed and reburied in the cemetery plot for the disconnected—exactly the fate awaiting her friend. How to ensure postmortem care for not only herself but the rest of her already dead ancestors is something she is pondering still.

....

As anthropologists have said about gift exchange and feminists about interdependence, no one can survive (strictly or forever) autonomously, and the movement—of goods, acts, care—between persons is what sustains life both materially and symbolically: the very ontological grounding of the social across the difference of arrangements it is given in specific places and times. Death is exemplary here; how can the deceased bury their own body or keep the memory of themselves alive into a future in which they no longer physically exist (Butler 2009)? The dead call on the caregiving of others. If they are to matter. Which means mattering to someone other than the self, into a temporality beyond the here and now.

But when caregiving is so narrowly circumscribed to a social unit and form of recognition tied to what Thomas Laqueur (2015) calls the necronominalism of naming the dead (by, in this case, paternal kin), those deprived of such bonds become uncared-for souls. A deficit in care that strains what has long been the icon of Japan's relational culture: respect for the ancestors, the grounding of the emperor system, a genealogy of sacredness running back a legendary 2,600 years. For some, this has meant challenging the necessity of funerals and burials, as does religious scholar Shimada Hiroshi, who finds these rituals anachronistic and a burden that weighs most heavily on those with limited financial and social means to launch them (see Shimada 2014). But what I am interested in here is how this very notion of caregiving the dead by a specified other—a contract between the living and dead that has been constituted through relations of work, locale, or kin—is being redesigned and reimagined but rarely totally abandoned in the contemporary sociological and demographic landscape of Japan.

Deploying feminist concepts of care, I consider how both care and the relationality attending it are shifting, sometimes quite radically, in Japan today. Extending Berenice Fischer and Joan Tronto's classic definition of care as "everything we do to maintain, continue, and repair our world so that we can live in it as well as possible in a complex, life sustaining web" (1990, 40) into the management of death, I track how arranging new sustaining webs of caregiving come to resemble and reassemble sociality in alternative forms. This includes opening up to new others for caregiving the self as well as tasking to the self the very job once assigned others of being cared for after death. But to what extent is the older social form of and for grievability—the genealogical principle—being critiqued and transformed today in the face of its failure to adequately care for the dead? As Lisa Stevenson has said in another context, when one moves away from categorical reckoning—as in not aligning with the categories that accord recognition—what is needed are other gestures of compassion. She cites the author-artist John Berger speaking about the nineteenth-century painter Théodore Géricault, whose portraits of men in an asylum depict something of beauty in them other than their clinical labels (schizophrenic, for example). Géricault sought to understand them by a different name, "the name of their soul" (Stevenson 2020, 10). A recognition which is otherwise, stemming from a gesture of care.

Maia, too, extended a gesture of care in visiting her friend in the grave. But in a system of recognition where only successors and kin "count" as legitimate grievers of the deceased, the dead are consigned to the fate of the ungrievable (*muenbotoke*) when the wiring of their social armature doesn't fit. But what would it mean for mortuary care to be designed differently—both the work itself and who does it? This is what I consider here.

CARING FOR THE ANCESTORS: OBON AT A RURAL TEMPLE

Looking at the ways in which the fabric of necrointimacy—the social warp and woof of managing death—are getting reshaped, I step first into more traditional terrain. This is Obon as conducted in a village where the tradition of welcoming spirits of the dead back to earth is carried out in the context of longstanding ties to ancestors, to a local temple, to land on which a family has lived for generations. While not an expert on village Japan or Buddhism (on which this story hinges), I describe one episode of accompanying a Buddhist priest on his rounds to the homes of parishioners during Obon 2018, kindly arranged by anthropologist Michael Berman and generously acceded to by a priest with whom he underwent interfaith chaplaincy training (*rinshō*) to listen to, empathize with, and spiritually treat victims following 3.11. This "practice of concern" of honoring the dead, in Traphagan's (2004) terminology, is illustrative of a model that makes care both the responsibility and keepsake of the domestic household linked to the village, the temple, and the nation-state. What happens to this model and how care of the dead shifts when the relationality on which it depends is no longer available or gets replaced by something or someone else is what I attend to in the rest of the chapter.

Nenge-san Ryōshinji is a beautiful Zen temple in Shimizu City, Shizuoka Prefecture. Having traveled an hour and a half on the *shinkansen* from Tokyo station, then taking a local train and a cab to our final destination, Michael and I arrive shortly before noon. We've prepared for what Michael has told me is a rare privilege: accompanying a priest on his annual visitation of parishioners and the altars they've set up for the dead in their homes. I've brought a straw hat for the sun; Michael has brought small treats for the ancestors and personal notes to their families all the way from the States. With a huge smile, joyous in the reunion with Michael, Katsuno Shubin greets us when we find him walking by a lovely Kannon statue next to a small columbarium (*nōkotsudō*) outside. He points to the columbarium, where a plaque reads "Residents of Shimizu City who honorably receive eternal memorial (*eitaikuyō*) from Kannon"—a sign that the deceased interred here lack successors to care for them. I'm surprised that, even here in front of the temple, this innovation on burial is so openly practiced. But, as we'll learn throughout the hours that we're in his company, the challenges of staying afloat and managing a small temple in the countryside are considerable these days. The times are demanding, calling for adaptation in a host of ways, including serving his community beyond just tending to the dead—the task with which Buddhism is primarily associated as the "religion of death." Accordingly, after he introduces himself by name, Katsuno hands me a business card with pictures of six activities his temple now offers, including *zazen*, yoga, and community meals. But the importance given the place of the dead, not only today but in everything we're told and shown of the temple's operation, is made clear from the start.

Effusive and smart, bubbly and warm, Katsuno keeps chattering all day long, even when we start the hard pace of our rounds. Forty-four years old and having undergone the rigors of Rinzai training for six and a half years after university, he took over this priestship from his father. After showing us the main altar in the *hondō* with its beautiful 340-year-old gold statue of Shakyamuni, then taking us to a back room that holds the black lacquered spirit tablets (*ihai*) of the ancestors (*senzo*), Katsuno tells us that his father was commissioned by his sect to become abbot (*jūshoku*) here at the end of the war. The temple had been left stranded when the previous *jūshoku*, ordered to serve in the military, died with no successor in place. His picture, along with those of other soldiers, line one wall. Among the spirit tablets otherwise lacquered in black stand a few in gold, marked by a star indicating they are heroic spirits (*eirei*) of war dead. They ought, Katsuno tells us, to be given a privileged position. Here, though, because he adopts the principle that all dead are treated equally, they are not placed in the front. Rather, they become part of what seems to be a community—row upon row of tablets embodying spirits—in this darkened room that nonetheless alludes to life: "living becomes a memorial service" (生きることが供養になる), reads a banner on the wall. As we watch the priest's son bring in small trays containing dishes of pickled cucumber, sliced melon, and rice, we see that all the spirits are fed special foods for Obon.

The ancestors dwell here, cushioned in the belly of the temple. Sitting on the other side of the main hall (*hondō*) where most services are conducted, across a wide-open room where activities of various kinds take place, is the altar to another kind of dead: the wandering "hungry ghosts" (*segaki*/施餓鬼). In contrast to the ancestors, these beings have no place of their own. Stacked with towels, bottles of oil, melons, and colorful pieces of material dangling from sticks, small trays of food have been set out here, too, along with *sotoba*—wooden memorial tablets written in Sanskrit for the dead.

3.1 A flag beckoning wandering ghosts to the safe haven they will find at Nenge-san Ryōshinji Zen Temple, Shizuoka.

At the border between inside and out, these gifts signal to all spirits that the temple is welcoming and safe. So does the flagpole outside whose colorful pennants can be seen from afar. During Obon many temples erect such beacons to signal to the displaced dead an opening even for those not tied to the temple through intergenerational membership. As Katsuno explains to us over a lunch of cold noodles, he is committed to extending the operations of the temple even further: to a clientele beyond parishioners and to treating issues of life, not only death. There are 150 parishioners here (30 without successors, some of whom will be buried in the Kannon *nōkotsudō* out front), but there has been a drop-off in both activity and offerings ever since the 2008 financial crisis. Without animating the temple in other ways, its continued viability may be at risk—a possibility that this progressive priest seems remarkably sanguine about (adding that whether or not his twelve-year-old son starts training to succeed him will be the boy's choice and not that of the parishioners).

But we are running late because of all our chatting and need to embark on animation of a different sort: the practice of communicating with the ancestors (*senzo to komyunikēshon*)—the heart of the temple, crystallized in the rituals of Obon, as Katsuno's mother puts it. Katsuno showers, then grabs three umbrellas and announces our route: forty households across three neighborhoods starting with the nearest, which is both the newest and most middle class. In drenching humidity that turns quickly into a downpour, the three of us set off in this circulation of parishioners' homes to greet the ancestors.

Katsuno announces our arrival at the front door of each house. "*Tera desu yo*," ("It's the temple"), he belts out, walking in after shedding umbrella and shoes. He reminds everyone that he's asked their permission ahead of time for the two of us (identified as American professors studying religion and Obon) to accompany him and asks again if it's all right (all answer yes), then marches to the altar. Sometimes these are the *butsudan* that stay up year-round, but more often they are the specially arranged *saidan* for Obon. Covered in brightly colored brocade with a Buddha centrally placed, the altars are inhabited by ancestors (signaled by photos [遺影写真] and memorial tablets) and assembled with items to both honor and feed them: lanterns and flowers to the side, tiered shelves holding stacked mochi, trays of other assorted foods such as nectarines, a glass of water or cans of beer, and a cucumber horse and eggplant cow (*shōryōma*/精霊馬) to help transport the spirits to and from the house.

Given a *zabuton* (Japanese cushion), Katsuno kneels in front of the altar. We sit similarly, off to one side or behind, with family members, and are soon told to put our hands together in prayer. Katsuno starts intoning the sutras. Ten, twelve minutes, speaking as if singing, the melodic sounds of Buddhist prayer. When finished, he lights incense and asks the family if Michael and I can burn some as well to the ancestors. All say sure, some adding that the ancestors will certainly be pleased. Inching over on our knees, we light incense, clasp hands together, and bow our heads, down and up again. When done, the two of us offer our small gifts, which are put on the altar for the ancestors, then we all get up. There is banter back and forth, usually the offer of cold drinks and possibly more (yogurt and blueberries; sushi at one house, which we decline), and exchanges about the details of the families assembled, which vary from elderly singles to couples of all ages and families with kids. Each household is different: some are deeply respectful during the ritual, but in the home of an older couple the man leaves the room as soon as we get there and the *obaasan* keeps the television on (which Katsuno has to ask her—twice—to turn off). With all, the priest is friendly and warm, complimenting the children at one house for practicing *zazen* at the temple and being kidded by an older woman for being so "splendid" (*rippa*) and "cute" (*kawaii*). In one home, we're taken to an adjacent room to see five photos of the ancestors, including one in a soldier's uniform. "They're with us now," the man beams. In another, we feel the presence of death; Katsuno confirms that the pretty fifty-year-old lost her husband this year. Two doors down, the stillness we sense stems from a suicide. But in another household, with stacks of food on the table and at least twenty people of all ages gathered, life abounds. "Join in!" they urge.

But the priest is on a tight schedule, having gotten a late start. He jumps up after a few minutes, saying "Gotta go, or I'll never make it." Handed an envelope of offering (or sometimes, just taking it from the altar saying "This, I'll handle it"), the *jūshoku* is ushered to the entrance, thanked, and given good wishes—as are we. Then, we're off again on this reverse pilgrimage: not visiting a sacred spot but taking it to parishioners in their homes, thereby sanctioning the sacredness assembled there with the ancestors during Obon. Anointing this most everyday of spots that, particularly today, feeds the dead as much as the living in a relationality that, repeating every year, is also intended to forever go on.

While Katsuno will continue, Michael and I leave close to 6 p.m. having completed sixteen of the forty homes on the route. This ends what has been, for me, an overwhelming experience: communing with the living communing with the dead. My knees are aching from all the kneeling and my body has been drenched by the hours of heat and rain on our trek. But beyond that is the intimacy shared, and shown, by everyone opening up their homes and ancestors to us strangers on this most revered of domestic occasions. An extraordinary day with an exceptional priest who made all of this possible by bridging the uneven temporalities of a present both continuous and discontinuous with the past (Harootunian 2019). Supremely energetic but uncommonly down-to-earth, Katsuno Shubin smiles broadly when bidding us adieu by the side of the road. His mother will be fetching us shortly for the drive back to the train station. But the temple priest heads up the road to tend to the ancestors waiting there.

PREPARING THE SELF FOR DEATH

On a blistering day in July, I board the first train on what will be a multi-step trip to the outskirts of Tokyo. Things slow down right away in a delay caused by a "human incident," meaning a suicide attempt by someone jumping in front of the train.[1] A foreshadowing of my mission today, which is to join a luncheon conversation on the subject of death held for members of what is essentially an alternative burial association. By rerouting when I get to Shinjuku and taking a taxi from my last train stop, I miraculously arrive where I'm going on time. These are the offices of Ending Center, situated at the edge of Izumi Jōen in Machida, a beautiful Buddhist cemetery studded with cherry trees where the burial grounds of the nonprofit are located. Inoue Haruyo, the founder and director of Ending Center, has been peering out the upstairs window waiting for my arrival and rushes out when she sees me, laughing at how sweaty and (almost) late I am. Offering to share her huge umbrella for the sun, we head off to One More Home (*mō hitotsu no wagaya*)—the converted house Ending Center uses for its get-togethers in a residential neighborhood two blocks away.

Perennially peppy and warm, Inoue has long been a critic, and reformer, of Japan's succession principle (*keishō seido*). A writer earlier in her career, her first book argued against Japan's policy that married couples must have the same family name. Then, when her mother died at age sixty-two without a grave to enter—her husband, a second son, had not yet purchased a grave for himself and his family, but she was prevented from entering her natal family's by having changed her last name—Inoue learned how *keishō seido* plays out at the time of death. Coming to see how it systematically makes women, and some men, "relationless" (*muen ni naru*), Inoue teamed up with Ogawa Eiji, the head priest at Myōkōji Temple in Niigata, who established the first alternative burial ground not dependent on *keishō seido* at his temple in 1989. Together the two ran the Association to Think about the Relationality of Graves in the Twenty-First Century through the 1990s. Inoue returned to school in sociology and has become a professor, a leading advocate for the "human rights of the dead" (*shisha no jinken*), and a practitioner helping those facing dying and time after death without the help of family—what feminist critic Ueno Chizuko (2015) calls "care refugees" (*kea nanmin*). To this end, in 1989 Inoue established Ending Center, a citizen's group aimed at the realization of a dignified funeral and death (*songenaru shi to sōsō no jitsugen wo mezasu*), which has now evolved into a registered nonprofit with burial grounds of its own (Inoue 2012).

Ending Center offers postmortem services called "cherry blossom departures" (*sakurasō*), held in a natural setting according to a calculus of inclusion independent of the succession system. These are the two most common reasons for those who choose to be buried here, Inoue tells me the first time I interview her. And the two logics blur. The dead commune with nature in a burial ground where this and other forms of companionship supplement or replace genealogical ties. The dead are never alone here, the Ending Center brochure points out, because they are accompanied by a network of relatedness that Inoue calls inclusive relationality (*ketsuen*/結縁) instead of the relationality formed by kinship (*ketsue*/血縁) or locale (*chien*/地縁). Unlike in public cemeteries and most religious cemeteries, which still stipulate that those buried within have a kin-based successor, the dead may be buried here alone or in other forms of relationship such as with a pet.[2] Inclusion also extends to a joint memorial service (*gōdōsaishi sakuramemoriaru*) that takes place annually in April (cherry blossom season) for those who died that year and for all those buried at Ending Center. Many of the to-be-deceased attend in anticipation of their own future there.

Today, the event is one in a series of symposia, activities, and get-togethers made available to all those who have registered to be buried at Ending Center (thereby becoming association members). As Inoue has told me, she conceptualizes the role of her nonprofit, and herself as its director, as a death midwife (*shi no josanpu*)—guiding clients through the emotionally wrought labor of preparing one's ending. For some members, as she relates on the walk to One More Home, this becomes a life sustaining activity. One man, a resident of Hokkaido, recently moved to Machida, in Tokyo, just to familiarize himself with the site where he would be buried and the "grave friends" who would be resting nearby. The luncheon today, organized as an open discussion with the director about any matter pertaining to death, attracts six women (three members plus Inoue, a staff person, and myself). The conversation will focus on care, as in how to care for oneself in preparing for death. This is how one woman explains her selection of Ending Center: Though married, she decided not to enter the cemetery of her husband's family, where her mother-in-law (with whom she had lived for decades) had been recently buried and where the resident ancestors "are distant and hold no meaning for me." Instead, she saved the small earnings from a part-time job for years to pay for her own site—a gift to herself. Her husband remains opposed but, since she paid for it herself, "*shikataga nai*"—there's nothing he can do. Inoue calls this act of becoming unrelated to her husband's family upon death "post-death divorce" (*shigo rikon*): a disconnection that, in this case, feels liberatory.

The second woman, who arrives elegantly dressed and carrying a beautiful vase for One More Home, is more concerned about the debilitating disease she has been struggling with for two years. It has stripped her of just about everything she once loved to do: going abroad, eating good food, enjoying alcohol, swimming long distances. Though never prone to darkness, she has wondered lately: is a life like this worth living? Once she begins, the words tumble quickly, going over—and over—what has been lost in an everydayness now so utterly bare. Finally, she sinks back exhausted in her chair and admits that she has never expressed these thoughts to anyone. Having listened attentively, Inoue now launches in. Rather than offering gestures of sympathy, she urges the woman to frankly address her feelings: to write about them, but not just in an effort to feel better through positive thinking. "Write about the dark feelings too," she advises; not turning away, but more mindfully inhabiting the present as it is. "Also, find an *ikigai* (purpose) for the day, whether doing the wash, taking a walk, or making lunch." Calling this "self-spiritual care" in English, Inoue explains by using the Japanese word *jikatsu* which, joining the characters for "self" and "activity," means self-sufficiency.

The emphasis here on both self and activity jibes with what I encountered time and time again in the course of my fieldwork on new practices and initiatives related to death management: *shūkatsu*, meaning literally the activity of ending. As if in a new way of conceptualizing the social contract, the object as well as subject of practicing concern for the dead is now the self. At once moralistic and caregiving, the expectation is for the self to do the work of "birthing" its death. This, as Inoue explained at another event at One More Home, has reorganized the work of the funeral.

Whereas once this was enacted as "proof" (*shōko*) that one was honoring the ancestors, today it ought to be more of a "wedding" with and for oneself. A startling idea, I remember thinking at the time, that embraces the beginning of a relationship, but not one with anyone else.

Speaking again to the woman, visibly wrought by the recounting she has given of the life she has so sorrowfully lost, Inoue exhorts her to turn her attentions elsewhere to become more accepting—by practicing daily "purposes"—of a life lived in the shadow of death. This makes death, as I take Inoue to mean, not an obstruction to life, but as a means, and method, for embracing the time any of us has left with care.³ Sitting at the table that day, a stone's throw from where everyone there (except me) would be buried, we are discussing mourning and loss, but also the everydayness of the present and how to spend it caring for and about something, including ourselves. That this is organized around the topic of death—what Inoue keeps exhorting us to face *now* by preparing—rather than avoiding it is what *shūkatsu* is all about. In this it is quite different from the sequestering of death that scholars like Philippe Ariès (1981), Elias Norbert (2009), and Anthony Giddens (1991) have said marks modern times: confining it to spaces (hospital, cemetery, morgue) that the modern subject encounters only when they wind up dying themselves, which is then a lonely experience.⁴ At One More Home, by contrast, a form of intimacy is being cultivated with oneself (and with grave friends) in the process of becoming closer to death. The practice, it felt to me, was one of "touching" (*fureai*), which is used often in targeting and addressing the loneliness of the aging in Japan these days (Nozawa 2015, 383), is coming less from another here than from the self.⁵ A relationship of togetherness; a marriage of sorts.

The third woman at the get-together—a lively seventy-five-year-old who has made today's lunch from homegrown vegetables and brought it here via over two hours on public transit—says that it is these friendships that comfort her when she thinks about time after death. "These are my friends. By becoming friends while alive, we can continue our friendship after death." One of those excluded from a family grave by divorce (her daughter will be buried in the family plot of her husband, an eldest son with access to his father's ancestral grave), she purchased a site at Ending Center eight years ago where she'll be buried alongside her favorite cat, whose ashes are already awaiting her in an urn kept at home. "I've had plenty of dark times," she tells me in our interview after lunch. She grew up poor, then struggled as a single mom in a job market that discriminated against women, but she now enjoys the small things in life: growing vegetables on her terrace and attending get-togethers like this. But when she dies, she wants to "become nothing" at all. As she puts it, "I wouldn't want to be a burden by making others remember me." Burdensome, she recalls, was the duty that befell her younger sister in tending to the *butsudan* of her mother-in-law for years. Rather than spread over time and between the generations, passing from ancestors to descendants, care for the dead compresses into something far more horizontal and presentist for her. A form of respect and honor that this woman is currying in the life she prioritizes in the present—"living is what is important"—and to ties of friendship that, cultivated now, will accompany her lightly into the grave. As we relish the okra salad, somen noodles, fresh tomatoes and basil, and shiso jelly she has prepared for us, we're told by a smiling Inoue that such a simple but delectable meal is what this woman standardly brings to outings at One More Home. Feeding us, instead of the ancestors, in a gesture of care.

One month later, in the heart of Obon season elsewhere in Japan (Obon in Tokyo occurs mid-July, instead of mid-August), One More Home is hosting its fourth "ending activity course" (*shūkatsu no kōza*) of the year. The twenty-five who attend (two-thirds women, the rest men), all members of Ending Center, are here to learn about "My Funeral, My Design." In a three-hour event, the main speaker is a member I had interviewed the week before in one of twelve conversations Inoue graciously set up for me in my summer of fieldwork. Tanaka's spouse is buried at Ending Center and she coordinates outings like this with visits to his grave.[6] Cutely dressed in red hat and blouse, Tanaka tells us how her decision to bury her husband here was made when he started getting sick almost a decade ago: liking the feel of Ending Center, she decided on the spot. But his family couldn't understand why she didn't follow the norms for burial in his family grave or for a more formal funeral (she chose a family-only one). Yet, as she tells us today, ending preparations should be done in a style that feels personally right; *jibunrashii* (one's own style) was her mantra throughout. As she shows us the scrapbook of family photos with which she has replaced the *butsudan* at home and the urn coverings she crafts as a hobby (urging any of us present to join her once a month), Tanaka treats the self-styling of mortuary arrangements as a practice of care as much as design.

This is also how the one salesperson there promotes her product (a line of ecological coffins): on the basis of not only its tri-wall pressed wood but the potential it offers for creative design. Lightweight and easy to maneuver, it can be artfully decorated, as she shows us by drawing messages all over the top, cinching the center with a beautiful obi, and wrapping the entire thing in skeins of batik. As she describes in the case of a friend who, lacking the money for a costly funeral, styled a coffin like this for her dying mother, the affective labor involved becomes a way of showing respect to the dead. A member offers her own bevy of design tips and invites everyone there to jump in as well. As the suggestions start to fly—small patches of cloth hand stitched with cherry blossoms, fabric tape in bright colors or more traditional blue—this is how the workshop ends. We all cluster around the display coffin that has become animated by the activity of preparing it, and those there, for future habitation. Is this a substitution, a stand-in, a fetish or icon for the others one no longer has for handling mortuary preparations (Roach 1996)? Like the mascot dolls soldiers wore during the war when they were far from home and deprived of other social arrangements when facing death (Schattschneider 2005), this coffin seems to perform work of both intimacy and care. And today, at least, it also provides another method of life to ease the ambiguity and anxiety of death in increasingly relationless times.

For the wrap-up to this workshop on designing "my end, my way," we're invited to try out the coffin for a test run (*nōkan no taiken*). As everyone there has done this multiple times, they all tell me to jump right in. When I do, the sixty seconds I spend inside feel decidedly long. But, once out, I am struck by the energy still resounding in the room of a group of aging seniors preparing for death in a social get-together with grave friends.

This is one response to the precarity of caregiving the dead in contemporary Japan.

REDESIGNING THE GRAVE

The grave is where the dead dwell in relationship to others. But given the danger today of being "without a place to go" (*ikiba ga nai*) at death—an expression I heard from a number of interviewees referring to the state of lacking a grave and kin to tend it—the social model that has sustained grave-tending in the past needs to be redesigned for necrohabitation. As design can be thought of as the tools and mechanisms adopted to inhabit and engage the world we live in, it not only responds to the conditions of the moment but also exerts what scholars of critical design studies call ontological and political effects (Escobar 2018). In speaking about anthropogenic climate change, Tony Fry, for example, has argued that the "defuturing" and "unsettlement" that all earthly beings are facing today due to human interference can only be countered by coming up with new designs for both habitation and being human. We "need to learn how to dwell another way, and to reinvent the collective structures that shape our lives and define our humanness" (Fry 2015, 88). Such a redesign of the human should be guided by an ethics of sustainability that, using a notion of care similar to that of feminists like Fischer and Tronto, Fry refers to as an ontology of care. That is, making more viable how a greater number of beings inhabit the world—in life but we could also say in death—versus upholding a system (prioritizing growth, accretion of material wealth, or genealogical belonging) enjoyed by only a privileged few.

Sustainability, as in opening up burial to those excluded from (or disliking) the succession model, is what an association like Ending Center offers its members. It does so on the basis of a new kind of collective, if transactional, sociality (the "flexible relationality" of others one accesses by becoming a paying member) and a different conception of care (more an accompaniment by lateral others than the performance of honor and respect by those vertically bound by kinship). This, too, implies a difference in the subjectivity given the deceased. Under the traditional system, spirits require time, ritual care labor performed by kin, and continuing attachment to a hierarchical family line to become ancestors (or, when inflected with Shintō, gods).[7] But those buried at Ending Center enter a state that is conceptualized in far more personal terms. Of the twelve members I interviewed, none had a firm notion of the spirit transpiring for long, or in a particular state, after death.[8] Yet all were comforted (*anshin*) in their plans to be buried in such a comfortable place loosely aligned with friendly others, whether nature, grave friends, or pets. Similarly, as anthropologist Kawano Satsuki (2011) discovered in her study of the Grave-Free Promotion Society of Japan, which since 1991 has promoted the scattering of ashes (*sankotsu*), the majority of those selecting this lack either a male successor, a family grave, or both. And while critics of the method see this as violating the ideals of family solidarity and continuity as embodied in the family grave, those who choose ash scattering envision that the soul or spirit returns to nature, thereby getting dispersed and absorbed into an entity far beyond the family and even humanity to which the individual belongs (Kawano 2011).

The same is true of tree burial (*jumokusō*), a practice that has gained considerable popularity of late (more than ash scattering, which, due to legal complications, has remained controversial) and has even been instituted by both public and private cemeteries as a nonfamilial, cheaper option than its family plots. Started in Japan by a Buddhist priest who, influenced by a similar practice in England, established a woodland cemetery named Ōhasama in the countryside that would also be invested in rehabilitation of forests (*satoyama*), tree burial involves direct interment of ashes into the earth in a hole that gets marked by a tree.⁹ As anthropologist Sébastien Boret learned in his ethnography on the subject, those who select this method are often, but not necessarily, without successors and find it appealing for the personal choice this gives them both in fashioning their postdeath dwelling and in offering new ways to bond with others. Despite its divergence from more normative practice, tree burial can be every bit as social. According to Boret, practitioners at Ōhasama are particularly serious about the philosophy of burial they adopt, and *jumokusō* has retained, by redesign, two core ideas of the generational grave and ancestor worship system: continuous bonds and collective well-being. Rather than bonds of kinship, practitioners form "intentional" relations (*shien*/支援) with each other and with nature: a sense of belonging that continues over time and is continually reasserted and restitched (through workshops, collective gatherings to rehabilitate the forests, joint memorials, and visits to the graves of others as well as to their own future grave sites). This also means that the to-be-deceased are actively involved in the care of their (own) mortuary arrangements. Settling on Ōhasama gave him great relief, one of his interviewees told Boret, both because this relieved his children from having to do anything and also because it ensured he would be buried and cared for in the way he wanted. For some, there is also the belief that being buried directly in the earth will incline their spirits (*reikon*) to rebirth as trees: a worldview reminiscent of Shintō to which 13 percent of Boret's respondents adhered (and 50 percent admitted wanting to believe) (Boret 2014).

A collective grave specifically for women who never married, due to the war and the high casualty rate for young men, and who would therefore be graveless was the inspiration behind Moyai no Hi (舫の碑), which is also an antiwar monument. Started in 1987 by Suzuki Shunichi, the former governor of Tokyo, as one of the first nonfamilial communal graves in Japan, it has a membership of over twelve thousand today, one-fourth of whom are already buried (Boret 2014). With a single stone marking all those buried there, and with a system of dividing ashes (*bunkotsu*) between an urn and the communal burial ground, both the space of the cemetery and fees for entering it (¥120,000, or a little over $1,000, for initial membership) are kept to a minimum. Onna no Hi no Kai, another communal grave association for women kept single by the war, similarly operates the "shrine of intentional bonds" at Jōjakkōji Temple in Kyoto. Here, as at Ōhasama and

Ending Center, members are encouraged to meet while still alive and to cultivate a relationality that carries through death—as testified to by the names of both living and dead members inscribed on the walls surrounding the cemetery (Boret 2014). Updating this for a contemporary demographic of women who, for reasons far beyond war, have stayed socially single and are facing the aging and death process alone, a new director took over Onna no Hi no Kai in 2000 and converted it into a nonprofit based in Tokyo.

Called SSS (Single Smile Senior Life), this is more a support network for women's "single old age" with a communal grave (*kyōdōbo*/共同墓) built in 2013. At the informational meeting I attended in 2016, Matsubara Junko, a lively senior with dramatic blue earrings, cajoled the audience into getting over any dreariness associated with socially solo death. "Why be so gloomy?? SMILE is our motto. And being single (*hitorisama*) is the fact of our lives." She lay out the three goals of the SSS network: support for the heart, coming together with people in the same situation, and activity around the collective grave. Urging everyone to be prepared by making death arrangements well ahead of time—Matsubara spun this as a "bright activity" about which one should be positive. Listing the many get-togethers for members, the two different mortuary plans on offer, and the annual memorial held at the communal grave for all those who have been—and will be—buried there, Matsubara summed up her message by noting the social and temporal fluidity of the grave.[10] "The grave is not just a place to enter when dead; it is also a place to gather around when alive."

POSTMORTEM SOCIALITY FOR THE SOCIALLY DEAD

In speaking about lonely death and the rise of those who "die alone without being noticed immediately," Shunsuke Nozawa notes how this condition "signals a limit case of kinship as a default model of sociality" (2015, 374). Solitude and indifference, he says, are the stakes of life today in Japan for just about everyone. Nozawa begins his article with the paradigmatic example of this is dying unrecognized: a possibility not only for those who live alone but even for those who live with families in family homes, as was the case of a 111-year-old mummy found "unnoticed" in his family house (after dying thirty years previously). The familial model of belonging is becoming increasingly unavailable and, as a mode of affiliation that anchors identity to a group in an institutional sense, it is also inadequate, undesirable, even uninteresting for more and more Japanese. As Nozawa puts it, this produces a longing and desire for something (else): for a connectedness that may be instantaneous, transient, a "kind-of relationality" (*nanika no en*) rather than anything full-blown. Something semiotically small: greetings between two people, or a note delivered to a housebound elder by a postal clerk knocking on the door to make sure they're still alive (a service some post offices have started as "postal touch" [*fureai yūbin*]). Not tied to the duties or roles of identity formation or to a belonging dependent on affiliation with a particular group, this is a sociality that performs itself elsewise—what Nozawa explores through the concept of *phaticity*.

Originating with the linguist Roman Jacobsen, *phaticity* refers to the rubric or form by which communication, as communing between self and other, takes place. Differentiating this from relationality (*en*) that links one to a group (e.g., a family or association like SSS or Ending Center), Nozawa points to a more basic or fundamental kind of relationality (*en*) of simply noticing that an other exists. Phaticity here does not depend on or get routed through statuses, contracts, or names. Rather, it is the staging, framing, gesturing of togetherness itself. But when this involves a subject who is dead, to notice and tend to these remains (if only minimally) requires something that both spatially and temporally exceeds the deceased. In the case of an alternative burial society, this is the corporate body of the association that, for all its paying members, guarantees a final resting place, annual memorial services, and (often) the thirty-three-year "eternal memorial" conducted by a staff priest. But when someone lacks the wherewithal or incentive to make such arrangements themselves and when kin (and family grave) are also unavailable, what other provisions might there be for, in Nozawa's terminology, a more phatic chronotope of sociality?[11] One for those at risk of "dying alone without being noticed immediately"?

Sanya, a community of aging day laborers near Minami senjū train station, is where a collective grave project was started in 2016 as an alternative burial project of a quite different ilk.[12] Once a postal waystation, then an executioner's site where 200,000 were killed by the end of the Tokugawa period in 1868, Sanya sat close to the Yoshiwara red-light district and drew in marginals and misfits of various kinds—wandering outcasts, funerary and leather workers deemed unclean, sex workers. Low-paid laborers from the countryside resided there during the Meiji Era. When Japan was ordered by the General Headquarters (GHQ) to build facilities for the poor following the Pacific War, Sanya became a tent city, then a hotspot for itinerant workers with rows of low-priced sleeping facilities (*doya*) that numbered 300 by 1961 and accommodated 20,000 people. The scene of labor riots in 1960 when workers joined with student protesters, Sanya thrived with transactional workers (employed in construction and dockwork through intermediaries) until the bursting of the bubble economy in the early 1990s. By 1999, many day laborers were living on the streets. Today these numbers are reduced (319 today compared to 897 in 2005) but so is the availability of inexpensive housing as well as opportunities for jobs. Of current Sanya residents, most of whom are men, 87.1 percent are on welfare (up from 44 percent in 1999); their average age is 64.7 (up from 59.7 in 1999) (Marr 2021).

The day I visit is rainy and bleak. Our tour, organized by my friend Matthew Marr (a sociologist who has done extensive fieldwork in Sanya) for a short research institute I helped run at Tokyo University, takes us across the span of a few blocks. Men wander about. A few are asleep on the ground, and activity feels minimal, limited to just a few arenas—health clinics, nonprofits, bars, a couple of shops, sleeping establishments, and the place where men gather to look for work (or eat noodles) during the day. It all seems to be a bruised sort of place where, as our two guides from the nonprofit Sanyūkai keep describing with compassion, the men who live here do so in isolation, loneliness, and shame. These are workers, few of whom can find work anymore as they age—a hard process at best. Most are estranged from family and want to keep it that way. While many are on welfare, some refuse to sign up, either because they lack an address or because they fear that, if they register, the police could inform their families where to find them. Sociability lies thinly here for men who may gather during the day but tend to scatter, hiding like hermits, at night. And yet the prospect of being buried alone, or disconnected, as *muenbotoke*, sits uneasily, we are told: a continuation in death of the bareness that has shrouded them in life.

It is to save them from that fate that Jean Rubeau, who lived forty years in Sanya after moving there from Quebec, started the Grave Project. Having founded a nonprofit, Sanyūkai, and in collaboration with Doctors Without Borders, Rubeau raised ¥2.5 million ($23,000) by crowdfunding and built the grave (with a granite headstone and the etched word *Sanyūkai*) to hold the combined ashes of fifty deceased in 2016.[13] When I saw the grave in 2017, the space was about half full and included the remains of Rubeau, who had died by then. Plans had been announced to build another collective grave, funded by money already being raised. "One day a full row" for all those living in Sanya who would otherwise have nowhere to be buried, our guide tells us. "We may think a grave is about bones, but it's really about being connected (*tsunagaru*): about making connection (*en*) in the face of a disconnected society (*muen shakai*). For us, nobody comes to pick us up after death. It is much happier if we can stay together in the afterworld." The mission of the Grave Project is uppermost in what our guides tell us about Sanya. They pepper their remarks with the words "dignity" and "hope," using them to reference a future, in the grave, where these aging day laborers are to finally find a modicum of belonging and respect.

Walking through the emptiness of streets with scattered residents, almost invariably alone, I am struck by how much affective weight has been put into the collective grave, promising a sociality that has eluded so many during their lifetimes here. A relationality stitched in bones, as Amade M'charak and Sara Casartelli (2019) say of the forensic care work done on the remains of unknown dead who drowned trying to cross the Mediterranean Sea from North Africa to Italy. A way of noticing and touching: humanizing lives by finding a place for those otherwise lonely dead. In both cases, I see this work as raising the potential of a certain vitality and recognition being generated not from the precarity of death but from efforts made to notice the precarious dead by according them care at the end.

CONCLUSION: OBON OTHERWISE

The precarity and erosion of a family-based model for burial and caregiving of the dead is the story I have tracked in this chapter: from those who will become disconnected souls because their graves are neglected by kin (like Maia's friend) to those who find the family grave either inaccessible or unpalatable for a final resting place at death (like members at Ending Center, single women at sss, or day laborers in Sanya). As I have shown, as new designs for mortuary arrangements emerge, so too do new sociological arrangements between the living and the dead. Traditionally, the relationship extended through time and reciprocal care and accorded belonging to a lineage of ancestors that the dead would join and become. But it was also a relationship that put those without such bonds at risk of becoming "homeless" at death: a prospect that inspires anxiety in even those who profess no religious affiliation or belief in the afterlife.

A single woman whom I interviewed about her mortuary plans admitted that the prospect of being unvisited in the grave made her feel at once lonely and sad in anticipation—what Povinelli (2011) calls a future anterior of, in this case, oblivion. This was why, even though there was a family grave she could enter, she was planning not to: as the last in her family line and the one now tending to it, the grave would fall into neglect once she was gone. Can you imagine, she asked me, almost incredulously, how untidy and unkempt it would become, a sign to all those passing through the cemetery of the voidance of a family line and of herself? Options she was considering included a new-style columbarium at a Buddhist temple nearby. Not only could her ashes be interred but so too could all those in her family's ancestral grave, should she pay the (considerable) expense to have them removed and reinterred. The premises would be kept beautifully tidy, all the remains well attended to (albeit interred in a small locker or underground crypt), and their spirits blessed annually for thirty-three years by the Buddhist priest on staff. Flowers would be put in vases and incense lit to the dead. To her, this all added up to something that would help her (and her ancestors) avoid abandonment in the end.

A number of Buddhist temples are now offering alternative services like this: mechanisms that open up their system of belonging beyond that of parishioners (*danka*) whose membership in a temple (and access to its cemetery) has often been passed down in families for generations. This is true of Kakudasan Myōkōji, a seven-hundred-year-old Nichiren Temple in Niigata that was the first Buddhist temple to launch new burial options in 1989. This was Annonbyō, a collective memorial mound "where one doesn't need a successor and can go alone," open to any paying members.[14] An innovation on the part of its head priest, it was motivated, as Ogawa Eiji explained it to me, both to give a place in death to those who lack a male successor (like him) and to give life to Myōkōji, which was at risk of becoming unsustainable and joining the trend of Buddhist temples downsizing and closing nationwide.[15] The gambit worked. The famous landscape architect Nozawa Shin designed a collective grave (*gōshibo*) to house 108 deceased, which filled far more quickly than planned and stimulated the life of the temple. The number of parishioners has risen, people have flocked here from all over the country to learn about Annonbyō, and a host of new activities related to death and beyond have been implemented.

All those who sign up here become members of the relational association in a temporality that is anticipatory, as Ogawa described; it relieves the anxieties of the living by actively involving them in, and helping them to finalize, their ending plans. One can ritually inoculate oneself in advance of death by, for example, acquiring a posthumous Buddhist name (*kaimyō*) while still alive. A new service offered by some temples, this was once an (often expensive) act of respect thought to hurry the spirit's passage to the other side left entirely to the energies and pocketbooks of surviving kin. But, as instituted in 2002 alongside a "living funeral contract" (*sōgi no seizenkeiyaku bunsho*), it can be among efforts made to serve those without anyone else to handle their funeral and burial arrangements.

In 2019, the summer I accompanied the remarkable priest at Ryōshinji Temple on his annual rounds visiting ancestors at Obon, I attended another memorable ritual to honor the dead at Myōkōji. A festival celebrating both the thirtieth anniversary of Annonbyō and the ritual of sending off the dead (*okuribon*) practiced at every temple every year, the temporality evoked was at once timeless and time bound. Just like the temple itself, steeped in seven centuries of history, but also a progressive innovator embracing the future. As I learned when I arrived, it has embraced ever more innovations. It has a new successor—Ogawa's daughter, with the priestly name Ogawa Ryōkei, became the fifty-fourth priest and first woman priest of Myōkōji in 2019—and has remade parishioner status to be based on the individual worshipper rather than the family (marked by calling parishioners *danshinto*/檀信徒 instead of *danka*/檀家). The mission, as the new priest expressed at the time of her succession, is to make the temple "in sync with changing times. We place importance now on it being a place for gathering that transcends family and kin ties, where we can talk together about matters related to life" (Kakudansan Myōkoji 2019, 38).

All of this is on display at its Thousand Lights *Okuribon*: a daylong event with activities catering to a diverse clientele including parishioners, those planning on entering (or already in) Annonbyō, and local residents (busloads of elderly people from nearby towns come in for the day). I'm here at the invitation of Inoue Haruyo of Ending Center, sleeping on a futon next to her, her daughter-in-law, and two adorable grandchildren. Meanwhile, assorted others join us as volunteers for the day. I'm struck by the utter heterogeneity of everything: the activities—a mixture of religiosity, arts and crafts, and civic engagement (a history tour of the temple, yoga and meditation events, a booth for making paper lotuses, a talk with youth and the new priest, and a lecture by a municipal official from Yokosuka City about new efforts to address the unclaimed remains of lonely death). And all those I meet during the day—a woman there for the third time because her father-in-law is buried at Annonbyō, a couple planning to be buried there, a young man whose parents are parishioners, two older men whose families have been parishioners here for generations, and a journalist from Tokyo who, having once reported a story on Myōkōji, returns every year because she likes the atmosphere and human interactions she finds here.

As the sun sets, what has been a day devoted to activity now turns to a ceremony of honoring the dead. Those attending gather around the river,

3.2 Priests praying for departing spirits at the Obon Ceremony (linked to the temple's thirtieth anniversary of its collective graves, Annonbyō) at Kakudasan Myōkōji—a seven-hundred-year-old Nichiren Temple in Niigata.

a source of vitality and life. Above it hang lanterns threaded on ropes, intended to guide the dead back home. This is the mission of the priests as well, about thirty of whom now form a procession that approaches from two directions—one from the temple, the other from the cemetery. Moving slowly in their ochre- and mustard-hued robes, they join up at the river and, lining up on either side to be led by Ogawa Ryōkei, intone sutras whose sounds reflect off the water, somber and low. Communicating with the spirits, the priests extend gratitude for their presence here on earth, then offer prayers for protection in their return journey back to where they usually reside. The chanting is steady and sure, spread along the river, echoing from water to air. As it fades, the energy moves to the entrance of the temple, where things pick up in an entirely different register. Standing astride a massive *taiko* drum, the master drummer calls sounds from the instrument meant to resonate with the depths of the earth. This is music with mythological roots, music that wooed the Sun Goddess out of her cave when the earth was shrouded in darkness; meant to ward off evil spirits, it is also thought to encompass the voice of Buddha. Shifting in timbre, moving in and out of rhythms, the volume scorches the air then retreats into the hollows of this sacred drum. The mood cycles: excited, transfixed, touched. Then it veers again into the mournful reverberations of a bamboo flute played by a man standing behind the drummer. Taking over from the drumbeats, the melody is piercingly sweet, a sonic lament. Puncturing, then dissolving into, the senses. Leaving us still. Echoing, and remaking, this communion between the living and the dead.

At the foot of Kakuda Mountain, this is the annual ceremony of returning the spirits to the sacred mountain. Enveloped in beauty and connectedness. A poiesis of belonging, and also farewell. In the cemetery, where lanterns are scattered throughout the three hundred graves (both communal and individual), people now wander in a darkness etched with small pockets of light. Talking quietly. Perhaps, but not necessarily, with the ancestors.

4

preparedness
a biopolitics of making life out of death

He's peppy yet smooth. A bachelor who lives alone in a high-rise mansion, aging parents and brother far away, forty-seven years old. His first job was in a wedding company; his next, arranging funerals. All of this he shares while warming to his subject: introducing us to Total Life Support, the business he started five years ago to serve people just like himself, as he admits with a grin. Those without anyone else to depend upon (*miyori ga nai*): the socially single, without family, denuded of others to tend to them at death. As he learned from the funeral business, and from the wedding business before that, the social ties that once sustained large rituals—whether nuptial or mortuary—have eroded in a country where life stages may well be faced alone. Hence, the service his company offers is a web of specialists—doctors, lawyers, tax accountants, priests—to help manage "living and life" for the socially precarious. Using a military metaphor, he calls the constituency that his company targets a reserve corps (*yobigun*) of aging singles. But where is the war here, and who is doing the killing? And in what terms is Total Life Support defending life, with its service aimed at postproductive, socially solo, aging but not yet dead Japanese?

On another day, another forum conducted by an entrepreneur in the ending business: The presenter starts up with his PowerPoint. Five minutes in, the screen fills with images of things: belongings left behind by the deceased. Stacks of newspapers and comic books, assorted umbrellas and caps, random slippers, doilies, and dolls. On to the next image: shelves of rice crackers, heaps of dust cloths, cascading mosquito coils, toilet paper, and tea. And yet another where the disorder is as evident as the decay: tatami mats strewn with half-eaten noodle cups, crushed beer cans, spilled soy sauce and grease. Grimacing, Mr. Yagi asks the audience, "Isn't this a chore—the cleaning up of stuff left behind by the deceased?" As nods of weary recognition circulate the room, he introduces us to his business, Recruit, a company that "sorts out and disposes" of possessions of the deceased—a genre of service in the ending industry that began appearing in the early 2000s. While once this was a task close kin would handle at the time of death, Japanese can no longer count on this in an era when families are busy and scattered and more and more people live on their own. In short, Mr. Yagi tells his audience, the cleanup of one's possessions is a task that the to-be-deceased should handle themselves while still alive (*seizen seiri*). Failure to do so results in the worst images he shows us today: rooms stacked with the garbage of hoarders who died alone, their bodies discovered when they were already putrefying—a phenomenon of lonely death (*kodokushi*) becoming more common in Japan today. Feeling distaste, we are being asked to ward against such a fate. But to what end and for whom, precisely? To save oneself from dying badly, or to save others—neighbors, landlords, the country itself—from the inconvenience of the mess we may leave behind?[1]

....

Preparedness for death is what I take up in this chapter. It is a motto I encountered repeatedly in the course of my fieldwork on *shūkatsu*—the ending business of initiatives, services, and products for managing mortuary preparations for twenty-first-century Japan/ese. Enjoined to "prepare now!" for the cascade of tasks that accompany death, the public is at once made nervous about, and given solutions for and remedies against, the prospect of a disorderly death in the future. Like job seeking for youth—the frenzy of competitive job searching that students embark on in their third year of college or high school to ensure they have secure employment well ahead of graduation—the ending market operates to give customers the security of establishing something now for the future.[2] Though similar in that both emphasize "anticipatory action" in the present to secure something desirable down the road (Anderson 2010, 780), the ending market targets not productive youth looking to secure employment for life, but postproductive adults looking to secure an orderly death. At work is not a biopolitics of productivity: making life by growing or strengthening a population as in interpellating youth into an activity of being or becoming productive citizen workers (Foucault 2003). Nor is it necropolitics per se: the letting or making die segments of a population discarded as expendable for their inutility to the nation-state (Mbembe 2003). Rather, the ending market is curating something in between: making the managing of death into a life activity intended to curb the ill effects of dying unmanaged (for both the individual and the public at large). Here, as in the national imaginary more generally, lonely death represents the worst-case scenario of dying badly, which, because cases of it are on the rise, also serves as a warning about what is treated as a social pandemic for the country as a whole. Why this gets addressed in terms of preparedness, with what effects, and for whom, are the issues I am interested in here.

Drawing on the work of Andrew Lakoff (2008), I follow what he considers to be a regime shift in the handling of the threat of flu epidemic from preventive medicine to a strategy of preparedness in the context of US public health. Though the events of COVID-19 have exposed the woeful unpreparedness of the United States in handling that pandemic, I nonetheless take his analysis to be useful for my own discussion of preparedness in managing ("family-less") death in Japan. As Lakoff describes, prevention was the strategy President Ford proposed in 1976 when, learning of a new strain of influenza that threatened to become a pandemic, he mandated a nationwide program to immunize the entire US population ahead of the next flu season.[3] But thirty years later, in response to waves of pandemic brewing since the end of the 1990s and also the national failures of preparedness exposed by 9/11 and Hurricane Katrina, the government came up with something quite different. Utilizing techniques initially developed in military and civil defense to pair national security with public health, the US secretary of health announced a $7.1 billion pandemic preparedness strategy in 2005. The new strategy became part and parcel of a more capacious form of planning that aimed to institute a norm of preparedness about public health and life more generally. As the assistant secretary of health at the time explained, "Preparedness is a journey, not a destination" (Agwunobi, quoted in Lakoff 2008, 400).

Similarly, preparedness for death has come to be orchestrated as an ongoing journey in Japan, one intended to militate against the rising ranks of untended dead. But, fueled by a number of demographic factors, the risk of dying alone is a problem of personal and national insecurity quite different from other kinds. Unlike the threats posed by terrorist attacks on sovereign territory or by disease in a population, neither national security nor epidemiology offers a corrective to lonely death. In the absence of the government or family protecting against this fate, it falls increasingly to the resilience and responsibility of the individual to be adequately prepared ahead of time (Heath-Kelly 2017). By bringing the "future into the present," anticipatory action aims to mitigate the possibility of a bad death, stranded, stuck all alone.

Anticipation is both the temporal and affective mode of our times, according to Adams, Murphy, and Clarke (2009), operating when the future is unknowable and indeterminable. Anticipation is how we feel, envision, and plan for the future, and its demand for action is what Adams, Murphy, and Clark call *abduction*. Constituting the strategies and courses of action we use to anticipate, but not prevent, crises and challenges in the future, abduction is productive in its own right (255). In new economies of vitality, biopolitics are intertwined with capital and serve to expand human capacities (for, in this case, living more fully in the present and securing one's postmortem conditions by pre-preparing for death) and also forms of capital open to speculation for individuals, families, businesses, and the nation-state. Abduction has its own temporality as well as politics. As a "means of determining courses of action in the face of ongoing contingency and ambiguity," abduction continually tacks between temporalities, "from data gathered about the past to simulations or probabilistic anticipations of the future that in turn demand action in the present" (255). As Adams, Murphy, and Clark put it, abduction is the work of living in anticipation, of being out of time. And, as they say of women cryogenically freezing their unfertilized eggs, it is one of deferral: waiting to bear children in the future, a "commodifying of time and hope" (258).

While *shūkatsu* is anticipatory, bringing the future into the present with work that is also a commodification of both time and hope, it is not organized around deferral. Quite the opposite, in fact. As action taken in the present to anticipate, by warding against, a bad, disorderly, future death, it is quite a different kind of abduction: not waiting for an undesirable outcome by bringing into the present an ending activity once managed at the time of death. How this works, in terms of temporality and preparedness, and what this involves, in terms of personal behavior as well as social governance, is what I look at in this chapter using two different examples of *shūkatsu*. One is commercial endeavors, such as the two businesses mentioned above, that help customers envision, and ward against, the possibility of dying unprepared by ordering their death preparations ahead of time. The second is civic measures taken by one municipality in Japan, Yokosuka City, to implement a *"shūkatsu* plan" for its precarious elderly to prevent them from becoming disconnected souls. This helps those at risk of lonely death as well as the municipality, which bears the mortuary expenses for residents whose remains go unclaimed; preparedness here melds the personal and the civic with a plan that registers citizens, in life, for death. Throughout I question in what form the future manifests in the present (Luhrman 1998, discussed in Lakoff 2008), and what work preparedness is doing, for oneself regarding others, in dealing with death. I also consider the affective currencies that are generated here. Unlike the fear Lakoff found accompanying the vision of uncertain futures, the affect surrounding *shūkatsu* can be quite different. It may be risk-laden, or tinged with unease and anxiety, but it also carries something else. It is purposefully animated, as if managing death has become a reason to live at all.

RESERVE CORPS OF THE SINGLE

The room is bustling by the time I arrive. It is early June and we have assembled for an event scheduled for three hours—a ninety-minute forum and the association's annual social gathering with food and drinks to follow—and the crowd seems eager to go. I scoot to the only seat available in the front row and join the group of fifty or more, all but two in their sixties or older, a fairly even mix of women and men. We're greeted by Inoue Haruyo, the founder and director of Ending Center, a nonprofit devoted to the respectful treatment of the dead that offers grave sites and support for "cherry blossom burials" open to anyone (not dependent on families or the succession principle). As part of an Ending Center membership, one gains not only a burial plot but also access to the association's menu of activities, which includes a variety of workshops, a plethora of get-togethers (lunches, craft sessions, chats) at a converted home close to Izumi Cemetery, and special events such as today's forum and gathering. Inoue-sensei (the term of respect she is accorded by members) is gracious and warm as she welcomes us to the event, then introduces our speaker: a crisply suited man there to speak to us about aging energetically, with a focus on dementia.

Striding to the front, bowing and telling us his name, Mikuni Hiroaki starts by passing out an article he has written about his company that captures the gist of his message to us.[4] "A total support team that relieves the anxieties ahead for those in the reserve corps of the single"[5] is the title and an encapsulation of the work of his nonprofit with its cadre of twelve experts equipped to tend to any matter from taxes and inheritance to funeral options and cremation for a clientele likely to be handling all of their own death arrangements. Upbeat and direct, Mikuni tells us right off the bat that he himself falls in this category. Beginning with the self-introduction that is de rigueur in talks like this, Mikuni relates how his family moved from Niigata to Yokohama when he was a child, bringing with them his father's parents. Mikuni started work in the wedding business, then switched to the funeral business in 1998, and—riding the currents of the times—founded Total Life Support in 2008, having become aware of new needs in the ecology of mortuary arrangements. When his grandmother died in her nineties, the temple back in Niigata refused to help arrange for a funeral and burial in the ancestral grave there due to its distance from Yokohama.

As stressful as this was on his family, even more issues arise when the deceased has no one else to depend on (*miyori ga nai*) for making arrangements: a situation that has become increasingly pressing in Japan in the last ten years. This is how Mikuni identifies himself: divorced and living alone in a high-rise, he has a brother and parents, but says he's basically socially single. Recalling the number of deceased he has encountered in his work who died alone and were not given funerals or even interment of their ashes by grandchildren or distant kin when contacted, Mikuni says he started imagining something similar could happen to himself. How to live safely (*ikiki kurasu tameni*) until death by relieving the insecurity of how one will be treated after death thus became his agenda for Total Life Support.

Jumping right in, Mikuni announces that we're here today to learn how to handle ending preparations not for others but for ourselves. As the secondary theme is dementia, he asks if anyone present is already showing signs of it (to which five or six stalwartly raise their hands). Laughing broadly, he says that making it here today must mean "you're all pretty healthy." Still, telling the crowd that 60 percent of Japanese will eventually become afflicted, he launches into a series of hypothetical scenarios illustrating various circumstances, adding helpful information along the way, and pulling people from the audience to role-play in front of the room. *What happens if we get dementia? Do we want to go to a facility or stay at home, and* who would tend to us if the latter? So, what if our cognition still works, but, sorry to say, we get a diagnosis of terminal disease? Do we want life support or not? Is this written down with a legal guardian (hoteikōken)? This is advisable, he mentions, in order to avoid the municipality assigning one if we don't have family or allowing family members to make decisions we might disagree with. Best to designate a legal guardian while one still has cognition—he recommends doing so right now and mentions that his company can help; he himself has been legally credentialed to serve as guardian. And what about ashes and burial? Have we made these arrangements, including where the corpse will be held (anchijo) while waiting for cremation—given the backlog at crematoria these days, this could be a considerable wait—and how, and where, ashes will then be moved for interment? What about funeral or burial plans, the forty-ninth-day ceremony, a kuyō memorial? If there is no family involvement, might we want to consider donating our bodies for medical research? (In that case, the facility would handle all of these arrangements along with the expense.)

Let's say all this is taken care of. But what about all the stuff one leaves behind? Telling us about the services of cleanup companies (ihinseirigaisha) he also reminds us of the endless chores that need tending to: paying final bills, turning off electricity, closing down phone service, and erasing the data on our computers. Should we still have money or property, who do we want to leave it to, and what about descendants? Is this in a will, do we understand about inheritance taxes, and what about anything that would constitute mementos?

Going through a litany of possibilities, Mikuni engages in a speculative exercise of getting the audience to imagine the future littered, as it will be, with a host of challenges, obstacles, and tasks. Imaginative enactments, as Lakoff discovered, became one of the measures adopted by US public health agencies to confront the country's unpreparedness for flu pandemics. In the absence of tools for quantifiable risk assessment, experts deploy role-play to bring the prospect of future crisis and disease into the present as an object of both knowledge and intervention. "Exemplary of the type of rationality that underlies the contemporary articulation of national security and public health in the United States," imaginative enactments have two functions, according to Lakoff: to generate an affect of urgency in the absence of the event itself and to generate knowledge about vulnerabilities in the present system that need to be addressed in "anticipatory intervention" (Lakoff 2008, 401). As with the highly effective Dark Winter—a tabletop exercise simulating a smallpox attack on the United States staged at the Johns Hopkins Center for Health Security in 2001—the aim is to anticipate dangers that could undermine the health and security of a population by identifying existing gaps. And to then prepare against the future anterior of a potentially calamitous outcome.

With boundless energy, remaining high-speed throughout, Mikuni keeps presenting scenarios as if a gameshow host. Throwing out a range of situations and asking what someone might do, or has already done, answers are tossed back: *Draft a will. Consider hospice. Sign up for a high-rise columbarium with eternal memorial as part of the service.* But things are never as easy as they may seem, as he relentlessly points out. Hospices, for example, are dauntingly expensive in Japan (the cheapest he knows costs ¥900,000—about $8,270—per month) and dying with dignity (as a show of hands says is highly desired, as is the intention to deny life support at the end) necessitates a living will (*songen sengen*) signed ahead of time or through a spokesperson or guardian. And, as Mikuni keeps demanding of the audience, who precisely will be there to help them out? *Let's say you have Alzheimer's or, regrettably, you're now immobile but want to stay at home* (as do half of Japanese today, although 75 percent still die in hospitals). *Do you think a spouse, if you have one, can really handle this?* That's unreasonable (*tondemo nai*)! he shouts. A spouse will be aged as well, after all, and possibly predeceased. And don't count on other kin (daughter, daughter-in-law, grandchild) who may well be unable, unwilling, or simply not there to help out. For women, he calls it "delusional" to imagine a husband could suffice as a responsible caregiver.

The take-away message is to plan ahead, think of everything, and make arrangements for and by oneself. Handling this with responsibility in the way one chooses (*jibunrashii*) will allow one to live safely and fully until death. The emphasis here is on how to "live before dying" (*shinumae no ikikata*).

By the end, I am frankly exhausted by the requirements laid out for preparing energetically for one's death. Yet this is not the mood I sense in the room, where an air of cheerful resolve persists among those lingering to chat. As if everyone now has a mission. This is similar, perhaps, to what Andrea Muehlebach (2012) found in the moral purpose accessed by retired Italians in carrying out unpaid welfare work for the state: an enterprise that gave them something to do and also a social place to replace that once provided by the jobs they are now beyond. In Muehlebach's study, subjects were working for the benefit of someone else. In *shūkatsu*, by contrast, the engagement is taken on for oneself: making (the making of) one's own death preparations a moral endeavor, an everyday practice, a method for living. As Angela Garcia (2010) wrote about in a very different context (sharing heroin needles between mother and daughter in the Española

Valley of New Mexico), the dance with death can be undertaken to sustain life in a certain form. Here, too, the activity of preparing can both relieve one's anxieties about the future and provide something to anchor one's life to the here and now.

For the social gathering following Mikuni's talk, a room has been set up with tables laden with food and beer. As everyone mingles, a number of people stop at the table where items made by Ending Center members in arts and crafts sessions are cutely displayed. As I purchase handstitched cloths, a lively eighty-year-old bounces over to introduce herself. She tells me to call her Chiyo, but next to the last name on her nametag is a number that I ask her about. "That's the location of my grave site," she cheerily answers. "We're all going to be buried here and this identifies me to my neighbors." Laughing, she drifts off, and a man comes up. A retired businessman, he tells me how he and his wife have started coming to get-togethers here—for lunch, making crafts, learning about various topics pertaining to aging and managing death. Here, he says as he gestures around the room, he meets with his fellow grave friends (*haka tomo*/墓友): neighbors at death and companions of sorts until then. A sociality, and activity, organized around preparedness for death. Bringing death into the present, where its anticipation generates urgency, but also a method for living until the end.

A CITY'S PLAN TO PREVENT STRANDED BONES

In *shūkatsu*, enterprises like Total Life Support sell preparedness for death by promoting a particular engineering of the self: the responsible subject, managing tasks that once fell to others (namely family and kin). That reliance on the latter is eroding in an individualizing society are the conditions for *shūkatsu*: bringing into the present and the purview of the to-be-deceased a matter that was once handled by others at the time of death. This is akin to what Nikolas Rose (2007) has called a "politics of life itself," in which citizens are both urged and expected to become active partners in securing their own well-being. With a definition of health premised less on disease prevention or cure than on an ongoing regime of daily preparedness (Dumit 2012), the management of well-being operates through a pastoral power orchestrated by a plethora of enterprises, from pharmaceutical companies to food retailers, capitalizing on the promotion of health. Like *shūkatsu*, this pastoralism does not simply entail a "priest-like shepherd knowing and mastering the soul of the individual troubled sheep" (Rose 2007, 12). Rather, it is far more relational, reverberating between guide and guided as affects and ethics that make the object at hand urgent, moral, desirable. As with Mikuni engendering scenarios of possible futures freighted with precarity and possibility, the appeal is to the subject who sees herself as a responsible agent in ensuring a well-managed ending for herself and her neighbors and community (by not leaving a mess behind when she dies).

In the case of health, corporeality is optimized by embracing overall well-being: a biopolitics that is also an ethopolitics, according to Rose. Selfhood becomes somatic as ethical practices devolve on the body as the principal site for work on the self. As individuals embrace techniques by which they "act upon themselves to make themselves better than they are" (2007, 18), ethopolitics converges around vitalism: decisions and choices made to enhance, prolong, and engineer life in what is at once the making of (biological) identity and the taking of (biological) responsibility. Needless to say, this is contested terrain: what counts as life, according to what values and rights, and under what conditions and with what ramifications for governance and access. As Rose notes, the philosophical status, "indeed, the very ontology of human beings is being reshaped through the decision of entrepreneurs as to where to invest their capital and which lines of biomedical research and development to pursue" (2007, 20). In the case of *shūkatsu*, it is not the well-being of the corporeal body but managing the decay of that (biosocial) body at the approach to, and endpoint of, death that is tended to. A vitalism of sorts in making death respectable and orderly: the work of care that once fell to others. In doing so, the deceased are embraced as something beyond mere biological waste—as human, ancestor, buddha rather than thing. I consider this work of humanizing the dead to be *necro-animism*. An ethopolitics of life that has increasingly become a task for the individual to accomplish while still alive, for themselves as the to-be-deceased.

But the politics of necro-animism change considerably when a subject who has no one else to depend on is unable or unlikely to assume responsibility for handling their ending arrangements on their own. This is the condition addressed by an innovative new plan instituted by the city of Yokosuka to "not let anyone be alone" (*daremo hitorini sasenai*) at the end. Here, the status of singular sociality takes on a decidedly different cast from the upbeat tone given it by Mikuni, who seizes on the potential it gives individuals (assisted by his company) to design their ending. Following the position of feminist Ueno Chizuko, who has written a series of books on how single people can live and age robustly, Mikuni titled his own book on the subject *Ohitorisamade yukō: Saigomade jibunrashiku* (Let's pass as single: Doing it our way until the end). By contrast, Yokosuka City has engineered a plan for a different kind of subject: those who, living alone, need an ethopolitics from somewhere else to protect them from winding up as mere matter at death (the fate of the disconnected souls in the public cemetery).

It is a crisp February day in what was to have been a ten-day intensive fieldwork trip to Japan. But with my departure delayed by a snowstorm in Toronto, I have missed the appointment I made months in advance with Kitami Takayuki, the person responsible for the progressive policies the municipality of Yokosuka City has been putting into effect to help its aging single population. As vice director of the independent support division of welfare for Yokosuka City, Kitami has been giving talks nationwide and is incredibly busy. But he graciously reschedules, and I wind up at Yokosuka City Hall along with Kobayashi Tsuyoshi, the executive vice president of the waste company I interviewed the summer before, who has kindly set up this meeting and agreed to accompany me there. A port city on Miura Peninsula, forty miles south of Tokyo, bordered by the mouth of Tokyo Bay, where Admiral Perry sailed into Japan in 1853, Yokosuka City has a population that is both aging and declining. Of 410,000 residents, 30 percent are elderly, 10 percent of whom are alone and at risk of dying that way. Greeting us in his office, Kitami is at once genial and disarming; telling me he has read my book on Japanese character merchandise, he grabs his copy from his desk and asks me to autograph it. But we quickly segue into the matter of precarity. For efficiency, Kitami asks if he can just go over the PowerPoint presentation he has been giving about their new city plan: its "ending plan support" (*endingu puran sapōtto*), instituted in 2015, and the follow-up "my ending registration card" (*watashi no shūkatsu tōroku*), instituted in 2018.

Kitami starts with a disturbing social fact: the rise of unclaimed remains. Literally "bones that are uncared for" (*hikitorite no nai ikotsu*/引き取り手のない遺骨), these stem from single dwellers who, dying alone, leave behind remains that go unclaimed even when kin can be located. Constituting 3.3 percent of all deaths in Japan these days, the number has been increasing; it is 10 percent in the city of Osaka. Though only 1 percent of remains are unclaimed in Yokosuka, it represents significant numbers: sixty deaths in 2014, thirty-six in 2015, twenty-four in 2016, and (the last set he has available) fifty-one in 2017. Living alone is one contributing factor. Single-person households constitute 35 percent of all households in Japan today, and, of people over sixty-five years old, 14 percent of men live alone, as do 22 percent of women (predicted to rise to 21 percent of men and 25 percent women by 2040). But dying alone with unclaimed remains does not necessarily mean that kin cannot be found (*mimoto fumei*), as it usually did in the past. But around 2005, this started to shift, for reasons that seem connected to both economic and familial decline; it is now more likely that kin are located but, when contacted, refuse (*kyohi, kobamu*) to accept responsibility for handling any of the expenses or arrangements for the dead. For the fifty-one cases of unclaimed remains they had in 2017, this was true for fifty of them. Given the Cemetery and Burial Law (墓地埋葬法), the local municipality (自治体) must assume responsibility for all unclaimed remains found within its borders. An incredible burden on the city's taxpayers, the cost comes to about ¥250,000 ($2,276) per deceased for cremation, burial, and transportation as well as for holding the corpse in a refrigerated container while seeking out possible kin (which may take two or three months and cost more than ¥10,000 yen or $92 per day).

The burden of unclaimed remains also weighs on those likely to wind up this way, of course: the prospect of being consigned to a public grave for the disconnected where, because of the law separating religion from the state, they will receive no funeral or memorial (*kuyō*). Unless they make arrangements ahead of time that get properly recorded (allocating responsibility to, for example, a nonprofit organization to bury and memorialize them, such as the Sanyūkai Ohaka Project in Sanya discussed in chapter 3), those without kin to handle these arrangements become, under the law, "disconnected."⁶ In the case of Yokosuka City, unclaimed remains are interred first in individual urns in the city's columbarium for the disconnected (納骨堂). When the columbarium fills, which happens about every five years, the ashes are combined and reinterred in the collective plot (*gassōbo*/合葬墓) for enshrined souls. Kitami was inspired to create his preparation plan to reassure those at risk of this outcome as well as to relieve the city of the management and payment of these cases. Aimed at residents living alone, without anyone else to depend upon, and with monthly incomes less than ¥160,000 ($1,539),⁷ this is a premortuary living contract (生前制約予納) made between the individual and a funeral company for arrangements (funeral, burial) to be paid for, at least in part (up to ¥250,000 or about $24,053), by the city. In what has been highly praised as a creative collaboration between private enterprise and local governance, ten of the forty-two funeral companies in Yokosuka City have signed on to the plan, which is considered mutually beneficial for the individual and the city. It gives the aging precariat choice and certainty in their mortuary arrangements by guaranteeing a funeral, a memorial, and burial in a plot other than that for the disconnected. And it allows the city, by aligning with cooperating funeral companies, to tap into national resources for three-quarters of the expense by supplying a third party (the funeral company) to perform the burial (Fukusawa 2018–19).[8]

In the first four years of operation, 38 residents of Yokosuka City had signed up for the Ending Support Plan, and 358 consulted about it. Considering this a relative success, Kitami tells me he is sure participation will rise. Further, the plan has generated wide interest among other municipalities beginning to implement similar programs. He gives sixty-five town hall meetings on this a year, Kitami laughs, adding that Yokosuka City, like other municipalities these days, is stepping in to replace the role of the family. And not just for the poor and socially single. Rather, due to a number of changes in the landscape that make communication and connection between people contingent and strained, the numbers dying today without their ending wishes or plans known to anyone else are increasing. The danger here, as he exemplifies with three recent cases in Yokosuka, is that, even with burial plans and places, the deceased could well wind up in the public grave for the disconnected if they aren't officially recorded ahead of time.[9]

Today, citizens need a new way of registering their mortuary wishes and plans in anticipation of death, Kitami asserts. Whereas once the family register (*koseki*) and residence card (*jūminhyō*) provided all the information needed, now—as people increasingly live alone without the same kinds of affiliation and belonging—a new kind of registration for death is required. This is what Yokosuka City initiated in 2018 with "my ending registration card" (*watashi no shūkatsu tōroku*). A form that is to be filled out while the to-be-deceased is still healthy, it includes eleven categories ranging from medical record and emergency contact to location of will, living will, and contracts for funeral and burial.[10] Dovetailing with the new national trend in keeping "ending notes" in notebooks sold in bookstores and stationery shops (to keep a running record of personal wishes, plans, and relevant information regarding one's death), this ending registration is to be kept not only at home and on one's person but also filed at the local municipal office (*shiyakusho*). Much as Chiyo's name tag at Ending Center identified her grave plot, the registration card, in registering a person by their death plans, embeds the individual ever more in a life-death connection with local governance. And the city is taking on an ever greater role in place of family.

Two additional innovative collaborations have been recently announced. For those wanting to donate their bodies to science but lacking a successor or stand-in who could give the requisite permission, the city will now serve as guardian. In this new collaboration with Kanazawa Dental University, the latter says that 30 to 40 percent of their donors now come to them this way from Yokosuka City (Kanazawa Shinbun 2016). The city has also implemented a collaboration with care providers and doctors to do home visits, which is reflected in the fact that Yokosuka City has one of the highest rates of citizens nationwide who die at home (*zaitakushi*): 22.6 percent (Sunday Mainichi 2018).

In its first year of operation, ninety-five people signed up for the ending registration card program. Taking as one's personal and civic duty to make premortuary arrangements that are registered with local government is a specific sort of vitalism. When I hear Kitami speak later that year at Myōkōji Temple's Obon and thirtieth-year anniversary celebration for its alternative burial plot (described in chapter 3), he spends most of his talk laying out the details of this new registration plan. The response from the audience of over sixty parishioners, members, townspeople, and public officials is enthusiastic. One woman says this resembles the handbooks all mothers of newborn children are required to possess in Japan (*boshi techō*), which record vital prenatal and postnatal facts of both mother and child (including body weight, nursing schedule, and daycare center). The mother carries this book to every doctor's appointment, and it also establishes her eligibility for "milk money" from her local ward. But the ending registration card registers not emergence of life but preparation for its end: a death identity card, as it were, for those still alive, indicating their vital information once dead. From a vitalism of birth to a vitalism around death, this reflects significant demographic and social shifts: the fact that Japan is now a high aging, "mass death" society where the number of people dying exceeds those being born every year. As Ogawa, the former priest of Myōkōji, mentions in response, his temple has instituted a similar registration plan, one copy of which is kept at the temple.

The point to stress in all this, as Kitami reiterates at the end of his talk, is being a society that accords its dead respect (*songen*). When bones lie unclaimed, there is no recognition or dignity given to the person just departed. Nothing social; just the bare waste of a disconnected soul in a community grave. To prevent this from happening in Japan, there must be collaboration between the to-be-deceased, the municipality, and private funeral businesses or other civic establishments like temples. A joint effort in necro-animism: animating the dead by mitigating ahead of time the risk of becoming unclaimed remains at the end.

THE EVERYDAYNESS OF TOUCHING (MY) DEATH

In their essay on anticipation, Adams, Murphy, and Clarke note that one of the defining qualities of our current moment is its "peculiar management of time" (2009, 247). Having lost the certainty of a progressively better future that was the promise of modernity, futurity takes on a decidedly different hue filtered through contingency and ambiguity. We rely less on definitive sciences of the actual than on speculative forecasts and probable outcomes. This means living with anticipation as an everyday affect-state. But this is hardly passive. Rather, anticipatory work—the work of abduction—is action taken in the here and now orienting us toward the yet to come. "Anticipation is a regime of time, in which one inhabits time out of place as the future" (Adams, Murphy, and Clarke 2009, 247). Attempting to gain control over a future whose unpredictability produces anxiety and fear, abduction is labor of "living in anticipation." Tooling oneself in arrays of preparedness, one gives this not only time but also shards of the self—as if, in preparing now, one can produce the becoming one seeks in the future.

In this last section of the chapter, I turn to the everydayness of *shūkatsu* in tracking how this anticipatory pursuit of preparing for ending while still alive gets mapped onto the quotidian landscape of urban life. A lived condition of daily life is how my good friend Yoshiko introduced me to *shūkatsu* in the first place. When I was finishing my last project on precarity (irregular labor and life triggered by the burst of the bubble in the early 1990s), she took me to a bookstore and showed me a shelf categorized as *shūkatsu*. Seeing that I was unfamiliar with the term, she plucked a blank notebook labeled "Ending Notes" off the shelf and told me that she had started doing this herself the year before and would show me later that night what it entailed. Thinking that this might be a fruitful subject for my next research project, Yoshiko insisted that we watch the documentary that inspired a nationwide fad of writing ending notes. Called *Death of a Japanese Salesman: Ending Note* (エンディングノート) and released by documentary filmmaker Sunada Mami in 2011, it documents the desire of her father, a retired white-collar worker (*sararīman*), to leave a personal note to his family—more intimate than a will—communicating what he had failed to share with them in life on the eve of his death from cancer. His intention

PREPAREDNESS 113

never actually materializes in an ending note. What transpires instead is a man paying attention to both practical plans (researching options for his funeral) and relational work (repairing relations with his wife as well making sure to see his three grandchildren living in America one last time). While busying himself in these affairs, Tomoaki succumbs progressively to the disease, all of which is captured in the intimate everydayness of the documentary. For this company man who devoted the bulk of his adult life to working hard away from home, cancer has come early, leaving him little time to explore a bevy of hobbies and interests and to spend time bonding with family he so thirsted for in retirement. As he philosophizes at the end, his ruminations are given kind regard by the filmmaker, who, in the form of the documentary, realizes her father's wish to leave a personalized note to his family and beyond, after he is gone.

A popular success, much like the film *Departures* from three years earlier about a New Age mortician, *Ending Note* inspired a nationwide trend of writing ending notes. As conveyed in the promotional poster for the movie, "This is the story of one man and his family. And what is left is a final story that anyone can visit."[11] This was the invocation by which Ending Notes became such a national fashion: scripting one's final life story so as to leave behind a personal legacy that could be "visited" by anyone. Yoshiko showed me her own notebook of pages with entries to be filled in by the user, some of which are strictly practical and duplicate those recorded by Yokosuka City's ending registration card: medical information, provisions made for funeral and burial, contact information for those to be informed at death, bank accounts, location of living will and legal will. But other pages open up into far more personal terrain: prompts for favorite songs and childhood memories; places for posting photos, poetry, trips taken with friends, religious passages, and reflections on life itself. Yoshiko adds to it routinely, almost like a daily journal, in a summing-up of how she feels in the present regarding the future and drawing on her past: a temporal hodgepodge inspired by the desire to be personally prepared for the ending ahead. But the social visitation ending notes invite is both curious and telling: these are "final stories" that can be "visited" by anyone. But who precisely will that be if the writer does not have a family? As Yoshiko admitted to me, the writing of ending notes itself constitutes a pleasure and meaning all its own, even if no one else winds up reading or implementing them when one passes. This makes the gesture of writing ending notes something that not only anticipates time—the future when she is gone—but also stands (in) for a sociality of "visitation" by others—who may not materialize.

Anticipatory sociality: personalizing one's final story by writing it ahead of time *as if* for others. Something that animates the dead in anticipation of dying otherwise unrecognized or unclaimed; this is what Yokosuka City's premortuary plan and ending registration card promise as well. And it is revealing that a national day to write ending notes has been established at a moment when stories of lonely death reverberate in the daily news. Not intended as a preventative strategy as much as one of preparedness: readying for the end as an endeavor to be practiced even by people in their twenties. The term used here, also the grounding principle of *shūkatsu* more generally, is *seizen seiri*: ordering (*seiri*) while still alive (*seizen*). Coupled to affect, this is said to relieve the anxieties and uneasiness of an unsettled future (*fuan*) with measures taken in the present that give one grounding, presence, and calm. Something similar is at work in another lifestyle trend popular today: *danshari* (断捨離), a philosophy about things originally started by Sasaki Fumio (2015) that, combining the three characters for judgment (断), throwing away (捨), and detachment (離), promotes minimalism in material belongings. In the hands of such tidying-up experts as Marie Kondō, emphasis is placed on affect derived from maintaining order of, in this case, space. As she instructs with her *konmari* method of evaluating one's belongings one by one, then retaining or escorting them out of one's life based on whether or not they inspire a spark of joy, touching one's things with care (a process called *teate*) is intended to both heal the self and give care to the object. A method of tidying one's dwelling as an aesthetics for living more joyfully, the focus is on a presentism that circles around the self (Kondō 2015).

A small café in the Sumiyoshi neighborhood of Tokyo offers the setting and service of tending to life-end preparedness with something akin to the KonMari Method. Called Blue Ocean Café and run by a company in the business of scattering ashes, it serves tasty food in a stylishly pint-sized room lined with a bar at one end and shelves filled with pamphlets and books on aging, lifestyles, and death. Blue Ocean Café offers a menu of events ranging from talks on dementia, aging in the LGBTQ community, and grief support to opportunities for writing ending notes and looking at yourself in the casket. Activities last one and a half to two hours, cost ¥1,500–¥2000 ($15–$20), and are run by a coordinator. The sessions I participated in were at once intimate and low-key, with participants clustering around a small table and sipping the drink that comes with the entrance fee. One, on scattering ashes (*sankotsu*), was spent tallying and assessing the fine points of this as a viable mortuary option. It was led by a staff member of the café's parent company who took us through background information (it is rising in popularity; the company did 6 such ceremonies in 2007 but 249 in 2016), legal stipulations operating in Japan (it has to be done at sea and is forbidden on land and in rivers and lakes), and the ways *sankotsu* is carried out by their company and others: it may be done on a private or group-chartered boat; ashes are scattered by a family member or staff who takes their place (*daikō*); the longitude and latitude where ashes are thrown are noted on a certificate). Interwoven with a playful quiz and questions and answers throughout, the session ended with a long discussion about the relative merits of ash scattering versus burial in the ground (which one of the two middle-aged women joining me said she frankly couldn't countenance). A pleasant afternoon chat about the consumer choice facing us in death styling.

Another event I attended was much more hands-on: crafting scrapbooks to "connect memories" while still alive (*omoi wo tsunagu seizen sukurappubukkingu taiken*). This is to be an activity of self-care (*kokoro no seiri*), the coordinator announces at the start. An energetic woman in her thirties, self-employed as a life-ordering consultant, she has laid out an assortment of papers, stencils, glitter, glue, buttons, and newspaper photos and instructs us in various techniques and designs for making "frames" to house memories for the family photos we've been asked to bring. Remember to caption with a phrase like "my happy childhood," or "enjoying an adventure," she instructs us.[12] We are anticipating memories of our lives that could be "visited" by others after we die. I am reminded here of a phrase coined by a cleanup worker who, on being commissioned to sort through the belongings of a woman who died in a senior facility, was told by her son to dispose of all the photos that were found of the two of them. "Mementos with no place to go" (*ikiba ga nai katami*) he called these photos, using a phrase ("nowhere to go") that also refers to deceased who wind up in the collective plot for the disconnected (Yoshida 2006, 47). As if to inoculate ourselves against such a fate, what we are doing today is making a place for our mementos ahead of time: a container for people living together, as Marilyn Strathern (1992) has said of the home. Sitting with me are two middle-aged women and a couple in their thirties, all of whom have brought pictures—strikingly, none of family members. One woman has a photo of herself in a bright red sari as a young adult, the other of a trip taken with a female friend when about forty years old; the young man has one of his girlfriend on a motorcycle, and she a picture of the two of them. Jabbering at first, we soon fall silent, each of us absorbed in touching personal memories. *Tanoshikatta!* (that was fun), my fellow participants say in leaving. Sending us off with a set of supplies, our convener urges us to continue scrapbooking on our own.

Tokyo People's Action Volunteer Center offers a far less boutique, more public and everyday venue for preparing for ending and holds events on this subject (and many others) free to the public. The central headquarters for volunteering in Japan, this is where I attended a two-part workshop on care sponsored by a nonprofit called Association for Making Connections in Housing and Living for Old Age. The first part was a presentation led by the director of Aladdin, a nonprofit creating support networks for caregivers. In a room of about forty-five attendees, most middle-aged or older, with almost as many men as women (which Ms. Makino, the coordinator, beams about), we are told that support activities (*shien katsudō*) geared up in Japan at the time of the Hanshin earthquake in Kobe in 1995. Before then, care had been primarily the purview of the family. But the crisis of the earthquake, which included large numbers of people who died all alone, ignited awareness of the problem of lonely death and also measures taken by community and municipal groups to address it. Today, more and more public, civic, and community initiatives have emerged operating as supplemental or "parafamilies" (*giji kazoku*). While once caregivers were overwhelmingly women, usually daughters and wives, today 30 percent of caregivers are men. And while 55 percent of those taking care of the elderly are over the age of 60, increasingly the trends in delayed marriage, lower childbirth, and singlification mean that it is not only, or necessarily, family members doing the caring, which is also increasingly taking place at home (*zaitaku*). Yet sadly, Ms. Makino tells us shaking her head, only 35 percent of Japanese are prepared for this process, according to a 2012 survey done by Asahi Seimei (Asahi Mutual Life Insurance Company) on family and care. (The woman sitting next to me, about sixty years old, leans over to say this is exactly her situation; she came from two hours away to start preparing for the next stage ahead.)

The rest of the presentation focuses on various facilities or initiatives that offer support by giving caregivers (or "carers," *keara-zu* as she calls them) a "place of their own" (*ibasho*) to decompress: community cafés, chat rooms, monthly get-togethers over coffee or beer. But how to plan care for ourselves is the subject we turn to next. Staff members of the nonprofit hosting the event organize us into breakout sessions according to the living arrangement we anticipate as we age: at home or in a facility, alone or with a partner or family. Having designated my own likely course to be at home with a partner, I am put in a group (the smallest in the room; the largest

PREPAREDNESS 117

are singles living at home or in a facility) with three others, all married men. The discussion, facilitated by a staff member, revolves around the dynamics of care and how we all are doing, at what stage we are, and what issues we are having now or anticipate in our future. One man, seventy-eight years old and retired from white-collar work, says he is in the throes of caregiving (*kaigochū*); his wife has been sick and, though they have an adult daughter who lives at home with them, they do not want to burden her with the chore. So he has been doing the bulk of it, all the while trying to maintain his own health to stave off the need for a caregiver himself for as long as possible. Another man, seventy-two years old and also retired from white-collar work, has a wife and two adult offspring at home; while both he and his wife are still fit, he is here today to start planning ahead. The third man, aged fifty, is concerned about reestablishing contact with his estranged children from a first marriage. When my turn comes, I tell them about what is uppermost in my mind: dealing with Alzheimer's, as my aging mother has recently developed it.

The coordinator is lively and adept, offering useful advice and facilitating a remarkably open and frank discussion. She concludes, as I've come to expect in the world of *shūkatsu*, by telling us to take care of ourselves and prepare for end of life as soon as we can. The affect, upbeat but moralizing, is familiar, too. Projecting a sense of possibility and equanimity as long as these ending matters are managed as earnestly and quickly as one can. This is what the mass marketing of *shūkatsu*, and the mortuary business more generally, both fuels and accommodates today: the desire, and sense of urgency, to make accommodations for (one's) ending in as efficient, competent, and comfortable a manner as possible. Accordingly, the physical environment, particularly of the cities, has become much more visibly marked by the means for doing this and by companies advertising their wares.

Proximate to the pathways and portals through which busy commuters pass routinely in daily life stands Lastel, for example, a huge new mortuary hall built five years ago in Shin Yokohama. With a name that stands for "last hotel," though the press has dubbed it a "corpse hotel," one of its services is holding corpses in refrigerated caskets until space opens up in a crematorium: a service necessitated by the high rates of death in Japan with long waiting lists at crematoria. Like the name taken for the facility itself, Lastel is the antithesis of discreet in announcing its provisions to the public. I see the large vertical banner hanging on the building from a good two blocks away when walking there from the nearest subway station, advertising in bold characters: "Corpse-holding and viewings. We'll fetch bodies from wherever."[13] Once at the building, there is a large sign by the front door listing all the services offered by floor (e.g., basement: large hall for big funerals; second floor: smaller hall for family-only funerals). On the wall is another chart displaying the options by glossy photos, much like the displays placed outside of love hotels. Menus for consumer choice of sex in one case and death in the other.

I expected something garish and cheap, but this McDonaldization of death comes neatly packaged. Everything inside is nice: newly refurbished, fresh flowers in the lobby, smelling sanitized and clean. And as I'm shown on my tour, the provisions it offers run the gamut. From the large "general" funerals (*ippansō*) that can host over one hundred attendants (¥930,000/$8,947) to family-only funerals (*kazokusō*; costing ¥560,000/$5,387, or ¥640,000/$6,157 if signing up to spend the night of the wake with the casket in a "living room") and direct funerals (*chokusō*; ¥290,000/$2,790) for which the body is kept at Lastel but is viewable until sent to the crematorium, each floor accommodates different stages and services.[14] There is also a floor stocked with a wide assortment of mortuary goods, from caskets and Buddhist shrines (*butsudan*) to clothes and portable memorial goods (*temoto kuyō*). This one-stop shopping extends to offering a bevy of free seminars to the public, such as the one I have come for today, on inheritance (*sōzoku*) and managing funeral and burial arrangements. It is run by a government-authorized consultancy group and is so crowded that extra chairs are set up to seat the more than forty people there. We are given tips about how much inheritance we can leave without paying taxes (¥30 million or $288,605); warned to gather all personal details ahead of time that will be relevant at the end, such as evidence of everywhere we have lived; and urged to consider signing up for eternal memorial if we don't have someone to assume the role of ritual successor. The message echoes what I have now heard time and time again: "Do everything one possibly can while still alive." Doing so, our convener tells us, will "relieve the stress" that death preparation provokes in all of us and will "make life enjoyable now."

The couple I take the tour with tell me they are extremely impressed with everything they have seen and not disturbed by the image of Lastel as a "corpse hotel"—something our tour guide says is an excellent service they offer given that the average wait to get into a crematorium in Yokohama now is four days. Having heard about Lastel when it was featured on a news report on TV, they had come today to see confirmed what they learned then: that it is doing really good business. That has been my impression as well;

everything seems bustling and efficiently run. "So much to consider, which we'll certainly be doing!" they tell me with a smile. They walk off with a big bouquet of funereal flowers they have been given, as have I, by the attendant at the front desk, who said, "Why waste these?" Why, indeed. Making fungible these flowers accompanying the living back onto the streets, just as they accompanied the dead in this mortuary facility called a hotel in the heart of an urban center. Making profane—or perhaps a new kind of sacred—this handling of death.

CONCLUSION

"My-home" was both norm and ideal in postwar Japan: of working hard enough to purchase one's own home and inhabit it with a hardworking family that would fill it with the newest of consumer goods. "My-robot" is what might be found in a Japanese home in the second decade of the twenty-first century, vacuuming or tidying rooms or offering companionship and care in the place of family members who may no longer be there.[15] "My-death" is the term I give to fashioning one's own mortuary plans, arranging ahead of time both a final dwelling place and its tending.

At once work and care, an identity but also a mode of being (and becoming), something personal but interpersonal as well, self–death making culminates in the ID cards citizens are being asked to carry around with them, identifying their future ending plans as connected (not disconnected) souls. It also generates activities of remembering in the present for a future dead self that may be forgotten by everyone else. Keeping a death planning journal (ending notes) or spending an afternoon designing mementos right now are engaging in abduction—"living in anticipation"—that is, activities done very much in the present to ward against becoming the kind of dead in the future that nobody wants (Adams, Murphy, and Clarke 2009, 247).

In the next chapter, I move to a genre of business in *shūkatsu* that deals with exactly this kind of dead. These are cleanup services that are commissioned to straighten up residences and dispose of all unwanted belongings of the deceased. As such, their clientele can be anyone looking to get rid of possessions of the dead, either after death or—as is increasingly the case—in anticipation of one's own death as part of the "ordering while still alive" process. But these operations also provide "special cleanup" for those who died alone, socially estranged, and not noticed immediately by anyone else. The detritus left behind in these cases can be intense—a materiality that gets imbued with the scent of unsociality.

departures

The work of a clean-up worker is basically sorting and carrying away. When you enter the house of the client, the basics to take are cardboard boxes, masking tape, Band-Aids, cutters, and disinfectant. Just looking at these tools, one can see that the work differs little from being a mover.

A clean-up worker should be able to identify what was of importance to the deceased, even in a house crammed with things [ごみ屋敷化した家/a house that has been hoarded]. When we say *hoarding*, it sounds as if everything is in disarray, but to the deceased, there was stuff that wasn't garbage. And within that, isn't there something that was the most important? A gifted clean-up worker can find this information from the remnants of the deceased: by [looking], for example, in a picture album.

Kimura Eiji, *Ihinseirishi toiu shigoto* (2015)

the smell of lonely death and the work of cleaning it up

(UN)SOCIAL SMELL

As cities modernize, they get sanitized in terms of scent. Reducing the stench from sewers and streets is a marker of civilization, as is reducing the miasmas thought to signify and spread disease. A matter of both manners and health, the body has been a site for regulation: cordoning those infected by epidemic diseases in special zones and demanding that individual citizens maintain standards of personal hygiene such as not spitting in public. As the slippage of these borders arouses odors, the malodorous are considered dirty and dangerous—a sign, as Mary Douglas (2003) has noted, of matter out of place. But smell, particularly that considered disturbing, is hard to contain. As dirt on the move, it augurs an unwelcome sociality of the person(al) intruding where it doesn't belong. Based on her work with homeless people in London, psychotherapist Gabrielle Brown has argued that, when someone is said to smell, "we mean they smell of themselves" (2015, 33).

Long associated more with the body than the mind, smell was considered the least rational of the senses by Kant, of a lower order (along with taste) than the higher senses of touch, hearing, and sight. Yet it carries an immediacy and unruliness that lends it a particular affective charge. And, once having entered one's nose from outside, smells may be hard to reject, unlike a foul-tasting bite of food that can be thrown up. Smell is a relationship; it is "loquacious in its effect upon the senses of others" (Brown 2015, 35).

Unsettling the boundaries between ego and self, smells may disgust or arouse. This is particularly true for the smell generated by a corpse, according to James Siegel (1983) in reference to Javanese practices surrounding death. When flesh remains, the body can't conform to idealized notions of the deceased, which are easier to conjure when the remains have whitened to clean bones. Devoid of life but "without the capacity to refer to death in any sense," the putrefying corpse is "not amenable to becoming a recognized sign" (Siegel 1983, 10). Striking the senses through aroma, the affect is terrifying. Unsettling and uncanny, one cannot "lock the odor in place" (9). Fearing it could kill them, Javanese ward off the smell with a special incense intended to block it along with memories associated with the deceased.

....

Smell is the sense most strongly associated with lonely death. In the many accounts I have read of it and in the interviews I have done with workers who clean up the mess, smell is a constant. The hardest part of the job, as many told me, it is often what triggers the discovery in the first place. A foul scent that neighbors or landlords notice in front of a door that has remained unopened—as they now recall—for quite a while leads to calling in the police. Who, when entering, discover a corpse that has lain in a residence sometimes for months. Where, amid belongings becoming rot, there is a materiality that spews maggots and bugs. The smell both lingers and spreads, seeping into tatami mats and plaster walls, then outward to houses and playgrounds next door. Depreciating property and angering neighbors, it is both difficult to take and difficult to get rid of. Unsocial as this feels, the smell itself bespeaks unsociality, stemming as it does from "death unnoticed by others" (*kizuite moraenai shi*)—those who die in a condition of isolation and estrangement in which they were likely living for a very long time. Then, when expiring, there is no one to notice they are no longer around. Until their remains decay, communicating the presence of something amiss. The language of smell signaling an untended death.

This is the issue I take up in this chapter: the entanglements between the sociality and materiality of existence in what is seen as the limit case of it coming undone. The border here—between life and death, order and disorder—is what I examine in terms of the sociomaterial complex of homes. I analyze how this border gets perverted in the stories of hoarding, decaying interiorities, and insufferable smell that accompany the reports of lonely death: a condition on the rise, as are loneliness and social isolation more generally in Japan these days (Ozawa de Silva 2021). My lens is a new genre of business that, starting in the early 2000s as part of the *shūkatsu* industry, sorts, disposes, and cleans up the belongings of the deceased. Differentiating themselves from garbage services, *ihinseirigaisha* promote what they do as showing discretion and respect to material possessions in escorting them out of the home (and into the dump).[1] Relieving family members from a chore once considered their duty, these companies are also commissioned by the to-be-deceased to handle this along with other death preparations: ordering by disposing parts of their selves and homes before they die. In addition, cleanup companies are increasingly hired to perform the job of eradicating the mess left behind by a lonely death. Called "special cleanup" and requiring full-body hazmat suits and ozone machines, this is a job usually commissioned by municipalities or landlords of rental properties where a corpse has been discovered long after death occurred.

As Josh Reno (2015) has said of garbage workers in the United States who move waste found disgusting by those who produce it to landfills far from their homes, the work of waste removal is a form of care. Relieving others of a job found to be onerous and bleak, *ihinseiri* workers are performing labor that is at once valued and reviled. Meanwhile, their proximity and exposure to something so socially raw—and all too imaginable these days as anyone's possible outcome—makes them dispensers of a very particular, ambiguous kind of care. How they both assuage and capitalize on the specter of lonely death inspiring so much anxiety (and curiosity) these days in Japan's public imaginary is what I track in the pages to follow. I follow them through media stories, ethnography with cleanup workers, and one cleanup worker's dioramas of the death scenes she finds, which she reproduces to outlast—but perhaps conjure anew—the smell. Of a disquieting (un)sociality. But the promise, too, as I suggest of these dollhouses, is of a connection beyond the disconnectedness of these lonely deaths. Being dead otherwise.

Since starting the first business in Japan to "straighten" (*katazukeru*) the remains of the dead in 2002, Yoshida Taichi has become intimate with deaths unnoticed by others. Working toward the prevention of such cases by establishing a nonprofit, Yoshida is considered a spokesman for both the dangers of lonely death and the advantages to clientele of a business like his. Here is his story about someone who ends up like this, done in manga (cartoon) form in one of his books, where it is accompanied by a DVD:

> A retired widower, Mr. Solitary (Kojirō-san) lives alone. Grumpy and sullen, he shuns the greetings of his landlord when venturing out to buy a cup of ramen for lunch and covers his ears to ward off the sounds of the kids playing next door. Sitting on his tatami mat listening to TV (where he hears the news of a sixty-year-old man whose body was discovered weeks after dying a lonely death), he lets garbage accumulate all around. Sunk into inertia, the thought of renewing his now empty medicine container is too much. When his son calls to invite him for an outing with his young child to a local temple, Kojirō makes an excuse not to go. Outraged that his father is never willing to leave his apartment and allow him to help out, the son vows to cut off relations.
>
> In this state, Kojirō suffers what appears to be a heart attack and collapses to the floor. Fearing he will die if nobody discovers him, he keeps hoping somebody will. But weeks pass and bugs start gathering outside his door. Realizing that he hasn't seen Kojirō for a while, the landlord calls his son. But, still disgusted, the son refuses to be involved and the landlord has to solicit the police on his own. Together they enter the apartment and find Kojirō dead on the floor, maggots and bugs crawling all over his body—and everything else. [The one photo in the story is inserted here, showing the remains of an apartment where a decomposing body was discovered weeks after death. Though the body isn't shown, the sense of decrepitude jumps from the page: stained tatami mat, a sock and chopstick strewn where the deceased must have lain, a greasy table stuffed with assorted foodstuffs and newspapers underneath.]
>
> The story zooms into the aftereffects of Kojirō's death: the wretched smell and lingering flies that the neighbors complain about, threatening to move out if the landlord doesn't start fumigation and cleanup as soon as possible. But the procedure is expensive and the son, not bound to take care of it because he is not the legal guarantor and has decided to forsake his inheritance, is disinclined to accept responsibility. Strug-

gling to come up with some solution, the landlord finally gets the son to share a small part of the costs. The agony of everyone—the irritated neighbors, the burdened landlord, the weary son who has started recalling happier memories of his father from childhood, including being given a cap he now clings to—is overseen by Kojirō, who hovers above as a ghost. The story ends with Kojirō speaking with newfound self-reflection: "I didn't know that after I died, my death would cause so much distress—to my son, my landlord—and so much inconvenience to my neighbors." Then, addressing the reader, he urges us to make connections with those around us so as not to wind up as he has. "Everyone, don't do as I have, but please pay importance to forming relations with others.[2] We need to do this in order to live to the fullest now and to not have regrets after death" (Yoshida 2010, 22–93).[3]

The story of Mr. Solitary appeared in one of several books Yoshida has written about the work of *ihinseirigaisha*.[4] As a composite drawn from actual cases, Kojirōsan is emblematic of those most at risk: 80 percent of the lonely dead are male; their mean age is sixty; most are retired, laid off, or unemployed (among the "industrial waste" of those who, once gainfully employed, have lost place and sense of purpose along with their jobs); they frequently live alone and are estranged from children, kin, and spouse, whether by divorce or death. Yet part of the book's message is that no one evades the possibility of finding themselves all alone at the end. In a dialogue between a newly married couple later in the book, the twenty-five-year-old wife realizes that, even if they have children and stay married, her husband could die first, and their children could live far away, and she would then become an aging single woman living alone. As the back cover warns in large letters, "Until yesterday, this was about someone else. But tomorrow, this could be YOU."

Solitary death is treated as a social problem associated with material disorder. We see Kojirō living amid disarray—signs of the hoarding (*gomiyashiki*) that often accompanies lonely death—and leaving a putrefying mess that burdens his neighbors, landlord, and son with its effects. Yet Yoshida's book pays ample attention to the complexity of socioeconomic factors giving rise to such a condition: shifts in residential planning toward more single-person or family dwellings in high-rise mansions (residential buildings) since the 1980s, which promote "islands of isolation" (*kojima*) (Yoshida 2010, 115); rushed, consumerist lifestyles that fixate on the person/al and downplay relationships and time spent with others; and the precarity and stress around economic security and jobs.[5] But for as sympathetic an account of the growing susceptibility of Japanese to just such a fate these days as the story is, the portrayal of Mr. Solitary is graphically shocking, with pages spent on the odium of his corporeal remains. Bugs hovering, maggots crawling, stench conjured by the haziness on the page. What to make of this?

THE ORDERLY MAKING THE UNMAKING OF A HOME

The smell, as Yoshida Taichi admitted to me, was hard at the start. Yet opportunity is what drove him into this business of cleaning up belongings of the deceased, including residences where corpses lay among decay. Forty-four when I interviewed him in 2017, he had already built a career as a compassionate entrepreneur: a successful businessman who also considered himself an activist for the prevention of lonely death. When Yoshida was younger, though, sports had inspired his dreams. Yoshida played baseball in college and imagined he would turn professional, but realized he wouldn't make it by the time he graduated. He started to become a chef and worked at a restaurant, but switched to a job at a moving company with better pay. But, cringing at the trajectory modeled by his senior coworkers—working year after year to pay off house loans—he quit at the age of twenty-eight to strike out on his own. With only ¥5,000 ($50) in his pocket and two children to feed, Yoshida borrowed a truck and started his own moving company. This became a moving and recycling business, the first in Japan. Then, using a small inheritance from his father and joining up with his uncle, the business morphed into Keepers in 2002: Japan's first *ihinseirigaisha*.

The name itself is unique. Written in katakana, the syllabary for foreign words, Keepers (*ki-pa-zu*/キーパーズ) signals something different and new. First calling it a disposal business that gets rid of the belongings of the deceased (*ihin shori*), Yoshida wanted to distinguish Keepers from the traditional *benriya-san* whose job of carting away unwanted possessions to a junkyard harbors negative associations with death and waste. Replacing "disposal" with the word for "order" (*seiri*), it became a service that tends respectfully to the "straightening up" (*katazukeru*) of belongings, emphasizing both the nature of the matter (that is "not treated as garbage") and the attitude given it by the workers (who "tend to the feelings" of the bereaved and "show respect" to the deceased).[6] For a service that still brokers the disposal of belongings, Keepers adds a labor of care that personalizes the work they do and the attitude they take toward the objects themselves. In this they are treating the matter they deal with as something other, and more, than the garbage that Wang calls the "corpse of a commodity" (2011, 340): objects that have lost their utility and value. As revealed in the motto for the company—"we help in your move to heaven" (*tengoku he no hikkoshi no tetsudai*/天国へのお引越しのお手伝い)—the attitude is of recognizing the person still lingering in the things being removed from a home: what Sasha Newell, in his 2014 article on hoarding, has called the "unfetish" of an object still animated by the memories, attachments, and energy of the life it once had for or with a human.

This makes the workers not only manual laborers but also, as mentioned in the company's promotional material, "professional mourners" (*puro izoku*) and "substitute family members" (*giji kazoku*) in the process of disentangling person from belonging at the moment of death. Kimura Eiji, another owner of an *ihinseiri* company who started the certification process in the industry, describes this attitude as the very reason he entered the business. Having hired a local *benriya-san* to cart off his father's possessions at death, he was so shocked at the disrespect the workers accorded the things that he fired them on the spot and took over the job. Realizing what a difference it makes to act lovingly toward belongings of the deceased even in their transport to the dump—and seeing this as a need now that families, once expected to perform this role, are increasingly busy, far away, or not available at all—Kimura started his own *ihinseiri* company (Kimura 2015).

As Yoshida explained to me, grieving is assisted by not merely removing the bereaved's personal belongings from their dwelling but doing so in an "orderly, respectful" fashion. ("When these belongings are given order, memories of the deceased can enter the bereaved.") Through the ordering of things, one's feelings get ordered (*kimochi no seiri*) as well. But what Robert Desjarlais (2016) calls the poiesis of "making the unmaking" of death—the work of mortuary rituals—is also intended for the deceased, helping to detach the person still lingering in their belongings and the home inhabited on earth. This is why Keepers added, for no additional cost, the service of Buddhist memorial (*kuyō*), which is conducted by a Buddhist priest for a number of customers about once a month in a special room for a few special belongings that were particularly important to the deceased (dolls, photographs, a computer or cell phone). Helping to dislodge the (dead) spirit from the thing, the item is then disposed of, ideally by fire, much like a cremation. Such rites of separation conducted for inanimate objects have a long history in Japan. Going back at least to the start of the Edo period (1603), rituals of *kuyō* have been performed for such everyday objects as needles, scissors, and dolls with the intention of bidding them farewell, releasing any residual negative energy within, and offering gratitude for their utility to humans before being disposed of (Kretschmer 2000, Gygi 2018a, Rambelli 2007). Today, a number of temples perform *kuyō* memorials for discarded dolls, needles, or other personal possessions. And, as with the *ihinseiri* profession, there has been something of a "*kuyō* boom" as if the animism accorded things is getting (re)acknowledged on the brink of death—death of material objects, death of the humans to whom they once belonged (Matsuzaki Kenzō, in Kretschmer 2000).

Kuyō memorials can also be done in anticipation of death when, as is increasingly the case, those who commission the services of Keepers are doing so not for a deceased family member but for themselves ahead of time, as insurance, as it were, for the orderly management of their belongings at death. With *seizen seiri* (putting affairs in order while still alive), one can have one's belongings thinned out beforehand, or readied to be done immediately after death, thereby sparing family members the responsibility. Or, when there is no one else to handle this duty, the to-be-deceased is ensuring that they don't leave a disorderly mess of their remaindered belongings, if not also a corpse, in their dwelling. By (pre)ordering the materiality of their remains, customers are according propriety to others and also a semblance of respect to themselves. As Yoshida puts this, "It is important to not only live like a human, but to die like one."[7] Rituals of humanism performed through the medium of (disposing of) things: another example of what I am calling necro-animism.

The counterexample of a human-like death is the case of Kojirō. Written for his book on solitary death, Yoshida shows the story with manga visuals to public audiences when speaking on the topic of how to avoid becoming solitary.[8] Pulling from the "special cleanup" (*tokushu seisō*/特殊清掃) cases that now constitute about one-fifth of all Keepers jobs (two to three hundred of about fifteen hundred jobs per year), Yoshida shares details of the decrepitude his workers find: putrefaction from long-undiscovered bodies that seeps into surroundings and produces a mass of organic waste, penetrating the very infrastructure of a home—tatami mats, concrete floors, even walls. The decay, as well as the smell, is notoriously horrific, requiring special ozone machines, high-octane cleansing materials, and full-body protective gear for the cleanup crew. The message Yoshida delivers, as reported in the newsletter of Yokohama, where he gave a presentation at a citizens' forum, is that "We can't let this occur—these deaths of people who die alone recognized by nobody surrounded by what becomes possessions of the deceased. In order to prevent this, it is important for us to be people who won't be discovered in these conditions" (Ātofōramu azamino 2015, 3). Using unrecognized death as a limit case of dying badly that could happen to anyone, Yoshida then provides recommendations for restructuring one's life to avoid leaving burdensome remainders (stranded possessions, an untended corpse) at the end. At the Yokohama Forum, these included signing up with a company like Keepers to declutter one's home in advance of death and computing one's finances to save only what is needed to live until the end and to spend the rest on enjoying a full life in the here and now. This is what a woman—admitting that she could imagine becoming a candidate for lonely death herself as it can happen even "in the middle of normal life"—gave as her big takeaway from the forum. Having cleaned her house recently and realized how much in her home would be "useless" (*fuyō*) to anyone else, and thus a nuisance that would bother others after her death, she has decided to pare everything down and to spend down her savings in "doing the things she wants to do" (*yaritai koto*) in the present. An ethos and ethics of self-management that reduces clinging to things—whether belongings, the future, or the genealogical attachments once so normative in Japan—to the end of a sociality of not burdening others and taking joy in present activity. This is the message delivered by Yoshida as a spokesperson in the ending market today about a biopolitics not of productivity but almost the opposite, addressed to aging, postproductive Japanese. And about not letting the inutility (of their belongings and themselves) reduce them to waste (like Mr. Solitary).

By all accounts, Keepers has been extremely successful. In 2016, when I interviewed him, Yoshida had twenty-five full-time employees (including nine women, all in the office), employed as many as thirty dispatch or contract workers for any one job, and had completed a total of 16,000 cases in its fourteen years of operation. It has also spurred an avalanche of other *ihinseirigaisha* nationwide as well as a certification system to raise professionalization in a sector that has had a number of reported scam operations. As he told me with pride, Yoshida maintains the highest of standards with his workers—what he says justifies the relatively higher costs he charges compared to other companies.[9] As the first of its kind, and reflecting the current lifestyle trend in decluttering (*danshari*, spread by such professional declutterers as Marie Kondō), Keepers and its originator have been given considerable media attention. Stories about Yoshida and the business have appeared on television and in the press, generating hosts of customers as well as a degree of pop cultural acclaim. A movie, *Ano toki no inochi*, and manga, *Death Sweepers*, are both loosely based on Keepers.

Yoshida has also published a number of books himself on topics ranging from case studies of what he has encountered as a cleanup worker (2006) to solitary death (2010), real estate and inheritance (2015a), and details concerning funerals, inheritance, and wills (2015b).

Yoshida greeted me warmly the day I met him in his office—really a home in a residential neighborhood with an office upstairs, a big warehouse in the basement loaded with stuff removed from the residences of clients, and a room with a small Buddhist shrine for doing *kuyō*. All of the elements of the business abut here: a home stuffed with possessions in the state of becoming waste awaiting the Buddhist removal of spirits first. A company doing the work of making order of and for things of the dead.

THE WORK ITSELF

To dismantle a home with precision and care is the work of those in the *ihinseiri* business. This much I knew after reading voluminously about this work and interviewing three different directors of *ihinseirigaisha* following my interview with Yoshida. But, being an anthropologist, and assuming I'd get a much better sense of what this process actually entails by visiting the worksite (*genba*) itself, I reached out to Yoshida to see if he might allow me to shadow a work crew. Curious as to why a foreign scholar would want to do this, he accommodated me nonetheless. Thanks to his generosity and the heads of two different crews who handled all the arrangements, I made three on-site visits in the summers of 2017 and 2018: two at homes within Tokyo and one on the edge of Yokohama, all jobs commissioned by family members (including the third, a case of lonely death). My expectation, going into it, was that the work would be carried out efficiently in an orderly and respectful fashion—this is how these companies advertise their service, after all. But what surprised me was the impression of the work getting done almost seamlessly, as if a gentle dust buster had been programmed to silently, automatically empty the house. As I stood there, looking on and being shown boxes getting piled up with stuff and hauled away, there was oddly little sound. Just a home dissolving as if going down a drain. Yet all this was carried out by manual laborers. I found this ordinariness of draining a home extraordinary: an activity of diligence and care to empty with order. A striking contrast to all the emptied homes (*akiya*) and emptied graves (*akihaka*) littering the country these days that stand as markers of decay and neglect (Holden 2017).[10]

P.1 Lanterns strung over the creek at Myōkōji Temple, showing the route back home for departing spirits during Obon.

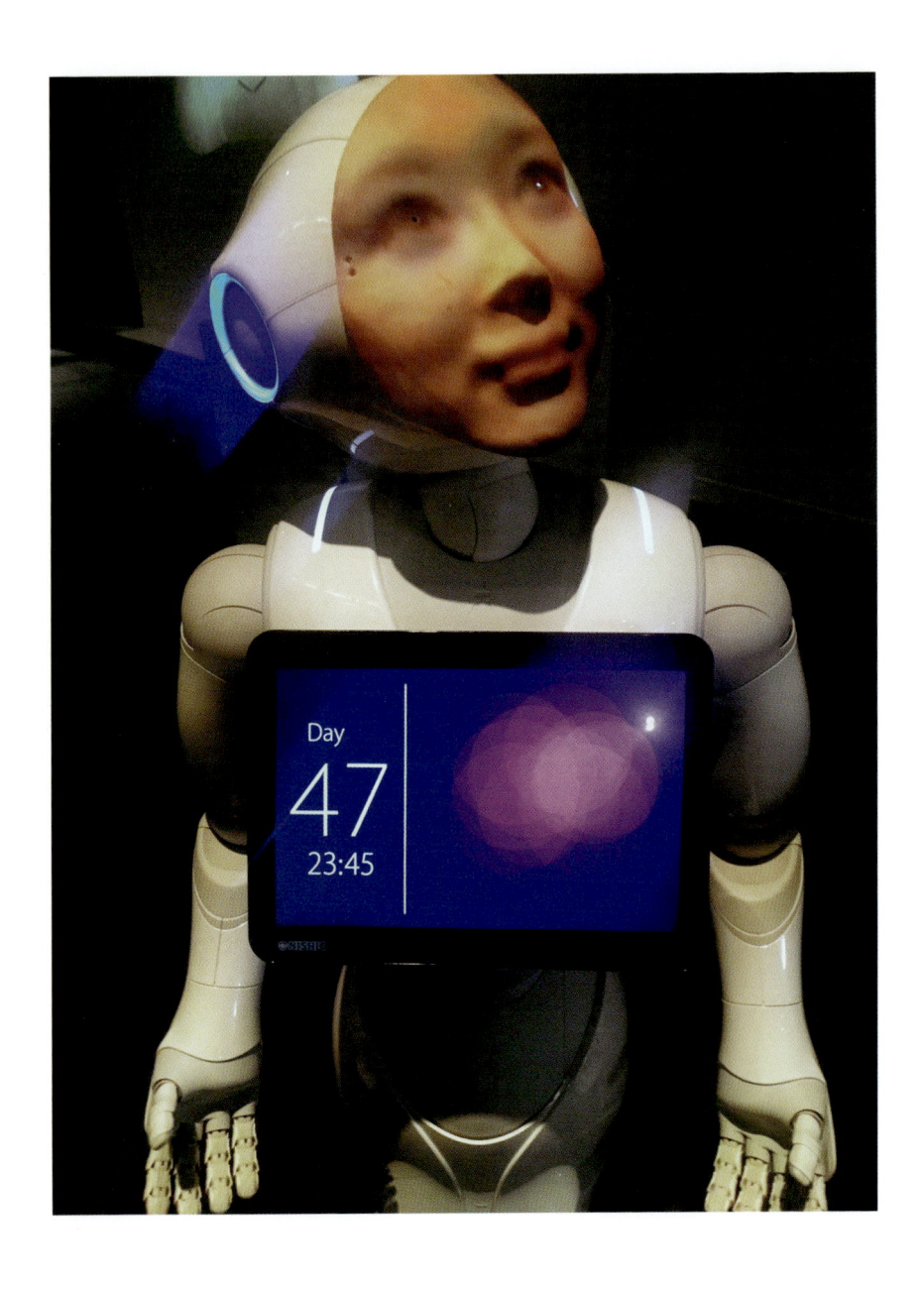

P.2 The *Digital Shaman Project*, an art installation by Ishihara Etsuko, displayed summer 2018. Meant to embody a deceased spirit for the forty-nine days of suspension between the two worlds, during which it is tended to by mourners.

P.3 An altar to the ancestors during Obon.

P.4 A composite of miniatures created by Kojima Miyu to commemorate rooms cleanup workers have been commissioned to clean after a lonely death.

P.5 Two of Kojima Miyu's *gomiyakushi* miniatures, crafted to reproduce rooms that she was commissioned to clean (such as the one on the right) following lonely deaths. *Gomiyakushi* translates as "hoarders."

P.6 Softbank's humanoid robot, Pepper, performing as priest during ENDEX, the annual convention for those in the funeral and cemetery industry.

P.7 A wake held at dusk during a monsoon in Tokyo.

P.8 Lanterns accompanying the dead back home. Kakudasan Myōkōji Temple, Niigata.

A crew of eight, an assortment of contract workers and regular employees, assembled in front of the house shortly before 9 a.m. and donned their company shirts and hats as soon as the Keepers truck arrived. The crew head, Yamanaka, who first checked in with the clients and confirmed they were okay with me being there, gave the workers their assignments.[11] Grabbing empty boxes and gloves, each worker walked into the house and started working in pairs in different places. They began sorting systematically through stuff, removing electronics from walls and cabinets from the floor, moving box after box of carefully managed waste into the van parked outside. A work done with quiet efficiency while I chatted amiably with the middle-aged couple (a professor of engineering and his wife) commissioning the job in this house that had constituted the middle-class dreams of the man's parents. His father had been an architect who moved to Tokyo from his hometown in Niigata in 1962 when he acquired a position here. The neighborhood was still a field in those days, but his father designed the house to accommodate the modern lifestyle of their nuclear family with bedrooms for each child and an office for himself. Fifty-five years later, Mr. Nishimura laughed at his father's wish that his oldest son would inherit the house. "It's a relic," he said dismissively, adding that the still-beautiful *tansu* in the house would be gotten rid of as well. He and his wife lived in a modern place with walk-in closets and had no use for them. But the books his father loved to collect, many of which remained on the bookshelves on the first floor, the son touched with more affection. Still, the only mementos they would keep of the father who had died three years ago and the mother who now lived in a facility close to their own residence had already been removed; everything left in the house was targeted for disposal.

As the dwelling was reduced to mere bones, Yamanaka smoothed out the entire operation, more as if he were kin than the overseer of a contractual job. Continually checking in with the Nishimuras, he advised them about what might have monetary value when the antiques dealer came (only a few coins, a sake set, and some vases for which they were given about $250 in cash) and brought to their attention items he thought were good candidates for the box intended for *kuyō*: belongings particularly close to the deceased. Having hired Keepers because they heard it had a good reputation, they were thoroughly satisfied with the job, as they wrote me afterwards. Similar dynamics transpired at the second job I observed, for Wada-san, a woman in her seventies who lived next door to the house of her parents, which she'd made little headway in cleaning since her mother died a year before. Here, too, was a warmly attentive crew leader, workers packing things up with silent precision, and a client grateful for the care and efficiency with which this job was getting done. Wada flitted here and there during the entire operation, laughing often and apologizing to me at the start of the day for the "mess" I would find things in (even though cleaning it up was the entire point of the job).

Telling me that everything left here would be thrown away (*shobun*), she was nonetheless incredulous that the antique dealer found so little with market value inside the house: a couple of necklaces and a wartime medal from Manchuria that garnered ¥4,000 ($35) in total. Rushing to him with armfuls of his mother's old kimonos ("they're beautiful, right?"), she is told there is no market for these. Just like the carcasses of empty houses dotting the country, the remains of this home fail to carry value to anyone else. Yet the crew treats all this stuff with a discretion that belies its status as waste. Split into teams, carefully categorizing items as they put them into different boxes for different orders of disposal, the workers seem to speak only when conferring about which box to put something into. Working steadily and softly, they produce the neatness of the house coming undone. All the while Yamanaka keeps Wada busy in talk, chatting about which of her mother's belongings should be given memorial before disposal, for example. The crocheted toilet paper coverings she made, for sure, and the clothing she wore in the hospital before dying. All go into what becomes two big boxes destined for *kuyō*. Wada's daughter arrives midmorning to help her mother oversee the job. They tell me that the *butsudan* still standing in the corner will be the one item preserved and carried by the workers to Wada's house next door. The daughter also relates that she's considering moving into the place herself. She, her husband, and their two middle-school-age children live in a high-rise apartment thirty minutes from here. It has been fine, but if this house could be renovated at a reasonable price, it would afford her family more room and a sense of slowness and spaciousness in the neighborhood as well, which she thinks might benefit her children at this stage of growing up.

Movement between different valences of value and different orders of temporality: between a past when this home was full (of people and things), a present when it is getting emptied of the trappings of the dwelling it once was, and a future of possible reinhabitation by reassembling the old in new form. To the degree that they facilitate these shifts, the workers are making the unmaking of this home bearable for those left behind—labor that is a form of poiesis. But what happens when the job involves a corpse that has decayed onto the remains, making what gets removed even less recognizable as human, and may not have social intimates overseeing the cleanup?

These were the circumstances of the third on-site visit I made. Having specifically asked Yoshida if I might be able to observe a case of lonely death, I receive a call the day before by Hashimoto, crew leader for the job, wondering if I can make it on such short notice. Warned that the circumstances will be bleak, I head off with mask and gloves early the next morning. Taking a cab for the last leg to the winding residential neighborhood, I see two young men waiting at the corner and surmise that they are workers. Indeed, they've been hired as *haken* (dispatch workers) for the job, having worked a funeral the day before. Besides Hashimoto, who has worked for Keepers for thirteen years and tells me he loves the job, only one member of today's crew is regularly employed by Keepers.[12] For one, it's his first day. He'll have a hard go of it and by midmorning will almost pass out from the heat.

5.1 A composite of cleanup workers from Keepers and Kojima Miyu (*top, center*), pointing to one of the miniature dioramas of death scenes she has re-created after cleaning it up on the job. The news articles are stories about lonely death.

LONELY DEATH AND CLEANING UP

The day is blistering. And the house, set off of a parking lot where the Keepers van and a truck for industrial waste (*sangyō haikibutsu shūshū unpansha*/産業廃棄物収集運搬社) will sit all day long, has no electricity and therefore no air conditioning. Showing signs of once having been sumptuous—as I later learn, it was over a hundred years old and had survived the Tokyo firebombing during the war—it is overlaid with a trellis of tangled vines in front and has an overgrown garden out back. Once I arrive, I am shooed into one end of the parking lot, where two relatives of the deceased interrogate me about my intentions and ask me not to post pictures on the internet or to use my findings for anything but research. After that, the older one retreats but the other, the younger brother of the deceased—a forty-eight-year old man cutting quite the figure in nylon shorts, T-shirt, stringy hair—darts here and there all day long but is willing to chat. As he tells me, he was the one who discovered the body (four weeks earlier, by this point) after it had been lying there for eleven days. The condition was so horrendous it shocked the firemen who answered the call. But Imura seems unbothered, adding that the two were totally estranged despite being physically proximate; his own residence is in an apartment building down the block.

This was the family home; his brother lived here with their parents until their father died five years ago, and their mother moved into a facility three years after that. An alcoholic who died at fifty-four from liver complications, what he has left behind are piles of disorganized stuff. Each of the four rooms downstairs are strewn with rotting garbage, empty bottles, old newspapers, and containers of half-eaten food. In the tatami room where he died, apparently sitting up on a futon beneath which blood has seeped (as Hashimoto shows me right off the bat), there are stacks of shoeboxes (as many as forty, most with athletic shoes inside), a picture on the wall, a calendar set to July, clothes (some of which look like suit jackets still in wrap from the cleaners), and a couple of old TV monitors. In the adjacent room are boxes of DVDs, cartoons of model dolls, and tons of Lolita magazines (some unopened). The place is a mess. The smell stings immediately and ramps up throughout the day as the heat intensifies and we inch toward the front room (which is handled last in the cleanup). Everyone stays masked and the workers keep up a steady pace despite the intensity of the job. But it is a hard slog. During the first break, the newbie of the team has flushed cheeks; Hashimoto asks if he's ok and orders him to lie down and drink plenty of fluids. Once back on the job, he moves slowly, I notice. Even the veterans take an occasional pause. One of the contract workers I'd met earlier simply stops at one point on the pathway in front of the house—catching his breath, gathering his thoughts? He stands there for a good five minutes before starting up again with the work.

The younger brother wants to keep nothing. When I notice a small wooden box in one of the rooms, he picks it up and tells me it's his brother's umbilical cord. But he doesn't keep this or a big album of photographs the workers find. There's no box for *kuyō*, either. Hashimoto confirms that Imura doesn't want any memento at all of his brother or the family home. But, don't worry, he reassures me, Keepers will perform *kuyō* on a few appropriate items back at the office on their own. Standing in for the social ties so fissured here and performing this ritual gesture in addition to the physical job of emptying the house. The younger brother seems to conceptualize this in strictly utilitarian terms—physical removal of life reduced to the bare minimum of the waste made by a dead body and his stuff. Bare death. Akin to—if the inverse of—the minimal biopolitics of maintaining bare life that Redfield argues is the humanitarian work of Doctors Without Borders (2013). Imura tells me that his brother's ashes have already been sent to a high-rise columbarium nearby. As for the house, he would sell it if it were up to him. But the decision will be his mother's, and he's not sure of her plans.

As I overhear the uncle say when a neighbor comes over in the middle of the day to complain about the mess the house has been in for years, with branches and weeds obstructing the path in front, "This is a case of lonely death. I'm only a distant relative and we're all doing what we can to just get rid of everything as quickly as we can." But, on leaving, I am shown again to the room where the man had died. Lifting up the futon and staring hard at the blood, Hashimoto murmurs softly, "This is how a life ended." Witnessing this unwitnessed dead. Responding to the body by giving recognition of sorts to the person once there (Butler 2009, 50).

ADDRESSING THE WOUNDS OF HOME

Getting rid of decaying matter as quickly and thoroughly as possible is the task shouldered by the cleanup workers: a job that is at once material and social, relieving the landscape of disorder and stench. In the process, it exposes disposers to human decomposition, yielding a smell of death (*shishū*/死臭, 屍臭) considered uncanny and strange (*ishū*/異臭). Pungency arising from illness and disease is often unbearable for family members themselves, as Julie Livingston discovered in her study of a cancer ward in Botswana. Nurses step in when tending to the open and rotting sores wrought by the progression of cancer. In standing in for family members, "one of the most crucial tasks of oncology nursing is to humanize patients whose bodies are undergoing profoundly disfiguring processes of decomposition" (Livingston 2012, 108). What Livingston calls "embodied work"—touching the wounds of others with one's hands—rehumanizes patients with neither sympathy nor pity but with empathy (110). An empathy driven by the belief that nurses can perceive another's suffering at the level of feeling and transform that into a phenomenology of care. A practice and form of care labor for patients that devolves upon "addressing their wounds matter of factly and gently" (112).

Though their job is quite different—eliminating the remnants of lives now decomposing rather than attending to bodies in the process of dying—disposers, too, are addressing wounds that they attend to with gentle matter-of-factness. It is in the practical labor of attending to material remains that care is performed, as Amade M'charek and Sara Casartelli (2019) have argued about the forensics done on the retrieved bodies of migrants drowned in the Mediterranean Sea. Carried out carefully, it addresses the bones—apart from or regardless of the identities they once were attached to. A forensics of care is how Elizabeth Davis (2017) characterizes the work done in Cyprus to piece together fragments of bones dug up from where they were hidden during the country's Civil War. Delicately performed, the technical labor becomes an act of "rehumanization of the dead" (229) in which workers stand in as "proxies for the relatives" (230) who can't be there because no one (yet) knows the identities of the remains. According to Davis, the relationship formed between the living and dead is one of "vital materialism" (239)—a vitalism reaching within and beyond the materiality of dead bones to an existence that transcends biological life in the here and now. This, too, I would argue, is the terrain of cleanup workers who, close in time and space to death, are exposed to the life still lingering in the objects of the dead that they are employed to cart away. Stuff entangled in homes that workers are there to disentangle in a labor of gently escorting outside.

Another figure in the *ihinseiri* business, Kimura Eiji, describes a worker who spent weeks listening to the memories of a woman who had commissioned him for the job of cleaning out her residence in anticipation of her death.[13] Aging and single, she knew that no one else would do this for her nor appreciate any of her belongings once she was gone. Carefully going through each item one by one while relating the memories attached to them before putting them into the box for disposal, the woman was "touched" by this worker behaving as if a "friend" (Kimura 2015, 185–86). In this job of removing matter, the currency was memory. Kimura advertises this to potential customers as the objective of his ordering and disposal service (Kimura 2015), which I was surprised to hear when I interviewed his associate director about what was, after all, a cleanup company. Under the motto "You'll never lose touch with your memories," this is what Kone Hideto told me their company's mission was: "trying to help customers think ahead of time of how to retain proof that they had lived at all."[14] As in, staying in touch with what has mattered in one's life, even while discarding one's belongings. Jason Danely, in his research on aging and loss in Japan, eloquently calls the home the place where memories are embodied and sheltered in possessions, noting how getting rid of things can feel like throwing away the person who once inhabited and possessed them.

As he relates about Mori, one of the subjects he tracked for years, whose "mountain of belongings" hoarded at home elicited disgust and pity from her grown daughters, the difficulty she had in paring things down was existentially painful (Danely 2014, 40–41). It took years, and endless battles with her daughters, before any progress was made. For, as with all of those in his study, Mori was facing the challenge of managing the loss and grief of aging. Some, Danely found, manage the task of detaching from their material things with remarkable grace. But for those unable to do so on their own or needing help to complete this task before they die, a cleanup company like Kimura's can offer assistance. To retain, as Marie Kondō advocates in her method for decluttering, only those things that spark joy in their owner, but to respectfully show gratitude to all possessions that are then escorted out of one's life.

To commission this for oneself in anticipation of death—what more and more customers of *ihinseirigaisha* are doing for themselves while still alive—is one thing. But, as Kone told me in an interview, the work of ordering and disposal reveals a microcosm of the conditions in which Japanese are living ever longer and dying disconnected in ever higher rates. The figures he quoted me for lonely death were 2.5 percent of those dying in 2016, predicted to rise to 15 percent by 2022, 28 percent by 2026, and a whopping 45 percent by 2030.[15] Special cleanup jobs (80 percent of which are cases of lonely death) now constitute one-fifth of all the work his company does, and the demand is sure to rise along with the pressure on certified disposers, only some of whom can handle the emotional and physical arduousness. As Kone admitted to me, he has done this work himself. "The toughest part is the smell. There's nothing like it. And it stays with you forever, this thing." But having just heard from him that his company's motto is "You'll never lose touch with your memories," I am reminded of an observation Yoshida made of a job he and his work crew from Keepers did to clean up a woman's room in a senior living facility. Her estranged son had commissioned the job and refused to take any of the photos they found, including a couple of him as a boy holding his mother's hand. Yoshida called these "mementos with no place to go" (*ikiba no nai katami*), recalling how difficult the experience was for his workers (Yoshida 2009, 49). As one put it, "I usually feel a sense of accomplishment when the job is done. But today it felt like we couldn't give anything to the old woman. I feel full of apologies to her" (Yoshida 2009, 52).

THOSE WHO TOUCH THE REALNESS OF BAD DEATH

In the wounds of the homes they are emptying, workers are exposed to the pain evoked by the carcasses of possessions. Meanwhile, they are scanning for signs of something else: what Kimura calls "information about the deceased," which he says any skilled worker should be able to find even amid the greatest disarray—a buried photo, an old sports award, drawings in a sketchpad (Kimura 2015, 74). If found, these mementos should be passed on to the bereaved (if there are any) or else simply acknowledged by the worker. Proof that the deceased once lived a life that mattered—somehow, in some form—given a semblance of recognition here. As Judith Butler has written, "Only under conditions in which the loss would matter does the value of the life appear. Thus, grievability is a presupposition for the life that matters" (2009, 14). And, keeping in mind Newell's (2014) concept of the unfetish of possessions where the personal spirit still lingers even in the detritus of a hoarder's stuff, cleanup workers may be the last to address the person who once lived in the mountain of belongings they are now ushering out of the homes of the otherwise unrecognized dead.

Given their intimacy with scenes of death, cleanup workers are uniquely positioned to offer not only final respects to the deceased but also commentary on the conditions of decomposing sociality they find on-site. As Yoshida (2010) makes clear in his book on solitary death, for example, it is based on what he has seen with his own eyes that he warns readers to do whatever they can now—be active, keep or kindle connections with others, make mortuary plans ahead of time—to prevent dying like Mr. Solitary.

Gathered from the "realness" of this kind of death, the material disarray itself is what Yoshida lays out—in graphic detail—in the firsthand accounts he gives of being a disposer (Yoshida 2009). This is also the tactic taken in a comic book series devoted to the gruesome extremes of the special cleanup work done by disposers. Framed as a kind of moralistic tale, with youthful cleanup workers taking on the work of tending to the dead in the face of their elders' and society's failure to do so (reminiscent of what Filip de Boeck [2010] has found in new mortuary rituals conducted by Congolese youth in Kinshasa), *Death Sweeper* (デス・スウィーパー) opens with the self-starvation of a once promising medical student.[16] Disillusioned by the lack of futurity offered him by his country's institutions, the young man dies. The decomposing corpse is found by his younger brother, Hiroyuki, five days later. In the malaise Hiroyuki subsequently spirals into, it is the memory of the cleanup worker who tended to his brother's remains that somehow moves him. He finds a job advertisement for the *ihinseirigaisha* and applies. Although the office woman warns him about the smell ("that never leaves you") and the boss figures he'll never be able to put up with the job, being a college type, Hiroyuki pleads, "Please hire me; I need to catch the reality of my brother's death." Given that it's summer and the suicide rate is sure to rise, requiring more workers, he is taken on.

The work starts immediately with a job where, with odors reminiscent of those he experienced with his brother, a seventy-year-old man has died alone, "dissolved" in a hot bath. Right off the bat, Hiroyuki is fishing out ears and other bodily remnants from the bathtub—after running out of the room to throw up. His partner reminds him that this "still is, or once was, a human." Afterward, when dragging him to a fried food restaurant—the only place they can go to eat where their own stink of decayed flesh is disguised by that of frying meat—he asserts that their job is tough but important; "Someone has to do this work." This is the story explored in the comic. Of cleanup workers absorbing, and tending to, the decomposition of human remains in cases of solitude or neglect (such as when a man insists that the windows stay closed during the cleanup to not alert his neighbors of the smell of his wife's death by suicide). For Hiroyuki, however, the work is animating. Over time he becomes not only used to the job but enlivened by it, as if the shock of dealing with the dead flesh of the socially wounded makes him newly attuned to the poignancy of life. Brought to a recognition of life in general, he is brought back from the precipice of losing it himself.

PRESERVING THE SMELL: DOLLHOUSES OF AND FOR THE LONELY DEAD

Something similar is at play in the extraordinary dioramas a cleanup worker has crafted of the scenes of lonely death she has encountered in doing her job. Kojima Miyu was drawn to this work because, like Hiroyuki, she personally experienced a family member who had a lonely death. Her father became estranged from his family and suffered a heart attack, but was found by her mother, who happened to go by that day to check on him. Though her father had been a violent man who had beaten her and her mother, Kojima nonetheless regretted the state of his death: socially broken with nothing tying him to anyone else. Twenty-two when she started working at To-Do Company in 2014—the only woman I have encountered in the business who works on site rather than in the office—Kojima began her miniatures two years later. She makes them in her spare time, in the garage that serves as the company's warehouse, out of a desire and intention she can't entirely explain. Never an artist before this, the impulse just came to her: "shrinking and condensing" the scenes she has encountered at the start of a job as a disposer (Kojima 2019, 8).

Kojima first displayed six of her miniatures at ENDEX, the national convention for those in the mortuary business, in Tokyo, summer 2016. Her display, called *mini gomiyashiki* (miniatures of hoarding) for the material clutter in two of the six dioramas, immediately drew media attention, but her models had become even more newsworthy three years later. At ENDEX summer 2019, visitors swarmed the To-Do booth, stacked as it was with Kojima's models and the book she had just published on the subject. *Toki ga tomatta heya: ihinseirinin ga minichua de tsutaeru kodukushi no hanashi* (Rooms where time has stopped: stories of lonely deaths as conveyed by miniatures) (2019) is something of a catalogue of these ENDEX displays.

Lined up in a row on the table, each with a note describing the circumstances of the person whose home is depicted, the dioramas measure the size of a medium cardboard box (about 12 by 18 inches).[17] The detail is uncanny. The smallest, titled "Died inside the Toilet," represents a Japanese-style water closet: two brown walls with white water tank affixed in-between, Japanese-style toilet on a two-tiered blue tile floor, roll of toilet paper strewn across the room, toilet brush fallen on its side, and pools of dark red blood inside the toilet and splashed on the floor. The story reads: "Discovered one week after dying. Seems to have collapsed when she was in the toilet. No ambulance was called. Lived in what was once a famous

5.2 One of Kojima's miniatures: a room where a corpse was discovered on the futon.

danchi [apartment complex popular in the postwar rebuilding effort of the 1950s and '60s] and wanted to die at home. As she had no one to depend upon, the landlord looked after the final affairs. Discovered in October—two months after death."

In another, there are three walls with sliding screens (*shōji*) and a fourth opened halfway onto a six-tatami-mat room with a television set in one corner, a small table scattered with an assortment of food containers and cans, two magazines on the floor, newspapers neatly wrapped for garbage set outside the room, and a beige futon soaked its entire length in the dark hues of dried blood. Under "Life Insurance Went to Daughter," the account is: "When [the man was] found, the daughter was contacted by the local municipality (*yakusho*). They had been estranged for twenty years and she renounced her inheritance. He'd been living a hand-to-mouth existence on welfare. There was vomit and blood on the toilet stool. He's likely to become a *muenbotoke* (disconnected soul). Hard to know what there was between parent and child; perhaps he thought of his daughter at the end. Cause of death: internal bleeding. Discovered in July, one month after death. The landlord will bear the cost of cleanup and refurbishing the apartment." Tiny dogs and cats populate two of the other rooms—one the site of a suicide where the dog, unfed for days, also died and was burned on the premises by the cleanup crew, who gave it a memorial service. In another, a bath (*ofuro*) overflows with a muddy avalanche: the result of a death caused by the shock of the hot water and a corpse that then sat there for the two months it went undetected while the heating device continued to ratchet up.

Intriguingly perverse. These scenes less of living than of death, all miniaturized and disturbingly still. Not toys to be played with but scenarios that, as Susan Stewart (1993) says of dollhouses, materialize secrets. Kojima is taking us into her world of cleanup and lonely death, exposing what the public doesn't see and senses only indirectly. What motivates her craft is to convey the misery of lonely death, which is hard to understand with a photograph. The feeling of realness upon discovering a corpse: this is what she hopes to pass on to others. It is not to shock those who see these models, but to transmit the feelings of empathy she experiences in the course of discovering and cleaning up the remains of lonely corpses. These feelings are better communicated, Kojima believes, through a medium other than photography, which, too "hard to look at," "hides the core of things," and thus fails to convey what she calls the "realness" of the scene (*genba*) (Kojima 2019, 6–7). But what precisely this is she doesn't quite manage to articulate. In my interview with her, she tells me that she is trying to communicate something different in each replica, but it is always about the humanness of the person who died.

With one of her most recent—of a twenty-one-year-old student who died by suicide—it is the tragedy of someone dying so young in such a normal-looking room. The room is tidy and sparsely furnished: a futon with a navy blue blanket, a refrigerator in the corner with a toaster oven on top, two bags of garbage ready to be taken out, a small staircase up to what looks like a loft for storage, and a low table on which are two newspapers and the suicide note. A noose, bloody at one end, is knotted high on the staircase, and ゴメン (*gomen*)—the word for "I'm sorry"—is written in large letters of green masking tape on the wall. The scene feels immediately, viscerally sad. It is the letters I can't stop looking at. An expression of regret, but made to whom, about what? Kojima and I wonder out loud together. That we don't know makes the scenario inconclusive, the miniature tugging at the unknowability of it all. The effect is quite different from what another miniaturist, the New England socialite and heiress Frances Glessner Lee, intended with her dioramas. Although they also miniaturized death scenes, Lee designed hers in the 1930s and 1940s to the end of advancing

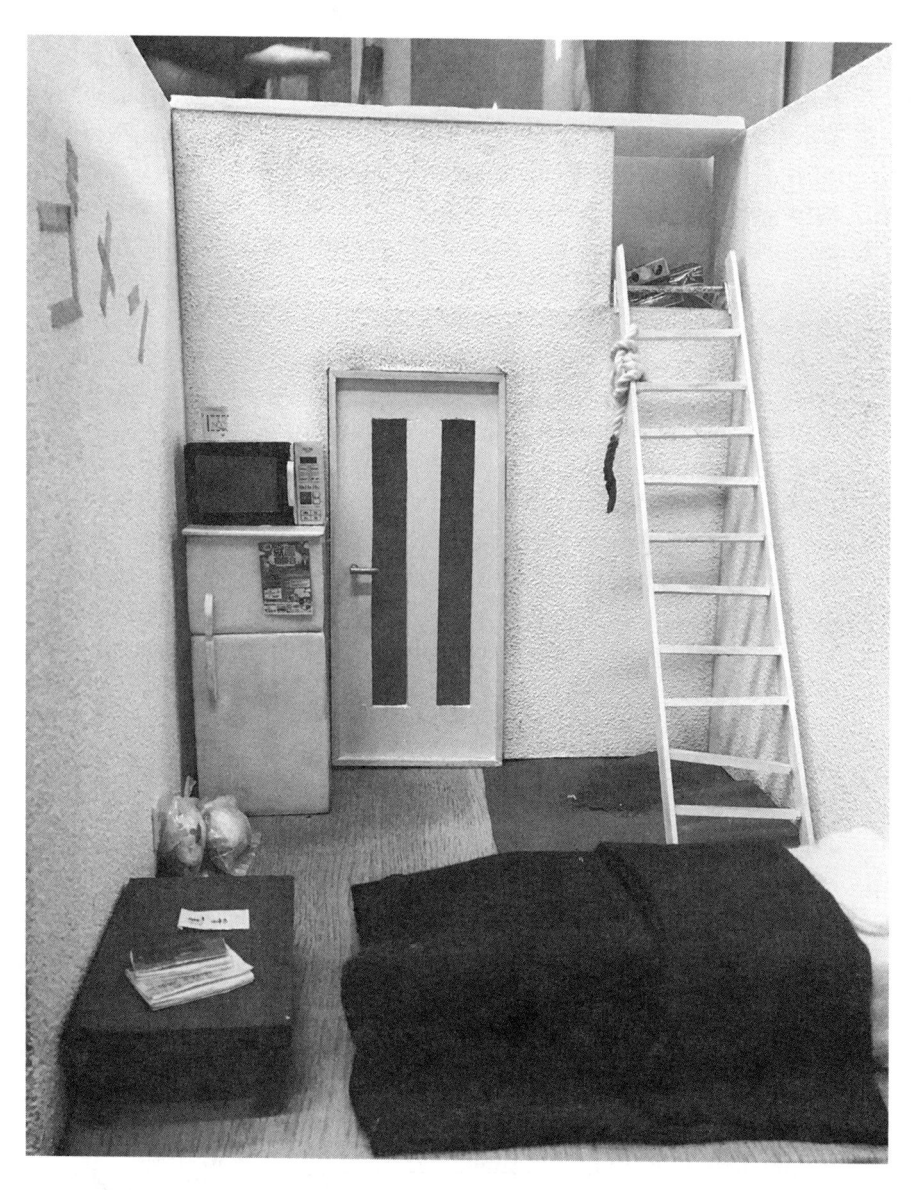

5.3 Another of Kojima's miniatures: a room where a young student committed suicide by hanging.

forensic science. Convinced that if only the setting could be properly seen, the truth would be revealed, Lee made her Nutshell Studies of Unexplained Death to teach those trying to solve crimes how to read the materiality of clues. Lee finished twenty before she died in 1962 and was honored by an exhibit of her work at the Renwick Gallery in the Smithsonian American Art Museum in 2017. Eighteen of the nutshells are still used by the Maryland office of chief medical examiner to train detectives in the forensic science of deciphering crime scenes (Zhang 2017).[18]

But there is no one truth that is being conjured by Kojima's dioramas. While one can read the signs for what resulted in death—a bloody bathtub indicating overheating, a dangling noose pointing to suicide—it is far less clear what life had been like for the deceased. As Walter Benjamin has said, the art of good storytelling is built not from information—what he decried in the 1920s as the "new form of communication"—but from human experience, which, far more layered and ambivalent than mere facts, defies quick and definitive conclusions (Benjamin 1969, 88). This is true, too, of Kojima's art, which, though accurately depicting the scenes of lonely death encountered by a cleanup worker, tells only so much of what the process of living and dying all alone was like. What makes these miniatures so powerful is the work demanded of the viewer in filling in the story—imagining, feeling, putting oneself in the place of this other, empathetically giving care. Taking in the uncanniness of these homes.

The detail is arresting: the pillow on the futon at an angle, a cup of noodles standing next to the toaster oven, the bloody noose over a blue mat soaked in matching red. Life arrested in death: the moment of discovery before cleanup begins. Kojima tells me she takes pictures of everything, which is vital for the accuracy she seeks in imitating the scenes—a process that takes her about one month each to complete. Which she does, as with the work of cleanup itself, with care. "I do this work feeling as if these are the rooms of my own family" (Kojima 2019, 138).[19] Care work as a form of communication. In communicating the realness of feelings in discovering a body, she is telling a story to those who will see her miniatures and also to the dead, hoping perhaps that they will feel her presence, as she had wanted her father to, even after the fact. Sinking deep into the death scene she cleans up with her hands, Kojima is trying to retrieve something in the remains that communicates—to her, to others, to the deceased—the humanness of the deceased. As she says of one of the cases memorialized in a diorama, body fluids had seeped out "quietly after death." Giving poetry to the decomposition of flesh, she sees an "eloquence about his life left behind in the remains." This, despite being a "father who couldn't communicate through words,"[20] as evidenced by the fact that the daughter commissioning the job had been estranged from him for thirty years (Kojima 2019, 26). Leaving Kojima, the cleanup worker, to address the wounds of his belongings. For only after the job was done and the room now emptied and clean did the daughter step into the home in which her father had perished.

"Up to the Ceiling" depicts the dwelling of a hoarder. "The job was commissioned by Chiba Prefecture. Someone had noticed stuff piled up to the ceiling and notified the landlord. The resident had been a man in his sixties living alone on the second floor. The apartment building was wooden and old, and many of the residents had moved away. He'd been living on welfare, and when the neighbors noticed a bad smell coming from his place, more moved away as well. "Cause of death—unclear. Died in February. Discovered two months later." This one fascinates more than possibly any of them with the volume and mixture of waste so minutely crafted and packed to the gills of this dollhouse of mess. Crumpled magazines, containers of half-eaten food, newspapers flung next to beer cans, and endless plastic bags, even a few garbage bags neatly tied up. On one wall a picture dangles precariously and the drapes on the window hang raggedly off to one side. Cupboards line the other wall, bringing no order to any of its junk. This is a scene of utter bleakness and rot. It is stunning to imagine someone inhabiting such a space. More stunning yet to see it reproduced here with such fidelity, down to what Kojima points out are tiny plastic bottles filled with a yellow liquid representing the urine she found, along with plastic bags of excrement: how this man handled his bodily waste as the toilet was stopped up. Picking his way along a single path like an "animal's trail" to live in what became the home of his death. Kojima cleaned this up as part of her job; when I ask her how difficult it was, she answers that it was hard but not disgusting. Part of the spectrum, she suggests, of being human these days. Of living as a hoarder, of dying all alone, of the challenges facing everyone in a country where the rates of lonely death, single households, and isolation are spiraling upward quickly.

Kojima states at the end of our interview, "Our job is to clean everything up. But the smell never entirely disappears." In her craft, so carefully wrought, of miniaturizing death scenes, Kojima would seem to be purposely holding on to this smell. Conjuring it, if not literally then imaginatively, in the reminders she gives of lives that ended all alone. Arresting the death in time, she preserves it: a "*repetition* of a death that is therefore not a death" (Stewart 1993, 69). As if to let this, at least, speak of the life she recognizes in and of the deceased. Touching the dead as if they matter, have mattered, somehow (Butler 2009). And making sure, in these replicas of death, that we don't—that someone doesn't—entirely forget.

As I stand in front of her miniatures in the garage where To-Do keeps its warehouse and Kojima crafts her art, I am dressed in my winter coat and Kojima is dressed in a down jacket. I am shivering in the February air. Not from the cold, I think. But from these traces, made into artwork, of a lonely kind of death. So ineffable and strange, disturbing yet utterly profound, these dollhouses hit me deep in the gut, stealing my ability to find the words for the interview I came here to conduct. Instead I stand quietly, looking at the scenes. Feeling much like I did on the day when, shadowing the Keepers crew to the house where a man had died sitting up, all alone, I also stood at a scene of lonely death. Taken there by the head of the work crew, shown the blood, addressing the life that ended on this spot. And putting up with the smell: unsocial, unruly, but all too human nonetheless.

CONCLUSION

Smell, as suggested at the start of this chapter, is promiscuous. Hard to contain. Even when policing against it has risen alongside modernization and urban living, those aromas that spill over nonetheless—particularly when the source is human—demand an involvement of sorts. Unwelcome, perhaps, as when we find the panhandler on the street to be smelly—smelling of themselves but inside our noses. Something too much about someone else, it can trigger anxiety about oneself. "This could be me," Gabrielle Brown writes about encountering homeless people on the street. "Loquacious in its effect upon the senses of others," smell is potent in arousing all sorts of things (Brown 2015, 35). Including a response of recognition in tending to the remains of those who died unrecognized by the intimate others they did not have or were long estranged from. As with Kojima Miyu, a cleanup worker, who not only bears the smell but re-creates the scenes where she encounters it. Giving care—to the dead and to the living whom she is inviting, by witnessing these dioramas, to care for humanity in a much more capacious sense than within the lines once drawn—and now falling apart—for belonging in Japan. In disaggregating care from the social hands that once provided it and according care to the "dead without family" these days, I call this "promiscuous care" (Care Collective 2020, 40). Performed in the register of smell.

In its immediate practices, burial involves the corporeal remains of kin. Yet from their very inception these remains are not just themselves. They become symbols and ciphers for what they are not. In death, the other is not simply there in his or her corporeality. She or he is not-there yet exists as *having-been*. This *placelessness* of the dead is crucial. The ritual will always be a care for *something* in the place of *someone* who has been, as a shaping and articulation of this being with the dead. This is its temporal & historical reality.

Hans Ruin, *Being with the Dead* (2018)

de-parting
the handling of
remaindered remains

On a quiet morning, stilled by summer heat, I participate in a "picking of the bones" (*kotsuage*) ritual. Following the funeral, which followed the wake the night before, this is an intimate gathering of those closest to the dead and takes place at the crematorium to which we have accompanied the corpse. Greeting what emerges from the furnace, all hover around the gurney before lining up in pairs to move a single bone fragment from one tray to another. Staying with the dead, witnessing the transformation, placing the pieces into what will be their new home. Once filled, the urn is handed to the chief mourner, who, as the descendant's successor, represents the family. Following the genealogical principle, the living survivors will now be tasked with the work of caretaking the dead spirit via daily and seasonal rituals at the grave and *butsudan* over a period of thirty-three years until the spirit of the deceased is absorbed into the ancestral collective. A material sign of the social bond of continuity embedded in handling the dead and remains.

Six months later I am standing inside what could be a broom closet for its darkness and size. This room, in the city hall of Yokosuka City, is where the remains of residents who died alone are stored while staff attempt to contact the next of kin. But, even when kin are contacted, these days fewer are claiming the remains, which rest on shelves collecting dust. In an era when unclaimed remains are on the rise nationwide, most of those here will be buried in the municipal grave for the disconnected after the prescribed six months of waiting. Then, eventually, the remains will be emptied from their urns, intermixed as collective ashes, and moved into an ossuary marked *disconnected*. And yet the majority are identified by name—a fact that makes their failure to be claimed all the more egregious, and sad, to the official whose job it is to oversee his city's unclaimed remains. A material sign of the social bond absented in handling the dead and remains.

That we live in relationship to others is marked at the level of the body—the material substance seemingly housing the individual self. Exposed to and dependent on other humans, our own bodies are not precisely our own. Considering this the ontological condition of human existence, what she calls precariousness, Judith Butler argues, "We can think of demarcating the human body through identifying its boundary, or in what form it is bound, but that is to miss the crucial fact that the body is, in certain ways, and even inevitably unbound. It is outside itself, in the world of others, in a space and time it does not control, and it not only exists in the vector of these relations, but as the very vector. In this sense, the body does not belong to itself" (2009, 52–53).

That the body is social is true in death as well as in life. What becomes of a corpse, and how and for whom it engenders affects, meanings, or practices (or fails to do so), depends on others. Referring to remains as "relational bones," anthropologist Elizabeth Hallam notes that they operate as relational entities in that they are defined, treated, and shaped within relations of various sorts—"relations which can be at once material and social, emotional and political, and which develop and change over time" (Hallam 2010, 468). Bones can be violently removed from a corpse to become a war trophy, museum artifact, or commercial commodity; or they can be lovingly washed and preserved as remnants of the departed in transit to a spiritual destination somewhere else. These are radically "different kinds of entities." And "how they become salient, how they are sensed as affective, emotive, or otherwise, requires examination in social contexts" (Hallam 2010, 465).

Hallam calls the work anatomists do *articulation*: piecing together bones to reconstruct the skeletal "architecture" they once inhabited as a living thing. A craft of relationality, articulation involves joining parts in the materiality of bodily remains and in the (social, religious, and medical) logic by which these are read or onto which they are mapped. In the case of anatomy, the enterprise is driven by knowledge: seeking to better understand how the body functions for medical or scientific reasons or to identify an unidentified body, whether for a criminal case, the exhumation of a mass grave site, or the retrieval of war dead in foreign lands (Wagner 2019). But even at the anatomical level, the ways in which bones link up to one another and the rest of the body are varied and complex. This is true, too, of how bones speak of or to the world outside. Dead bodies are indisputably there, Katherine Verdery (1999) has said, making them a thing that is always more than a thing. But along with their *thereness*, corpses also materialize the *not-thereness* of (a) being no longer alive. That bones make present what is absent increases their efficacy as symbols, she suggests, but it can also make the material of corpses charged with something beyond or outside meaning altogether—what I am more interested in here.

This relationship between the materiality and sociality of dead body parts is what I take up in this chapter, questioning how changes in the sociological composition of the living population—the downsizing of the family system, increase of single-person households, high aging and low childbirth demographics, lifestyle trends toward expedience, speed, and individual responsibility—impact the treatment of decomposed human matter. With diminishing numbers of social hands to move the dead through mortuary rituals, what happens not only to the handling of this matter (and for and by whom) but to the materiality itself and the lines by which it is distinguished and regulated? At one end of the spectrum (as discussed in chapter 5) one sees alternatives to the familial or intimate hands that are not so readily available these days for tending to (someone's) bones: cleanup workers, for example, who, in performing their job carefully, accord a form of care to the deceased whose belongings they cart away. At the other end of the spectrum are shifts occurring in the processing and handling of the materiality of remains. A notable one here is downsizing. Mimicking the overall trend toward simplifying mortuary practices (as in the popularization of family-only or direct funerals over more formal, expensive affairs), there is a reduction in the quantity of ash retained as well as in particle size. Keeping a smaller amount of ash allows handheld or wearable urns (a pendant, for example). But what motivates these new fashions is not necessarily the absence of social hands. Rather, in at least some cases, it is the desire not to abandon death making but to make it more in sync with the lifestyles of twenty-first-century Japanese—carrying the grave around one's neck, as it were, instead of having to make an arduous trip to the countryside to visit it twice a year. I often heard about bringing the dead "close" from those both promoting and consuming such new-style products as "at-hand memorial" (*temoto kuyō*) goods. Yet, in such new trends involving the reduction or alteration of cremains, there are other implications to consider as well, such as what happens to the increased amount of remains now designated as waste, and what is the attitude of grievability toward the dead when the vehicle this is encased in is a diamond, a robot, or a technological gamescape?

These are the questions I ponder in this chapter. I do so by a rather simple exercise: tracking the ontological shifts bodies undergo as they depart by different procedures tended by diverse sets of hands. In the four venues I examine here—a ritual of bone picking, unclaimed remains in a municipality, the work of a crematorium producing both cremains and "leftover ash," and a bone-crushing business—I follow the particles themselves as they move according to different scripts and on different trajectories. Throughout, I consider who is handling these different parts and with what kind of posture or relationship to the dead. And, given how rapidly a system once dependent on the family is changing these days, what are the tensions or ambiguities of these shifts in the ecology of dead material itself? For this is a particular kind of matter that, even when treated as waste, remains entangled in the life just departed. Demanding a response of some kind.[1]

I draw on recent research by archaeologist-anthropologist Shannon Dawdy, who looks at the "afterlives" of new-style commodities that memorialize the dead in the United States. With ashes transformed into portraits, diamonds, or glass sculptures in order to commune with the deceased after they are gone, these "commodity relics" are ontologically ambiguous. Inviting ghosts to reside in commodity form, they are objects that are also subjects intended to extend indefinitely the ambiguity (presence and absence) of the corpse (Dawdy 2019, 207). Using Shannon's term *unsettled entities*, I contemplate how dead matter is formed and re-formed in various combinations, questioning what happens to the relationalities between self and other, person and object, and living and dead in the course of doing so.

PICKING UP BONES

In the middle of August, on a day steaming with heat, a small group of intimates accompanied the corpse to the crematorium.[2] This came at the end of a farewell ceremony (*kokubetsushiki*) that had been exceptionally grand. Over six hundred relatives, acquaintances, and business associates showed up the night of the wake for the deceased—president of his own company, father and grandfather of multiple offspring, a budding politician, and member of a golfing league. Held in an upscale funeral hall, the place was well curated, with photos of the deceased spread throughout, a wall of white chrysanthemums at one end, tall fans blowing air across sculpted blocks of ice. Having streamed in past tables where they deposited envelopes with funeral money (*kōden*) at the start, mourners were ushered upstairs to be served drinks and small snacks after the service. While there, the ritual successor, the deceased's eldest son, gave formal greetings thanking everyone for their attendance.

The next day, a sizable if smaller number of people showed up for the funeral, where two priests recited sutras and a friend performed a song he had written himself. Coming up to the altar in pairs, mourners burned farewell incense (*shōkō*) to the deceased, nodded respects to the family sitting up front, and filed past the body in the coffin, adding a single flower to what became a floral blanket. Then, waiting outside, given final greetings by the chief mourner, everyone bowed as the casket was carried to the hearse by six attendants. Showing respect, sending farewells, moving things along.

At this point, most of those attending left. Remaining are just a few of us: intimate family and friends who have chosen to accompany the body to the crematorium. After one more farewell ceremony in front of the furnaces, we are shepherded upstairs to a room with cold drinks and hot tea. People chat lightly and relax as we wait for an hour. Then, fetched by an attendant, we return to the furnace room, where, bracing for my first *kotsuage*, I am not sure what to expect. But the mood has become quite matter-of-fact as we greet what has emerged from the furnace on the trolley-cart. Standing at its head, the attending staff guides us, describing what we are seeing and what this process of picking bones entails. Strewn in front of us, still hot from the furnace, lies a substantial amount of ash and bone fragments: what the lower temperature of cremation in Japan is meant to retain. Though not recognizable as the person, they signify the dead nonetheless—the remains of the deceased that are called "bones of the deceased" (*ikotsu*) or sometimes just "bones" (*kotsu*).

People seem curious, peering at the remains as if in an anatomy lesson, commenting on the color and sturdiness they see. One woman says, "These are fine bones" (*rippa desu ne*) and another agrees. For a man who died of cancer at age sixty-eight, this strikes me as an odd pronouncement. But, as I am told, the bones of even sicker, more fragile elderly can appear yellow and brittle. Those of children are so sadly small. Someone else murmurs that they look a tad reddish, an effect, she surmises, of the fact that he insisted on wearing his favorite red bathrobe into the furnace. (Better for him not to have done so in order for the bones to be whiter now, she whispers as we leave.)

Not letting us linger too long, the attendant soon picks up key fragments. The ear bones, pieces of the cranium, and—of most significance—the *nodobotoke*: the hyoid bone from the midline of the neck, which is thought to look like a sitting Buddha. Putting these aside and arranging the bigger pieces in one section of the cart, he invites us to join in the ritual of *kotsuage*—picking up the bones. Lining up in pairs, we approach the table and use special chopsticks to move single pieces of bone into a special tray. A ritual that is also a form of work, moving the bones. All the while, we look at and touch the dead. As if eating the deceased. This is not to feed us, but to caretake the dead: a supreme act of sociality, as Beth Conklin (1995) has written for the endocannibalism that, once practiced by the Wari in Amazonian Brazil, was intended to wrap the deceased within the warmth of their loved ones' bodies. Absorbing flesh into flesh, this mortuary practice was considered to be preferable to disposing the dead in the dankness of cold earth. It was also thought to help the living more quickly process their grief by eliminating remnants of the dead; in contrast, burying them in the ground would remind survivors constantly of their loss. Though hardly consuming the dead in *kotsuage*, there is a tactility here, too, at once intimate but with a substance already moving into a different state. Bones rather than flesh; fragments instead of a corpse. Sensing, in our hands, the becoming-something-else that death triggers (as captured in one of the Japanese expressions for dying, *jōbutsu suru*—becoming a Buddha).

Once we are done, all of the fragments and ash go into the urn in a process the attendant manages resolutely, pounding pieces with a small mallet to fit in as much as he can. Talking to us the whole time, he sweeps up the remaining ash on the table and scoops this in as well. Lastly, he retrieves what he had earlier put aside and places these on top: the ear fragments, one on either side, a few cranial pieces on top, and, at the center, the *nodobotoke*—the sitting Buddha. Then a pair of the deceased's eyeglasses, sitting as if on his head. We all smile. A human touch to this pile of bone fragments and ash. But the lid is quickly put on, the urn now closed.[3] A container for what once was the living; the physical remainder that indexes the dead. After putting the urn in a ceremonial cloth, the attendant hands it to the chief mourner. He will now lead a small procession out of the room, accompanied by the wife of the deceased carrying the memorial tablet (*ihai*) inscribed with the man's posthumous Buddhist name and a daughter who holds the memorial photo (*iei*) taken well in advance of his death when still in relative health).[4] These three objects encapsulate the dead: the urn with physical remains, his image when living, and the memorial tablet containing his spirit, signified by the new identity he has assumed with the designation of a posthumous name (*kaimyō*).[5]

From the concreteness of the corpse, visible during the wake but covered in flowers by the end of the funeral and now reduced to bones, the deceased is moving into the state of spirituality. After remaining on a temporary altar at the home of the deceased for forty-nine days, the urn will be buried (in a columbarium or grave), at which stage the materiality of the body assumes less importance than the sign system in the *butsudan*, where the *ihai* and *iei*—now treated as channels for communicating between the living and the dead—will continue to reside. The spirit assumes an ontological condition that Joshua Irizarry calls transcendentally ordinary as it is believed to retain much the same agency as the deceased did in life: the same personality, same tastes, same likes and dislikes. Yet, now free-floating, it can also occupy different places simultaneously, such as two *ihai*—one at the temple and another at the household *butsudan*. "Multiplicity of immanence is *hotoke*'s most transcendent quality," according to Irizarry (2014, 178)—a quality of sacredness that arguably comes into being through the ritual care given the material remains and spirit in transition by social hands like those gathered here today.

With the *kotsuage* now completed and the procession having made its way to the parking lot outside, aqua minivans are waiting to take everyone for a ceremonial meal. The priests will accompany us, as will the *ihai*, the *iei* and the urn. A meal, sharing food with the dead.[6]

A funeral like the one described above is expensive and socially dense. Put on by the family, it is attended by those variously related to the deceased by kinship, friendship, or work—the three categories by which those gifting flowers are listed on a huge board during the wake. Grievability conducted by those enacting their relationality to the dead. Yet traditional funerals like this—called general (*ippan*) by those in the business—are on the decline, constituting about 20–30 percent of funerals in Japan today. The trend is toward family funerals (*kazokusō*), which only immediate family attend (50–60 percent of funerals today) and direct burial (*chokusō*) when the corpse goes immediately from hospital to crematorium to burial without ceremony at all (currently 20–30 percent of funerals, but rising) (ENDEX 2017). Even further along are the deceased who, in the wake of what Mori Kenji calls an era of the "absent" or "refusing" other that serves as the social relations willing to tend to the dead, become "abandoned corpses," which he sees precipitously rising these days (Mori Kenji 2014, 152). These include more and more urns that get left behind on trains, abandoned without the certificate (*shibōshōmeisho*) that would normally identify them. This permit, which legally must be obtained from one's local municipality, allows for cremation and is to stay inside the urn. But to avoid contravening the Law Governing Cemeteries and Burial (*bochimaisōhō*) against abandoning corpses, those abandoned like this—whose caretakers may be motivated by lack of funds to pay for burial—are left without their paperwork. They make their way into a train station's lost and found, where, alongside forgotten umbrellas and backpacks, they sit on a shelf awaiting possible reclamation before being moved to a grave for the disconnected in a local cemetery or temple.

A similar fate awaits corpses of deceased who die alone "without anyone to depend on" (*miyori ga nai*), people living alone who have not made mortuary arrangements and who lack a responsible other willing or able to do so (whether that be family, friend, or a commercial or civic organization the deceased has signed up with prior to death). Often such people have been socially estranged for a long time and, once dead, leave bodies that go undiscovered for days, weeks, even months. When no family member is willing to assume responsibility for tending to the remains, the burden falls on municipalities, where cases, and costs, of lonely or isolated deaths (*kodokushi*, *koritsushi*) are rising rapidly (as detailed in chapter 6).

The room I am taken to at the end of our interview is dim and small. It is the waiting room inside city hall where urns of unclaimed remains are held awaiting kin. But kin rarely show up, I am told by Kitami Takayuki, the person in charge of these matters for Yokosuka City—a city of 400,000, with an American military base, an hour and half south of Tokyo. As mentioned in chapter 5, where there is a fuller discussion of Kitami's work in Yokosuka City, the incidence of unclaimed remains is on the rise across the country (now representing 3.3 percent of all dead nationwide and a much higher proportion in some places, such as Osaka, where it was 10 percent in 2015). But equally noteworthy, as Kitami stresses to me, is the fact that the identities of these unclaimed remains tend to be known. This differs significantly from the past, when unclaimed remains were mainly of persons dying unidentified with their family's whereabouts unknown (*mimoto fumei*/身元不明)—travelers, for example, who died far from home. Today, by contrast, the circumstances are less likely to involve kin who can't be located than kin who refuse to accept responsibility.

In 2015, when the city had fifty cases of unclaimed remains, staff were able to make contact with kin for forty-nine of them; all refused (*kyohi*) to accept any responsibility for the dead. This represents a shift that accelerated in the early 2000s—a time when the rise of digital media and smartphones facilitated contact and identification but the economic downturn accompanied a neoliberal trend toward individual responsibility (*jiko sekinin*). Since 2003, the number of unclaimed remains has tripled. Financial strain may be a factor, Kitami surmises, but the reasons more likely involve distanced relations: the divorced wife hasn't been in touch for years, the child grew up never knowing his father, the sister hasn't heard from her brother for decades, and they feel no obligation or motivation to step up to the plate now.[7] This leaves the dead with a name but no place.

Urns packaged in boxes and cloths, all with their names clearly written on the outside, sit on the shelves. "Here is a name; here, too, is a name. See, they *all* have names," Kitami said, shaking his head. In this room, the urns are stored for up to one year; corpses are also stored before cremation—usually in private facilities paid for (quite dearly) by the city—during the time of doing due diligence in trying to locate next of kin (usually two or three months).[8] Called storage (*hokan*/保管) by the authorities, this is both a process of governance and an ontological state for the corpse. For while the law mandates that local government assume the responsibility and cost for handling the corpses of unclaimed deceased, it also dictates that—due to the separation of religion and state established by the 1947 constitution—the municipality cannot perform the ceremonies honoring the spirit of the departed. This includes *kuyō*, the Buddhist ritual standardly performed for the deceased by close family members, Buddhist practitioners, or (increasingly) a commercial and religious conglomerate that takes over this practice for the (absent) family.⁹ Thus, those without family to claim them or the money to pay for attended burial and memorial for themselves after death are relegated to the status of disconnected souls (*muenbotoke*). These are the ones who wind up as corpses in refrigerated containers awaiting cremation, then as cremains in urns in a dark storage room inside municipal offices awaiting burial, then deposited in a city repository (*nōkotsudō*) for the disconnected dead, and finally—when the city repository fills to capacity every five or six years—as intermingled ashes in a collective grave (*gassōbo*/合葬墓) in a city-run cemetery for all the disconnected others.¹⁰

The waiting room Kitami takes me to feels neglected. The atmosphere is quite unlike the response generated by the compound crisis of earthquake, tsunami, and nuclear meltdown of March 2011, when an incredible outpouring of volunteerism galvanized the country to attend to the bodies and souls that were lost, went missing, or were found but remained unidentified. This was a gesture of sociality that expressed a sentiment of national belonging ("hang in there, Japan," as signs all over the country read) that is far less often extended to the bone shards of lonely dwellers.¹¹ And yet, these numbers are rising in what Kitami sees as the death of Japan's collective spirit. Less than ten years after 3.11, he called the collection of unclaimed remains he was showing me evidence of Japan's relationless society (*muen shakai*).

Yet the unclaimed remains in Yokosuka City do receive attendance of sorts. For all the deceased interred in the city's columbarium and grave for the disconnected there is an annual secular memorial service, attended mainly by municipal staff and officials. Other cities, like Kyoto and Osaka, also stage interdenominational ceremonies co-run by nonprofits, as do a number of public cemeteries, such as Tama Reien in Koganei, Tokyo. Yet none of this makes up for what Kitami laments as the status of spirits whose material remains never get claimed. Destined to be *muenbotoke* forever, this is how they enter and stay in the ground. Which is why, in endorsing a "0 *muenbotoke*" manifesto for Yokosuka City, Kitami crafted a new municipal plan to ensure that the residents most likely to die and be buried unrecognized make arrangements, while still alive, to have proper funerals and burials.¹²

In the three times I heard Kitami lay out this plan, he emphasized the need to listen to the bones of unclaimed remains. In what I found to be strangely worded at the time, he titled one of his public lectures

"Unclaimed Remains Speak," referencing three cases in his city that year of deceased wrongly interred in the municipal plot for the disconnected because their wishes or plans for a more social burial had gone undiscovered at the time of death. (Two were widows who, because of Alzheimer's, hadn't informed anyone before their deaths of where their husbands had been buried; one, a single man, had left both a note saying he wanted a funeral and proper burial and sufficient funds to pay for them, but they weren't found until six months after his death). In what is now a second municipal initiative to get all residents to make their mortuary plans ahead of time and to keep a copy of their plan in the municipal office, this "ending registration card" (*shūkatsu tōroku*) is an "unsettled entity" in Dawdy's terminology. These are identity papers for the dead that serve as a social contract, mortuary insurance, even quasi ritual that protect one from becoming disconnected ashes in an unidentified urn once deceased. And, just as in the case of Dawdy's commodity relics or Kojima's dollhouses of the dead, ghosts have triggered this as well. Here, though, the temporality is more anticipatory, as in not waiting for the ghosts of *muenbotoke* to inhabit one's urn. In listening to "unclaimed remains speak," Kitami has devised the ending registration card to ward off the future anterior of the rise in the numbers of unclaimed urns and interments in mass graves for the disconnected. By signing up for "my ending plan" and registering their plans at City Hall, residents are protecting themselves from winding up there as urns gathering dust. A plan that stitches individual responsibility to municipal governance, it promises a modicum of sociality at the end: one prized from dependence on—and potential abandonment by—kin.

AT THE CREMATORIUM: MAKING AND CLASSIFYING REMAINS

According to the law, the dead must be treated properly. But this only pertains to remains classified as human. Animal remains are not legislated by law, and remainders of human bodies designated as matter can be readily disposed of or even sold. "Proper" treatment thus depends on the categorization of human versus matter: a terrain undergoing rapid change today alongside shifts in mortuary culture, marketing, and practice. This is what Didier Fassin (2009) calls *biolegitimacy*—what legitimately counts (and doesn't) as human life—taken into the realm of death.

By law, a corpse must be treated in a specific, regulated manner. A death certificate is to be issued by a doctor, then a certificate to permit cremation must be obtained from the local municipality, although at least twenty-four hours must elapse between death and cremation at a certified crematorium. The cremation certificate must remain in the urn with the cremains. Remains are to be entombed at an officially sanctioned place for burial or deposit—cemetery, temple, columbarium—and are not to be abandoned, destroyed, or stolen as if mere garbage or waste; to do so is to commit the crime of abandoning a corpse (*shitaiikizai*).[13] It is on the grounds of violating one or both of these laws that some of the newest mortuary practices have been contested for failing to properly treat human remains as human. This is true for scattering ashes (*sankotsu*) and direct burial in the soil ("natural burial"/*shizensō*), both of which take place outside of sanctioned burial grounds. Yet, while trying to press for changes in the law to better accommodate the shifting lines in mortuary trends, advocates of new practices also argue that these fall—or can be made to fall—within the letter of the law. The long-standing customary practice of retaining some ashes at home, not burying them in a certified tomb or cemetery, has never led to the prosecution of anyone, for example. And the law doesn't prohibit as much as not extend to burial at sea, as proponents of *sankotsu* have argued (Tsuji 2002, 190). But those seeking new methods of disposal are also turning to the parameters of the biolegitimacy of remains themselves. Manipulating, as it were, the very calculus by which *human* and *waste* are designated in the infrastructure by which corpses are remade into cremains. Wrinkles in the relationship between the materiality and sociality of tending to human/dead, conducted in the currency of ash.

In midsummer 2018 I am given a tour of a public crematorium in Kanagawa Prefecture. Situated in the city of Yamato, on the outskirts of Tokyo, Yamato Saijō (大和斎場) was established to "serve in death, all those living in the four adjacent cities of Yamato, Ebina, Zama, Ayase" (as advertised in its promotional pamphlet). Though somewhat older than other crematoria—it was built in 1982, with a ceremonial hall added in 1995, and a separate building for wakes under construction when I visit—it has an excellent reputation for being "easy to use" and affordable for local residents, according to my guide, Mr. Hida, the head of facilities.[14] Indeed, the price for cremation is surprisingly low: only ¥10,000 ($95) per body for residents of the four cities, but ¥50,000 ($473) for nonresidents. Usage is up, reflecting a national trend in Japan's "mass death society" (where the number of deaths per year exceeds that of births). The number of cremations for the four cities has increased to 4,993 in 2017 from 3,648 in 2008. With eight furnaces (*ro*) that run from 9:00 a.m. to 3:30 p.m. daily, and by running three batches in each and staggering the batches in thirty-minute intervals, the *saijō* can manage twenty-four cremations every day. The crematorium also offers other accommodations. For those wanting to do memorial services (wakes, staying with the body overnight, a farewell ceremony), it has four memorial halls (*shikijo*/式場), which are reasonably priced at ¥30,000–¥50,000 ($274–$473) to reserve from the wake one night to the funeral the next morning, depending on the room selected. Even cheaper is a direct funeral with a bare-bones farewell ceremony in the furnace room at no additional cost.

The process of cremation itself is technologically modern and clean. No black fumes or noxious odors are emitted as in the past, as Mr. Hida laughingly points out. So different from "all those pictures one sees of prewar Japan with the crematorium blowing its ominous billows of smoke." But this doesn't mean that neighborhood residents are eager to have a crematorium in their midst. As I know from the news stories on local opposition, building a new facility for processing dead remains (whether a crematorium or a facility for holding corpses until cremation—so-called corpse hotels) is a hard sell. Negative associations with death linger still. And yet the process here is highly refined and carefully run. The burners (*bānā-*) go up to 1,000 degrees centigrade and can be adjusted to produce remains of different sizes. Operated by two workers at a time, the process can be witnessed by family members via a window at the rear.

For the first hour of the tour, I am taken through all the affordances the crematorium offers the bereaved for memorializing the dead: the waiting areas, memorial halls, the variety of altars (*saidan*) available in different religious styles (Shintō, Buddhist), and rooms where one can stage a meal and gather the gifts of money that mourners will bring. As advertised, everything seems user-friendly and serenely pleasant and neat. But it is the raison d'être of the place that interests me most. On entering a large open room divided by the clean machinery of the ovens, I am struck by its aesthetics of efficiency and the stillness accompanying the cycling of bodies to and from the furnace doors. The two workers on duty, both uniformed and in their mid-thirties, show me the mechanics of running the burners. This is a job that takes a month to learn, involving both technical and interpersonal skills: ensuring the body burns (using long poles to rake and push the body) while maintaining the high temperatures of the machines under the watching glare of family members. One of the two workers always acts as the person in charge (*tantō-san*) assuming responsibility for organizing the remains, making sure they are correctly identified, and guiding families through how to pick up the bones. Sometimes the process needs readjustment, as when fragments that don't initially fit in the urn are pounded down into smaller sizes. When I ask them how they find the work, they tell me the hardest is when the remains are those of a child. "This is just sad," one of them says in barely a whisper.

Jobs differ by size, Mr. Hida elaborates as we stand by the burners. In general, the larger the body, the more time required, which is also a factor in cost. The cremation of full adult bodies costs ¥10,000 ($94) each, but children under twelve cost ¥7,000 ($66) and fetuses are ¥5,000 ($47). Yet a single body part costs ¥10,000 (the example given was a finger), and *kaisō*—reburning ash for reburial, done at a higher temperature to produce a smaller sized ash particle—is ¥7,000. Then, when handing cremains over to families (or whoever is retrieving the remains), quantity can vary by custom: more are preserved in the eastern part of the country (Kantō), but less in the western region of Kansai. The remains collected (*shūkotsu*) by family members and carried away in urns are one form of matter: what Mr. Hida refers to as bones, indexing their human classification. Yet there is also a remainder at crematoria, which Hida insists is leftover matter (*zanhai*) rather than human bone (*zankotsuhai*) when I ask him about it, having recently learned that some public crematoria sell this remainder for its metallic content. In their case, he tells me, *zanhai* is routinely collected and "appropriately sorted" by a reputable disposal company that fetches it at the end of each month. Whether or not they profit from it, he didn't say, when reminding me that "Yamato Saijō is public, remember. We serve the public here."

Zanhai is categorized as industrial waste partially as a result of a Supreme Court decision in 1910 that acquitted a defendant who had paid to obtain it based on its customary use as fertilizer. Article 190 of the criminal code that was promulgated in 1907 and partially revised in 1947 classifies it as "leftover ash," not "human bone" (*ikotsu*)—more like dust than bone, as was argued in the court case (Tsuji 2002, 190). Accordingly, businesses that traffic in the sorting and recycling of *zan(kotsu)hai* have been in operation since the start of the twentieth century. Hanshin Material Corporation, with its main office in Osaka, has existed for eighty years. Today, one of its newest divisions, Japan Environment Management Association (JEMA), is devoted to doing research and development related to the "appropriate disposal of bone/ash remains from crematoria."[15] What drives this business today, as I was told by Kobayashi Tsuyoshi, the vice director of the company, is not the use of *zanhai* as fertilizer but the metallic content in human remains: a shortage of silver and gold beginning in 2008 greatly increased their market value. And given that crematoria legally own this spillover matter (meaning that it becomes the property of the city in the case of public facilities), a marketplace has arisen around the sorting and reselling of salable remains. A crematorium will outsource this work to a private company that, winning the bid for a contract, will then initiate the various steps of dividing bone (*kotsu*, human material) from ash (*hai*, nonhuman material, such as metal) and processing the two different contents. What is deemed material (or dangerous, impure items) is sold or disposed of; what is deemed human is interred in a burial site and paid respects to at an annual *kuyō* ceremony.

Of fifteen hundred local municipalities (*jichitai*) in Japan, five hundred now commission what are called disposal services (*shorigyōsha*). While some, like Kyoto, abstain from this business on the grounds that, no matter how carefully the sorting is done, it risks dishonoring the dead, others, like Yokohama, actively pursue it but utilize the revenues for civic projects. This offers an interesting twist on the accounting given life and death. Ash as matter is commodified while profits from its sale are deployed to "making life" for public benefit. This makes for an unsettled entity of another type altogether: not a commodity relic, but a commodity of remains subtracted of the human/self that can now be sold to generate a resource to serve the public. At both ends, this process of subtraction is carefully attended to in his own company, as Kobayashi described to me. Their new model factory deploys high-tech techniques in separating ash from bone. And JEMA's governing board includes religious specialists who advise on how to show courtesy to the human dead buried in the cemeteries where the company inters its nonhuman waste.

The border between human and waste is also rejiggered in another context. By remaking the size of ash to be categorized as matter rather than human, one evades the regulations imposed by the law for disposing of remains. This method—of pulverizing cremains to be smaller than usual—is commonly used by those seeking such alternative disposal methods as scattering ashes. It is also useful for those who desire to use the convenience of urban columbaria (*nōkotsudo*) with their lockers and boxes for what may be the contents of entire ancestral graves, which are then closed down and emptied. By compacting the ashes into finer granules, ever more dead can be kept within a container the size of a large shoebox.[16] But here, the process of recomposing dead/remains is done not to eliminate what is human (in order to sell the matter for its metallic content) but, rather, to make the remains more convenient for ensuring grievability (whether

DE-PARTING 163

by scattering ash or depositing in an urban columbarium where visiting the dead will be more convenient). In the latter case, the work is done not by a waste company but a bone crusher, whose methods are as technically refined as caringly performed.

THE BONE CRUSHER

On a gray February day in 2019 I am on my way to visit a "bone business" (*hone ya san*). In Tokyo for a short fieldwork trip, this is the first of four interviews, all at locations I am navigating for the first time. For someone with a poor sense of direction (*hōkō onchi*), this is quite the challenge, involving endless legs of bus and train travel, and then trying to find the street address on foot or by cab. Today, the taxi driver drops me in the general area of my destination—a residential neighborhood of small houses, factories, and shops in the old downtown area (*shitamachi*) of Tokyo. But neither taxi nor GPS has left me at the door of the place, as street numbers follow no linear order in Japan. Only after asking three people do I find one who can help me find the location by noticing the parent company written on the mailbox outside—without any descriptor of it being a "bone company."

I have arrived miraculously on time. But the man answering the door greets me with surprise. "You're the professor? We were expecting you yesterday." He graciously ushers me in nonetheless, and we go upstairs to the main office of his company—a lovely two-room space lined with Hokusai woodblock prints on the walls, glass-door cabinets filled with new-style memorial goods, a long table in the center, and a tatami-mat room with *shōji* screens tastefully embedded in the wall. Painted in white, it feels more like an artist's studio than a bone-crushing factory. Kai Koji starts narrating the company's history immediately after telling me he designed the premises himself. Called *ikotsu sarai* (Serai Remains), it started fifteen years ago as a business for scattering ashes at sea (*kaiyō sankotsu*).[17] The first of its kind in the country and still the largest today (when more than two hundred businesses have joined the field, including tiny mom-and-pop operations), they manage up to five hundred cases a month. But this represents only about 20 percent of their current clientele. What has grown in the interim, constituting about 80 percent of the business today, are services related to "closing graves" (*hakajimai*), though Kai prefers to call it "moving graves" (*haka no hikkoshi*). This involves digging up the remains in (usually rural) ancestral or familial plots, to the end of closing up that grave, and reinterring the remains in a more convenient urban place (often a high-rise columbarium). The process, though often laborious and expensive (because Buddhist temples, fearing the loss of annual revenues, impose burdensome regulations and fees), is intended to avoid the abandonment (*muenka*) of ancestral graves now pervasive in the countryside due to family lines dying out or the inconvenience and expense of maintaining them for city-dwelling Japanese (Kotani 2018). This has brought much business to Serai Remains. Accordingly, it has now diversified to being an "ashes cleaning service," "ashes powdering service," "ashes technical service," and "ashes eternal prayer support" (永遠の祈り).

We sit at a wooden table stacked with porcelain urns, postal boxes surrounding us on the floor. "Doesn't this say it all?" he gestures to the room, giving me a cup of coffee and laughing. Animated and pint-size, he talks fast, conjuring up Joe Pesci as a Japanese artist with his fuzzy blue sweater, stylish goatee, and mop of disheveled hair. But the business is about technique as much as artistic touch, as he describes over the next three hours. As one of the promotional brochures announces, Serai was started with a single mortar and pestle—implements of grinding by hand more commonly associated with cooking. With this image, Serai promotes how it approaches bones "with a memory still unchanged today."[18] Kai shows me a large white marble mortar filled with small marble balls in the lab downstairs—still used to complete the final stage of grinding ashes to fine powder. Ashes are ground to a particle size of 2–3 mm, which reduces the total volume by about four-fifths. The rule in pulverizing (*funmatsuka*/粉末化) ashes is to make them no longer legally recognizable as human remains.[19] In this form, an entire ancestral grave can fit into a single box in a high-rise columbarium in Tokyo, thereby enabling urban dwellers—at least theoretically—to visit with far more regularity and convenience than the laborious trips required by plots in the countryside. Pulverizing ash to maintain grievability of the genealogical line is one end; pulverizing leftover ash to extract metallic content from something rendered not human but thing is quite another. Unsettled entities where the lines of materiality and sociality fall out differently: one, not social at all; the other, maintaining a social lineage of ancestral honor and respect.

Things circulate multiply here. First, ashes arrive, usually by mail in a packing service (*yūpakku*) that costs ¥1,500 ($14). Inside, urns are taped shut with the name of the deceased clearly written on the top. On the outside of the box, the contents must be clearly identified as "bones" (*goikotsu*). The image is a bit jarring: bones traveling through the mail like an Amazon order, yet clearly marked as honored and human. Boxes arrive from all over

6.1 The stone mortar and pestle that bone crusher Kai Koji uses as the last step in pulverizing ashes to a smaller particle size.

the country—some are huge, with as many as twenty urns inside—almost daily. Disappointed that none come in the day I am there (despite three other deliveries on this Saturday, a sign of good business), Kai takes me through the next steps. Depending somewhat on what service has been requested, the first is usually bone washing (*senkotsu*). Done to remove the mold, mud, and smell that have accumulated from being in the ground for what may well have been a hundred years or more, this cleaning is also clearly affective. A form of caregiving that mimics the washing done to corpses when first dead: making clean, restoring order, managing matter.[20] The price of ¥21,000 ($193) for remains of up to four deceased includes disposal of old urns but not the cost of new ones, a nice selection of which Serai sells in a variety of colors alongside the ceremonial cases (*zushi*) that

6.2 Fragments of bone set out to dry after being washed and before being pulverized.

they are put inside. Customers are told the wait is fourteen days for the process to be completed: what takes Kai—in a job he had to learn and still does himself—two hours using alcohol and water. Once cleansed, the cremains are put into a low-heat oven to dry.

This is what I am shown when we head downstairs to the lab. The racks in the oven have big bone fragments in one pan and smaller particles in the other. Everything is neatly packed in this converted garage where the machines are glistening and clean, all is white and smells fresh, and dead matter, once cleaned and compacted, gets repackaged into assorted boxes and containers that fill the cabinets. The feel is designer high tech, but our talk ricochets off various body parts—those in front of us but also the imaginaries by which corpses have been diversely particularized in the past. "Hair of the deceased" (*ihatsu*/遺髪), for example: what, during the war, was sometimes cut from a soldier's head and sent back to his family to stand in for the corpse. This is one of the categories of "deceased matter" that Serai works with, as announced in the company's informational brochure. It doesn't specify fingers, though Kai tells me that these, too, have stood in for an entire body in various circumstances—not only during the war but also when cutting off a digit takes the place of giving one's life for an infraction in the yakuza. The old infiltrates the new here, as with a pile of remains set out on the counter that Kai has recently been sorting through. Enmeshed in all the bone chunks and ash are a number of metal nails and old coins. The latter are from the Edo period and are easily three hundred years old.

While the lab isn't running today, Kai takes me through the steps of pulverization. There are twelve in all. The process starts with removing any metal content and putting the rest into the "pot mill rotator" for slow rotation and ends in hand-grinding with the mortar and pestle and vacuum packing the cremains in an aluminum envelope that is then put into a "cosmetic bag." The time involved is two to five hours, price depends on quantity (¥7,000–¥15,000 or about $66–$142), and the end result is shipped back by mail at a set price of ¥1,500. A customer can also choose to have the entire process done by hand (*tesagyō funkotsu*) using mortar and pestle. Reminiscent of the touching done when social intimates are washing the corpse or picking the bones, such cases often involve the bodies of children, and parents may also request to witness, or even participate in, the procedure themselves. I find this to be quite extraordinary, the intimacy a grieving parent would be able to bear, even welcome, in not only touching their child's remains but assisting in the transformation of their corpse.

A tactile engagement, taken to the limits of materiality—resembling, perhaps, the eating of a beloved's body parts in the ritual of endocannibalism of the Amazonian Wari' described by Beth Conklin. Staying with the dead, down to—and beyond—the bones. A material intimacy quite at odds with the trend of dematerialization elsewhere in the death-making scene in Japan: toward more robotic, digital, or automated services for grieving and depositing the dead, as taken up in chapter 7.

When I ask Kai how he feels about his work, it is the cases involving children that are the hardest, he tells me. But otherwise, this is a business he utterly loves. Even when young, he always had an interest in death; being useful to others in managing it is what led him away from the nuclear business to this. This extends to the array of new-age containers for cremains he has shown me upstairs—everything from pendants and bracelets to small egg-shaped holders and white marble boxes. He sees these, as he does his work in general, as providing means to stay better connected to the dead. For times have changed and burial in the ground, with its costly and laborious upkeep, is no longer in sync with people's lifestyles. If Japanese are not to abandon tending to the dead altogether, new methods for doing so are called for, Kai announces to me at the end. Such as the necklace around his wife's neck, which he points out seconds later when she walks by. Her father's ashes are inside and she carries them everywhere with her. Forever in touch, a portable grave. "*Temoto kuyō*, such goods are called: "on-hand memorial."

CONCLUSION

De-parting takes place in various ways with the particles treated differently in each. From picked bones to unclaimed remains and from ash pulverized to extract its metallic content or done so for reburial of ancestors in an urban columbarium. In all this, the absence of the departed arrays differently in the presence of material form. But the lines of sociality and materiality are not always, or necessarily, neat. And while the touch of social hands makes both a literal and symbolic difference—giving care to the remains, according grievability to the deceased—something falls outside, even here. Leftover ash at the crematorium and neglected bones in rural family graves lend themselves to ontological ambiguity and unsettlement between the living and the dead. The tension already inherent between the thereness and not-thereness of mortal matter slips further here: between what once was a human and the signs of that human being no longer being alive, but also the thereness and not-thereness of social connectedness in relational bones that can be derelationalized in fact.

As Hans Ruin has said of mortuary rituals, "The ritual will always be a care for *something* in the place of *someone* who has been" (2018, 61). But, in keeping with the notion that bones are relational, might we conceive of rituals emerging in Japan today as caring for not merely the deceased but also the departed relationality that once enveloped the dead? The maintenance company JEMA certainly attends fastidiously to the leftover ash in its care, as if the attentiveness to its very materiality is a stand-in of sorts for the absent sociality. This possibility is what I turn to in the next chapter, on urban columbaria, where a highly technological system is set up for ritual visitation of the grave—that most social of ceremonies, iconic of sociality itself. Yet the ashes sit in a warehouse and enter the grave only when or if someone comes to visit them. Do bones still speak even when the others who once cared for them are no longer doing so? If so (or if not), what work is this new-style grave park performing, how and for whom, and with what new lines drawn in the ontological ambiguity between living and dead, materiality and sociality, human and thing?

machines

Hayakawa Chie's [film] *Plan 75* depicts Japan as a necro-political dystopia where the elderly are encouraged to euthanize themselves in order to assuage the nation's economic distress. People 75 and older who apply for the "Plan 75" program, as operation driven by uncannily pragmatic end-of-life protocols, receive 100,000 yen, or approximately $800, for their self-sacrifice.... With stinging precision, Hayakawa reveals a culture that seems almost mobilized to push corporately assisted suicide on those who are a burden to health care and financial systems.

Diego Semerene, "*Plan 75* Review" (2022)

The names of the dead in any form, and specifically their names on lists.... are there to be remembered, forever; others—not on the list—are forgotten, either purposely excluded or, more commonly, having never counted in the first place. Lists of the names of the dead that matter like churchyards, cemeteries, even rivers into which ashes are thrown, constitute communities of the dead that live from generation to generation.

Thomas W. Laqueur, *The Work of the Dead* (2015)

automated graves
the precarity and prosthetics of caring for the dead

On a warm summer evening, I meet two Japanese friends, middle-aged women, for a drink. One, coming from her office, stopped en route to pay respects to an aunt and uncle interred nearby. Single and with family issues that kept them from entering the ancestral grave, both had made plans ahead of time to be placed in a high-rise columbarium. This is where my friend visits them once or twice a year, always like this: when she has another appointment in the area and has a few minutes to spare.

Laughing, the other friend says she is considering the same arrangement for herself. Single, with parents now dead and no siblings, she has no one to tend to her grave as she currently tends to the ancestral plot. After she is gone, it will fall into disarray. Without annual fees paid and maintenance conducted, the plot will be designated as abandoned by the cemetery, which will then remove the contents and rebury them in the collective plot for the disconnected. To avoid this fate for herself and her ancestors, the woman aims to find an alternative long before she dies.

At a dinner party the following summer, the topic of new-style columbaria comes up again. A man in his early sixties says that they suit him to a T. Single, with no interest in entering the family grave in the countryside, he has already signed up for one. He likes the feel of the place, finds it convenient and well-run, and if a friend occasionally comes by to visit—or even if not—it seems like a good final destination. A couple sitting at the same table say they are currently closing up the ancestral grave of the husband's patrilineage in the countryside and will be moving the contents (pared down and cleaned up) to a high-rise columbarium in Tokyo. They, too, say the new venue appeals to them for the setting and the convenience it affords.

Later the same summer, I'm on-site with a cleanup crew handling the remains of a case of lonely death. The estranged brother of the deceased is on the premises and is adamant about not wanting to keep anything in the way of his brother's possessions. When I ask if his brother is to be buried somewhere, he says yes, he's already there: interred in a high-rise columbarium nearby. Not, I take it from his comments, a place he ever intends to visit.

....

Being anchored—somehow, somewhere—conjures up home: what Gaston Bachelard (1992) describes as not only a material dwelling but what shelters our daydreams, "allowing one to dream in peace" (6) of the world beyond. That this extends to being dead was conveyed to me time and again during my fieldwork by people who shared their anxieties about not having such a place—either not knowing where their own remains would go or not sure what would happen to those in ancestral graves when family members died or moved away. The sense of unsettlement this evoked—of being stranded, disconnected, out of place in death—seemed visceral and deep. Bereft of shelter for one's material remains and also for dreaming, perhaps, of the world beyond (where one might hope to already be). A state of homelessness in the future, anticipated in the present, kindling unease, even dread.

Nailing down her final resting place brought incredible relief, one eighty-year-old told me in an interview. But why, precisely, this mattered so much, Takeyama couldn't precisely say. By her own admission, she had never liked visiting the ancestral grave of her family, would never consider entering it (even if she could), and did not believe in a spiritual afterlife following death. "I imagine becoming nothing," she told me when asked how she envisioned time after death. And yet making final arrangements was important to her nonetheless. Divorced when younger, the last in her natal family still alive, and with a daughter now married who would be entering the grave of her husband's family when it came time, she was socially solo and without a predesignated place to be buried. Out of a desire to tidy things up, perhaps, and to not leave a burden for others, particularly her daughter, Takeyama investigated possible options once she turned seventy. She learned about Ending Center and had a good impression when she visited and started attending their events, so she signed up for a plot in their alternative burial society. Having done so brought a considerable sense of both security and calm. That she could also be buried with her beloved cat (whose remains were already awaiting her) and get to know in advance those who would be "grave friends" in death were added benefits. A home, of sorts, for the dead times.

Anticipation is a driving force here, as I have shown in this book. Anticipating an uncertain future, being stranded and disconnected once dead (epitomized by the specter of a disconnected soul), kindles a disquieting anxiety that the booming ending industry both addresses and ignites. Being relieved of this worry is what a preplanned burial affords: what Takeyama and so many others I interviewed recounted about the plans they had made, or were considering, for their future home after death. The temporality at work and the planning in the face of it are symptomatic of the moment. Peculiarity of time marks this moment of rapid-fire change, apocalyptic dangers facing the globe, shifting borders and dimensions of life—such as the downsizing of Japan's population, leading to (as often reported in foreign news) a market in adult diapers larger than in infant ones. Time management drives what Nicholas Rose (2007) calls a dependence on optimization within the politics of life. Knowing how to organize ourselves for the inevitable disasters that are both feared and predicted leads us to construct "pre-constituted futures" (as Marilyn Strathern refers to the anticipatory audits erected in the academy in the United Kingdom these days to measure accountability) (Strathern 2000). This brings the future into the present, and structures the present as if the future is what matters most. Anticipation engenders affects—of fear and urgency, but also excitement and hope—that are "lived and felt by those dwelling within this time, binding collectivities of nation, class, and globe" (Adams, Murphy, and Clarke 2009, 249). At work is a moral economy in which the future sets conditions of possibility for action in the present. In the case of worrying about one's future resting place after death, this both signals and stands in for an anxiety much more generalized in life today. Fixating on, as well as handling it through, mortuary planning gives this a focus—arguably why so much attention is paid to preparedness conducted while still alive (*seizen seiri*).

In this chapter I consider one of the newest designs for confronting the precarity of mortuary care today—automated delivery system columbaria that are techno-futuristic but nonetheless organized around a grave. Many who are customers are purchasing a slot for themselves ahead of time: anticipating, in the present, what once was mortuary planning handled by others at the time of one's death. Yet, in this case, a particular form of temporality is at the very core of grave habitation itself. The basic model is a building-style columbarium where remains are stored in boxes or lockers in a storage area but delivered by automation to a handful of beautiful graves when required by a visitor. Once the visit is complete, the boxes are returned to their shelves in an Amazon-like warehouse. The technology that runs these is "just-in-time" automation: the same apparatus that fueled the Japanese automobile industry's rise to global stature in the country's postwar leap to industrial heights. Serving to minimize the space needed to house large-scale industries (always at a premium in Japan), lean production or Toyotism (after Toyota, where it was first implemented) cut down on the spatial requirements of a large factory by syncing up production and demand. A lynchpin in Japan's double-digit industrial growth of the 1970s and '80s, just-in-time production is now being tuned to a different era with new sets of needs and demands in Japan's current moment of postgrowth and socioeconomic decline. At issue is a scarcity of space—what these automated columbaria respond to by compacting thousands of cremains into a relatively small urban structure. But more pressing is the scarcity of care in Japan's aging, increasingly single population for whom the rates of lonely death in the cities and abandoned ancestral graves in the countryside are accelerating quickly. How precisely these new-style grave parks work as an option—for those anticipating dying alone and also for families seeking to relocate ancestors closer to urban homes—is the issue I address in this chapter. It is perplexing at first blush that, unless someone arrives to visit the deceased, cremains stay in a warehouse. How, then, is just-in-time care working: for whom, to what end, and in what kind of temporality?

Based on their ethnographic study of automated columbaria in Tokyo, Uriu, Odom, and Gould characterize them as "a mixture of a gravesite, a luxury hotel, and a goods distribution warehouse" (2019, 748). From this description, one gets a sense of the dissonance between the storage bins where remains sit next to strangers and the upscale memorial hall outfitted with diligently tended granite graves. This tension represents the spectrum of death making today: at one end, winding up in a depository as mere matter; at the other, being secure in a final resting place attended by someone, somehow. Mediating between the two is the apparatus of a just-in-time delivery system: a device that both enables and exemplifies circulation into the grave *as if* that is where everyone winds up. I engage here in something of a thought experiment regarding automated columbaria: is technology performing death care? Designed to enable and also mimic the human-to-human exchanges so critical to social ritual (of, in this case, intimate others visiting the dead) automated graves are readied for visitation (Hertz 1960). Open seven days per week, 365 days per year, the grave can be visited any time. But what if it isn't? Or if the practice of visiting—now done primarily by Japanese of older generations who were brought up with the custom of ancestral graves—dies out over time, making these urban grave parks more repositories for cremains than sites that get visited by others? In that case, does the automated apparatus do a work all its own, humanizing—with the potential and performance of a grave system—what otherwise would be the mere materiality of deposited remains? If so, might that mean that sociality itself is becoming technologized? Or in the process of transitioning into something different altogether?

This is the thesis I consider by way of the concept of the prosthesis: a device, external or implanted, that substitutes or supplements a missing or defective part of the body. The automated grave works as a social prosthesis where, as Sandy Stone has argued, "Prosthetic sociality implies new and frequently strange definitions of space, volume, surface, and distance; in prosthetic sociality the medium of connection defines the meaning of community" (Stone 1994, 7). Besides performing Buddhist memorials for those without kin to do so, automated columbaria instantiate the grave system with its gears circulating *as if* for visitation even when that does not literally take place. Stretching different temporalities—rooted in a mortuary system from the past, moving toward something different in the future—this new mortuary design is in the midst of becoming, as Peter Boxall (2020) has said about facial prostheses that waver between reproducing a visage now lost and crafting another, familiar but new. The task, as he says of the prosthetic surgeon, is not to still life but to animate it by bringing its wearer into a relation with "time still to come." Animation, in the context of the automated grave, extends the presence—or remains—of the dead into the future and maintains a system of death making beyond the limits of its sustainability by family members, and perhaps beyond humans altogether.¹ Explicating how this works not only for those who are interred there but also for Japan at a moment of shrinking sociality and anxieties over abandoning the dead is what I undertake here.²

A VISIT TO THE AUTOMATED COLUMBARIUM

Out of Shinanomachi train station, down a hill, surging traffic nearby, construction everywhere; the temple is barely noticeable. I can't imagine this is the place. But a kindly woman assures me it is. And, up close, it augurs another world. The building is beautifully subtle: low roof with slanted stones, a front façade of wood inlaid with glass panes, and plaques on either side of the door that read Sennichidani Jōen (the name of the automated columbarium) and Ichigyōin (the name of the temple to which it is attached). Inside, the elegance continues. The walls are covered in handmade paper from Nepal, the carpet evokes a stream with its design of embedded pebbles, and the entire interior is built with hundred-year-old cedar trees from Yamaguchi Prefecture. The famous Japanese designer Kuma Kengo designed everything here, including the selection of materials. It is as breathtaking as it is incongruous, this tranquil, high-end temple to the dead situated in urban traffic.

The lobby hosts small tables and chairs. Mourners here to visit tap their card at the monitor on the counter (the "prayers' buzzer"), which directs them to a designated viewing booth on the second floor. If just there for a visit, they can go immediately up the elevator, encountering no staff (nor, possibly, anyone else) in the process. But in my own tour of the place, I am shown the main hall of the temple (*hondō*) on the first floor, which is beautifully outfitted with wooden floors, altar tables, seats, and the golden Buddhas that survived the Tokyo air raids during the war. The temple is Jōdo (Pure Land) Buddhist, and Kuma was commissioned to design the "Sennichidani Jōen" project to commemorate the four hundredth anniversary of the temple. Though I am not told this when I visit, the name "Sennichi" also evokes the grueling religious practice of walking for one thousand days (*sennichi kaihōgyō*) undertaken by some Tendai Buddhist monks at Mount Hiei as part of their training. One such "marathon monk" lived in this neighborhood and, because the trek is done at the risk of death (if one stops at all, he is expected to commit suicide), survivors become living Buddhas. So the name taken for this high-tech columbarium is that of a death-defying practice undertaken to seek enlightenment.

But one need not be Buddhist to be interred here, I am told in my interview with Ueno-san, the director of Sennichidani Jōen, who works for Hasegawa, the conglomerate that manages it under the banner of the temple. (As my tour guide at another Hasegawa-run automated grave describes this relationship, "The temple runs it and Hasegawa sells it"). As I know from other joint ventures such as Tōchōji, a Sōtō Zen Buddhist temple in Shinjuku that I visited the previous summer, many Buddhist temples are in danger of shutting down these days due to dwindling numbers of parishioners and loss of the revenues they brought in. By pairing with a business and opening up to nonparishioners with an option that comes with the service of eternal memorial given by a Buddhist priest on staff, Tōchōji has managed not only to stay afloat but to significantly increase both its clientele and revenue. Though he doesn't give me figures, Uneo confirms that Sennichidani Jōen has also been successful in advertising itself as a "peaceful, indoor, grave park" (*yasuragi no okunai boen*). A quite different image from the spacious sprawl associated with cemeteries in the United Kingdom or United States, but given the scarcity of space in urban Japan, where traditional cemeteries have long waiting lists and exorbitant prices for plots, this new-style indoor design makes interment both affordable and accessible in the cities. Using time-space compression with just-in-time automation.

Effusive about what Kuma Kengo has wrought here—a designer sanctuary for the dead—Ueno points out his handiwork and its natural aesthetics on our tour. Laughing, he says they were lucky to get Kuma before he was commissioned to design the stadium for the Tokyo Olympics; now they would be priced out. But Ueno is even more proud of the high-tech delivery system. This model takes only forty seconds to transport remains from storage to the gravestone after triggering the system with the buzzer downstairs. Urns are put into black storage boxes (*nōkotsu shūzō zushi*) that are stenciled with the family name on the outside and come in two sizes, large or small. For ¥900,000 (about $8,000), the remains of up to eight deceased can go into the larger container, if they fit. Efficiency reigns here, too, as Ueno explains. Remains can be powdered to reduce their volume in order to accommodate more deceased in a box. Plenty of ancestors could be included by keeping just a few of their ashes (with the rest respectfully disposed of following Buddhist conventions): an entire ancestral grave, he chuckles. But no pets, he replies when I ask, knowing that some other New Age cemeteries have begun to allow this. There are members here who wouldn't like the idea, but including mementos or personal possessions like eyeglasses is just fine.

When we embark on our tour of Sennichidani, Ueno starts on the second floor. Bypassing for the moment the beautiful black gravestones, each in their own viewing booth to accommodate visitors, he chooses to take me first into the warehouse, accessed at the very end of the floor.³ When we open the door, the space is cavernous; five stories high, filled with rows of metal shelves, everything latticed into tiny units for the storage of contents as indistinguishable as they are inert. The underbelly of the entire operation, the warehouse (*kōsō no shūnōdana*) is orderly, mechanical, and clean. Stork cranes operate what is called a conveyor belt system (*konbeyabun*/コンベヤ文)—the high-speed automation that has transformed the intimacies of everyday life in Japan from electronic toilets and smart home appliances to automated parking garages and conveyor-belt sushi restaurants. When asked to demonstrate, Ueno's assistant presses a buzzer on the wall, triggering a set of hydraulic arms to fetch the set of remains that she has requested. Cranking into place, the apparatus retrieves the designated box and brings it swiftly four floors down. Then, with the box inserted into the back of the waiting grave, the engraved name of the deceased will appear on the other side, Ueno tells me. Smoothly efficient, this is a warehouse like any other except for the human ashes it contains.

Taking our leave of the storeroom, where the deceased get processed like goods, we return to an entirely different scene, at once soothing and warm. This is the only part of the automated columbarium that most visitors will see. The row of black graves sits beautifully serene, each with fresh flowers in place, incense electronically burning, and tasteful wooden screens that can be pulled shut to ensure privacy during visitation. It is here, seconds after the prayers' buzzer has been triggered downstairs, that the remains of the deceased will be waiting in what becomes their temporary grave. To the right of the booth is a digital display, a computer operating system where data about the departed (photos, name, and any personal data the family has inputted) can be called up on an interface. Personalized for the duration of the visit, the grave is made to feel special and kept immaculately clean. But once visitation is done, signaled by pressing the buzzer to the right of the booth, the grave is emptied and readied for the next set of remains. While visitors tend to leave now, the facilities offer other affordances: a small worship hall, an art display, a room for hosting catered meals on special anniversaries, and a Buddha-outfitted alcove for all those whose remains get combined (*gassōbo*).

As Ueno tells me, Sennichidani is open 10 a.m. to 6 p.m. every day of the year. Visitors can drop in anytime without calling ahead unless it is to make arrangements for a special memorial or meal. Because no flowers or incense needs to be brought in, and no tidying or cleanup of the grave is required once there, visits tend to last no more than about five minutes. But grave visits (*hakamairi*) and Buddhist memorial (*kuyō*) still depend on human labor, Ueno explains. Given the convenience of things here, I wonder what labor he means. Well, walking up the hill from the train station and making the effort in the first place, he suggests. But there is only one group visiting the day I am there, and no one at all at the automated grave I visit in Kyodo, Tokyo. Such downtimes are common, Ueno admits, but during ritual times for visitation (Obon, New Year, fall and spring equinoxes), far more visitors show up. Business is good, I am told. Clients include parishioners with long-standing ties to the temple, but far more are new users who pay a one-time fee to be interred here. And rather than requiring family ties and a successor to maintain the grave financially and ritually as required by the family grave system, the new style of interment is utilized by a range of customers: single adults without family or children, married couples or others choosing simplicity in burial and visitation, and families seeking to move their ancestral grave here from the countryside ("closing up the grave," *haka jimai*, and "reburying" it elsewhere, *kaisō*).

TECHNOLOGICAL DESIGN: JAPANESE-STYLE AUTOMATION

Arising from the conditions in which people exist, technologies are the tools deployed to make life better or accommodate the dead. As Walter Benjamin understood, technology enchants by slipping newfangled inventions into conventions already established, promoting change by mitigating the loss of what gets left behind (Buck-Morss 1989). In doing so, technological design remakes the world and how we inhabit it, which means that new innovations not only respond to particular needs and demands but exert their own transformative effects on the landscape.

Design has from the outset "been inextricably tied to decisions about the lives we live and the worlds in which we live them; how we structure such everyday practices as tending to the dead involves 'normative questions' that are central to ontologically oriented design" (Escobar 2018, 33).

For Arturo Escobar, this is particularly true in times like ours, when sustainability—of the world, of humanity—is so much at risk. Figuring out how to survive and not give up on providing a semblance of security and respect for the dead are political in the sense of maintaining, by reinventing, the "collective structures that shape our lives and define our humanness" (Escobar 2018, 122). Care figures in this politics: what Escobar names an "ontology of care," borrowing on feminist theorists such as Berenice Fisher and Joan Tronto, who view care as a "species activity that includes everything we do to maintain, continue, and repair our 'world' so that we can live in it as well as possible" (Fisher and Tronto 1991, 40). As extended by feminists like María Puig de la Bellacasa (2017), caring is feeling and feeding the liveliness of all things, and animating what otherwise becomes uncared for as inanimate or dead.

....

Technological innovation led Japan on its recovery following the war. Out of the trauma of military defeat and devastation, Japan rebuilt itself by recalibrating national strategies and strengths. The country committed to domestic production and focused on manufacturing and services geared to lifestyles: consumer electronics such as Mitsubishi televisions, Toyota automobiles, and the Sony Walkman. People flowed from the countryside to jobs concentrated in the cities in a huge urban migration. Leaving village society behind, city dwellers adopted the rhythms of work now devoted to the company and the family life intended to shore it up with industriousness on everyone's part. This output, based on the efforts of citizen-workers, relied on both the individual and a nuclear family (rather than extended family as in the countryside). Rooted in a home run by a gendered division of labor (women running the home, men bringing in the paycheck, and children studying hard to reproduce these roles), this also constituted a consumption unit pursuing the latest domestic appliances.

A source of national pride, Japanese manufacturing catapulted gross national production to record highs throughout the 1970s, making Japan a global power and its economy the second largest in the world by the 1980s. Investing in new technology and management styles, Japanese industries became known for both the quality of their products and the innovativeness of their production methods. First adopted by Toyota, "just-in-time" (lean) production, also called Toyotism (or TPS, the Toyota Production System), was one of these. Updating Taylorism, the system Henry Ford deployed to make car manufacturing as efficient as possible, Toyotism replaced the mass production of Fordism with a more flexible syncing up of production and demand. Rather than storing large quantities of raw materials for future production or stockpiling already-assembled cars, production awaits customer demand before initiating (and adjusting) the process. Reducing waste in terms of space, Toyotism also ensures quick production by eliminating "unnecessary" steps on the assembly line and by relying on suppliers to deliver requisite parts in record time (Monden and Ohno 2011, 3). By implementing a post-Fordist strategy of rotating workers and making them multiply skilled rather than assigning them to only one job, Toyotism can better respond to shifts in consumers' desires and tastes, enabling a business to repurpose and redesign its lines of manufacturing with relative ease. Toyotism is considered a cornerstone of Japan's "economic miracle" and aspects of it became studied and adopted worldwide, including by many US automobile companies by the end of the 1980s.

Established in 1957, Daifuku is a material resources company that built its business on making conveyer belts for Toyota's just-in-time delivery system. By the 1990s, however, in response to changing times that included the bursting of the bubble economy and the ensuing nagging recession and industrial downturn, it innovated its operation. Calling itself now a "logistics solutions" company, it entered a new market: an aging population seeking different provisions for mortuary care than the family grave. In 1996 it designed the first mechanism implemented in Japan for automated graveyards. By retaining the form of the conventional grave but circulating remains in and out on a just-in-time basis according to the demands of visitation, the number of graves needed (as well as the cost and labor required to inter and visit the deceased) was significantly reduced. The first "automatic delivery style columbaria" (*jidō hansōshiki nōkotsudan*) in the country was built in conjunction with Banshōji Temple, but there are now over thirty nationwide. The largest, an expansion of the one at Banshōji Temple, houses the remains of twelve thousand deceased.

Interment within buildings is not new in itself. Columbaria, called *nōkotsudō* or *nōkotsudan*, have long been part of cemeteries. Following Tokyo's great earthquake in 1923, which, in destroying much of the city, including many of its cemeteries, offered the opportunity to innovate in burial design, a new law was instituted that allowed temples to construct walled-in sites one-third the size of their former graveyards to hold ossuaries. This relieved the pressure on space within temple cemeteries, which, despite efforts made by municipal officials to urge residents to bury their dead elsewhere, were still housing the majority of the urban deceased; of

AUTOMATED GRAVES 183

80,000 people who died in 1941, 10,000 were returned to natal villages, 17,000 were buried in municipal cemeteries, and 53,000 were interred in temple graveyards. A number of temples took advantage of the new law, creating stylish new ossuaries that could fit ever more cremains in less space by containing them differently. Now, instead of randomly burying cremains in the earth, temples had to seal them in concrete storage spaces, neatly lined up in tight rows. Recognizing its merits for not only spatial efficiency but also temporal durability, a newspaper article in 1929 praised a temple in the Fukugawa neighborhood of Tokyo for its modern ossuary with the observation that it would last "for eternity" (Bernstein 2006, 128).

Daifuku's website identifies the sociological crunch in caring for the dead these days as the issue its mechanized columbaria are intended to fix. According to Daifuku, the trend toward a population without successors and graves getting abandoned (*ohaka no keishisha ga inai toiu keikō*) is one of the biggest crises facing the country today. But, as sociologist Nagai Yoko has observed, such a situation stems from not only a deficit in care; it is also due to the temporal and spatial demands of the old(er) system being out of sync with the times. As she sees it, plenty of Japanese would still be invested in attending to the dead if doing so didn't involve traveling long distances (to ancestral graves in the countryside), unending obligation (for eternity, when this involves ancestors), and the daily intensity of tending to a household shrine (Tsukamoto 2019). Such issues are what Daifuku addresses by fashioning urban columbaria with an automated just-in-time contraption that retains the symbolism of the traditional grave but retrofits it to operate quite differently in terms of the spatial, temporal, and care work alignments of the familial model of mortuary care. This makes grave visitation and maintenance far easier and more convenient for living survivors. But it also serves those in the population without successors and those in graves getting abandoned in the countryside.

Spatially, automated grave parks provide a physical space for housing the dead. For all those interred there, their cremains will spend most of the time on a shelf in the warehouse. And yet those who will inhabit the temporary gravesite are assured of never getting thrown out—for as long as the facility operates, at least. Given the service of eternal memorial by the resident priest and connected to the durability of a Buddhist temple to which such hybrid operations as Sennichidani are attached, the sense of eternity associated with a final resting place is maintained. This temporality was once dependent on the ongoing practice of concern rendered as care work by living successors: visits to the grave, special memorials on ritual and anniversary occasions, and daily offerings at the domestic shrine, done for thirty-three years (after which time the dead transitions into an ancestor). But in an automated columbarium, this care comes as part of a commercial contract, exchanged for a one-time fee paid by users who are customers rather than kin (including the to-be-deceased, who sign for and by themselves in a living contact, *seizen keiyaku*). The relationship of care is now contracted with a religious and commercial corporation in an agreement that, anticipating a lack of caregivers in the future, wards against it by insuring that no remains of the deceased here will ever be abandoned. This contrasts with the situation based on the familial model of succession in conventional cemeteries and temples, where annual fees must be paid; when they are not, the grave is designated "abandoned" (after as little as one year and no more than five years) and the cemetery has the right to remove the contents and rebury them in a collective grave for the disconnected.

Care, too, attends to the grave. Kept continually glistening, replenished with fresh flowers, with incense perpetually (if electronically) lit, the grave site is given the honor and respect of a sacred spot: what once symbolized the patrilineal line. But those who visit their dead at Sennichidani will do so with the remains temporarily occupying it in a vehicle that is serially shared—more communal (or corporate) property than a spot privately owned by a family. By not having to pay for the grave or be responsible for its upkeep, the burden of care is distributed—away from the individual and onto the corporation or collective. This also means that occupancy is at once fungible and replaceable: one set of remains goes in and, once out, the grave is readied for another. With rotating occupancy, the grave is repeatedly emptied and can remain empty for quite a while. And yet, unlike the emptying of ancestral graves in the countryside—which is taken as a symptom of current times and a sign of abandoning the dead—the graves in automated columbaria are cared for and attended even when empty. This makes them a rather different entity than an empty signifier, as Roland Barthes (1982) once famously said about Japan, calling it an "empire of signs" where form is perpetually empty. Here the form of the grave is upheld even when emptied of contents. This arguably stands for an adherence to some notion, or desire, for ritualization of the dead even in the waning flow of caregivers to support it. But, with graves wired with just-in-time automation, it is also something in—and a sign itself of—transition. The state of becoming something else. Clinging to the old, apportioning it with the new, a mishmash of things in-between.

An urban deathscape proffers a solution to the dead getting abandoned in the villages (once the site, and the roots, for social tradition). The sacred remapped away from the model of social reproduction (based on the patriarchal, patrilineal family line) that can no longer sustain it. To something else that can also save the dead, and possibly the living as well, from "no future" (Edelman 2004).

AN URBAN COMMONS FOR A RE-RELATIONAL FUTURE JAPAN?

Completed in 2014, Rurikō-in is a new-style Buddhist burial ground in Shinjuku, Tokyo, just 170 meters from Shinjuku Station, the most crowded urban commuter rail hub in the world. Designed by Kyoto-based architect Takeyama Kiyoshi, Rurikō-in sports an automated delivery system engineered by Toyōta L&F Corporation that operates much like the one at Sennichidani Jōen. The system retrieves containers held in one of two columbaria (one above ground, the other below, both 800 cubic meters holding a total of 7,500 containers), and delivers them to the provisional graves in "meeting rooms" after a visitor has pressed their "griever's card" at the electronic monitor in the entrance hall. As at Sennnichidani, the storage units are kept hidden from visitors, and the mechanical system operates speedily and in silence. With remains delivered to the grave by the time someone comes to pay their respects, this is just-in-time memorialization in a space crafted to be at once architecturally beautiful and convenient for urban commuters to reach.

In their study of it, anthropologist Michael Fisch and designer Erez Golani Solomon see the logic of Rurikō-in's design as driven by remediation: remedying the precarity of tending to the dead in contemporary Japan with a high-tech, urban design. Shoehorned into the dense real estate of Shinjuku, Rurikō-in announces itself with a bold structure: a convex and concave concrete mass sitting atop a pedestal base like a stone chalice. Strikingly at odds with the high-rise buildings surrounding it, the temple projects "a totemic and primitive presence" with "an autonomy of form that conveys sensibilities borrowed from different times and different places" (Fisch and Solomon 2018, 147). Quite intentional, the architect envisioned his task as constructing something at once part of, and removed from, the bustle of urban traffic. "I wanted to create something that would seem to float, separate from the ground, and separate from its surroundings. Something that could be a part of this world but also contain another world, another kind of space, a sacred space" (Takeyama, quoted in Fisch and Solomon 2018, 137).

A renowned architect who built his early career on designing a number of traditional hotels and inns, Takeyama was hired by the Toyota L&F Corporation when it was commissioned by the Jōdo Shinshu Buddhist sect to build an automated columbarium in Shinjuku. Given license in the design, Takeyama crafted Rurikō-in to be architecturally novel, distinct from traditional temple conventions and also from the hyperurbanization of Tokyo's built landscape. Designed to be both sparse and sublime—an entrance between black granite stones over water, a waterfall cascading down one wall that is viewable from the inside when sitting on two Mies van der Rohe leather benches—Rurikō-in was meant to induce an air of serenity in visitors. "When you enter the building, you enter into a silent calm and your mind is washed free of the bustling energy of Shinjuku" (Takeyama, quoted in Fisch and Solomon 2018, 141). Offering a sanctuary of time and space, as does a traditional cemetery, it was similarly built to last an eternity: four hundred years, Takeyama has said is his aspiration. This is a temporality strikingly at odds with the average lifespan of the buildings surrounding it (currently fifty-six years for Tokyo's concrete buildings) and also the instantaneity of the automatic delivery system—the technology at the very heart of Rurikō-in and what inspired its creation in the first place.

This is the tension and the logic of the automated columbarium. Encased within the beauty and hypermodernity of a Buddhist temple built to last forever, a warehouse for dead remains is turned into a sacred graveyard for the deceased, operating with both accuracy and speed. By placing a barcode on the lower right side of each container and a small granite plate at one end with the name of the deceased, users are assured that the remains delivered to the provisional grave are actually those they are there to visit. The grave thus becomes data as well as a highly efficient portal for containing and emptying contents upon demand. As serviced by the advanced Toyota L&F storage and retrieval system, a "frictionless circuit" is produced between warehouse and grave (Fisch and Solomon 2018, 146).[4] Gauged to operate as silently and quickly as possible—to hide its machinery from clients and to minimize waiting time at what can be surges of visitors around holidays (especially Obon, New Year, and the vernal equinox)—the technology is highly rationalized and efficient.

With what Fisch and Solomon (2018) call its "logistical architecture," Rurikō-in operates beyond capacity with its just-in-time delivery system: the reason it can fit 7,500 "graves" into a relatively small lot in the heart of Shinjuku. Remediating the space and time of a traditional gravesite, the dead here are enfolded in the tempo and accessibility of urban living.

As the head priest at Rurikō-in has said, "We'd like people to come here as part of the light feeling of shopping in Shinjuku rather than for the express purpose of visiting the grave" (quoted in Ukai 2016, 96). But remediation goes beyond this for the dead who lack others to visit their grave and who might otherwise wind up as disconnected souls. As a single woman in her fifties told me, being interred in such a beautiful columbarium would give her peace of mind. And it would be far better than her alternative: entering the family grave where her parents and ancestors are buried, which will lack someone to tend to it after her own death as last of the line. She, as well as all her ancestors, would be in a grave becoming unkempt and abandoned like so many others dotting Japan's landscape today. Though she had no religious concept of an afterlife, this woman imagined that belonging, somehow, somewhere, in a repository for the dead was a better outcome than either the ancestral grave or nothing at all. Places like Rurikō-in, Sennichidani Jōen, or Tōchōji were options she was considering: places where the care she gave to her ancestors would be preserved and performed, albeit in alternative form. Even if no one came to visit them in the grave.

But visitation does occur. As Ueno told me of Sennichidani Jōen, visitors come to pay respects to the dead: mainly older Japanese who, buoyed by the convenience of being able to visit graves now in the city, sometimes linger for quite a while and make frequent visits. But there are also periods when few visitors come at all and a number of cremains that never make it out of their storage containers. Yet even then, as he said with a smile, the place operates as a "peaceful grave park" in the heart of the city. A commons, of sorts, where the graves become shared property rather than being inhabited and owned by individual families. Driven by the difficulties facing present-day Japanese in tending to the dead in times of sped-up, socially downsized urban lifestyles when a carryover of some kind is desired nonetheless, people have designed the automated columbarium as a new kind of final dwelling.

The idea for an eternal burial spot not dependent on kin is hardly new. This was the vision of Hosono Ungai, who proposed in 1941 the building of huge eternal tombs in the city (*fumetsu no funbo*) where everyone would be buried and mourned and that would simultaneously serve the living as civic centers and gyms. He was disturbed by the spread of abandoned graves at the time—one-third of those even at the high-end Aoyama Cemetery in Tokyo—and blamed it on entrusting care of the dead to the family.[5] With his Marxist politics of necro-utopia, Hosono envisioned local governments running these eternal tombs instead, though the idea never came to fruition. Given that automated columbaria are commercial and only open to those who can afford the membership fees (albeit at a price far lower than what a family plot or grave costs at a Buddhist temple or private cemetery), the operating principle is hardly egalitarian, as Hosono had intended eternal tombs to be. Instead, as with Rurikō-in, the final dwelling place they offer is framed less in civic than commercial terms: as part of the consumerist landscape (aligned with shopping) rather than as facilities serving the public.

Still, like Hosono's designs for his eternal mounds, automated columbaria are constructed to be worlds for the dead that are sustainable over time and announce this in their very structure. Built for eternity and with eternal memorial provided to all the dead within, the automated columbarium is a monolith collapsing and condensing sociality with an architecture intended to be as peaceful as it is bold. A far cry from the labyrinth of individuated ancestral plots, dependent on families to tend to them, that stretch on and on in rows increasingly punctuated by emptied, abandoned graves, automated columbaria would signal something otherwise. A shared home of sorts, a dwelling assembled around a collective just-in-time resting place. A commons for those otherwise without. And a sign of social redesign for (remembering, retaining, rerelationalizing) the dead of Japan as well.

CONCLUSION

Technology figures variously in relations between the living and the dead. It both compensates for humans and shifts their relations in various ways when assigned the work of caring for dead/remains. As did the virtual pet Tamagotchi (animated as if alive while a player expends labor but converted to a mere thing once the interaction stops), this raises questions about the parameters of life and the dynamics of interpersonal interaction. Can a machine ever stand in for the sociality of human-human interactions and, if so, what are the ethics, politics, and ontological implications for doing so? That children came to think of their personal Tamagotchi as entities they could bring to life or kill at will (as in the death sites that some kids posted for their pets online) was one of the critiques raised against them: that the toy was desensitizing children to the humanity of life (Allison 2006).

But there is a different way of reading the ontological implications of such technological designs: as offering a semblance of humanity to those already, or at risk of being, treated as inanimate for lack of social recognition or care. This is the argument I make for the automated grave. That, due to a model of mortuary care dependent on intimate others that more and more Japanese are precariously without, anyone and everyone might find themselves stranded in death, as public discourse continually stresses. While the rates of lonely death are higher in the cities, those in the countryside are also affected, and the incidence of abandoned graves is sharper there due to the fact that that is where familial roots tend to rest (Kotani 2018).

All of this raises the need—which is also an opportunity—for devising a deathscape that can house and grieve the dead in a more equitable and sustainable fashion, thereby reducing the rate and fear of (becoming) disconnected souls. My argument is that automated graves offer a technological solution to this imperative: a way of mass housing the dead in a manner that maintains the symbolism of the traditional grave by using a just-in-time mechanism that allows thousands to share it, if only prosthetically. Compared to other grave alternatives now on the market (including some run by nonprofits), this mechanism is arguably unique in its capacity to serve such high numbers of dead in a relatively limited space, which, being an urban development, also means it becomes a cipher for drawing in those (otherwise) abandoned dead from the countryside nationwide. Whereas once urban dwellers returned to rural homes to honor and perpetuate the sacredness of ancestral graves, now remains from those graves are being sent to automated columbaria in the cities in an attempt to rescue them from becoming abandoned materiality and souls. An interesting reversal, with the technosocial apparatus provided by automation—an ontological entanglement between humans and machines—making the urban deathscape the new environment, and promise, for sacralizing the dead in Japan. This offers, as Escobar has said of design, an ontology of care.

Certainly, this prosthetic apparatus also shifts the calculus of what it means to be human after death, pushing it in different directions by borrowing from, but redesigning, the conventions and practices once counted on for caring for the dead. No longer demanding a successor or kin to give care, or a grave in the ground to be tended to for thirty-three years, or even that the deceased assume a discrete individuality,[6] the dead today are being variously reconceptualized, as is the sociality surrounding them, by new mortuary designs in Japan such as the automated grave. While feeding a booming marketplace, this impulse is also being fed by something else: a desire not for mere management of dead remains but for something that accords a semblance of humanity by maintaining some social ritual for the deceased in the process. The automated delivery system columbarium is one model for doing this.

Hoping as a cognitive practice may require us to think in terms of both tendency and rupture, to reconcile the future as emerging from and linked to the present, yet radically unrecognizable. But hopefulness as an affective disposition requires a great deal more: to will both (self-)affirmation and (self-)overcoming; to affirm what we have become as the ground from which we can become otherwise.

Kathi Weeks, *The Problem with Work* (2011)

epilogue

February 2022. On the day Russia invaded Ukraine, two years into the pandemic times unleashed by COVID-19, in a season plagued by the climatic oscillations of global warming, I gave a talk on my work to the local chapter of the Japan-America Society of North Carolina. Invited by two expatriates of Japan interested in my work, longtime residents in the United States, who had requested that my presentation be not altogether bleak (as was suggested about my last book, *Precarious Japan*), I focused on the anticipatory preparedness (*seizen seiri*) so much at the heart of endingness in Japan today. Describing such examples as designing one's own coffin, keeping a daily journal of ending notes, and prearranging interment alongside "grave friends" or a beloved pet, I noted how such initiatives are fueled by (and fuel) a booming ending market that runs on the erosion of a family-based death making system. As more and more people face the prospect of nowhere to go and no one to tend them at death, we see an explosion of ending activity geared to planning ahead. But as remarkable, to me at least, was the energy pulsing through so many of the activities and events I attended in the course of doing fieldwork on *shūkatsu*. Like the buoyant head of a burial society for single women who, exhorting her audience to plan well in advance of their final days with a bevy of chores and tasks to manage before then, shouted with gusto, "What's so dreary about facing death alone? Let's engage all this with liveliness!"

The emphasis on the activity involved in this new necro-animism, as reflected in the name given to the ending industry, *shūkatsu*, which combines the characters for *end* (終) and *activity* (活), prompted the first two questions following my talk. The first was about why I call this a crisis. As I had mentioned at the outset, with such demographic and social shifts as an aging population, decreasing marriage and childbirth rates, an increase in irregular employment, the economic decline since the 1990s, and an ebbing of familial and other sociological ties, some consider there to be no future for the dead in Japan—a country where more and more people are living and dying alone with no place to be buried and no one to care for their remains or spirits after that. Despite such precarity (reflected in the rising incidence of lonely death in the cities and abandoned ancestral graves in the countryside), the counterexample is what I spent the rest of my talk laying out. Resistance to the death of ritualizing the dead. In a flurry of animation notable for the electricity with which it sizzles the air, this engagement with death planning—so unlike the dismissal or neglect with which it is treated in the United States—feels like a social phenomenon in its own right. Which is what the sociologist Émile Durkheim (1947) said of the effect and affect of ritual: orchestrated in recognition of something beyond one's biological or ephemeral self, it takes the individual to another plane. And registers like an electric current circulating between and beyond persons in what, for Durkheim, was the social. Might the culture of necro-animism in Japan today be inspiring not only death making of a new, self–death making type but also—and through this—a different mechanism for generating a sociality seen as so imperiled these days? While not saying quite this, I did stick with my claim that a shift in an older system of relationality was a major factor in the emergence of, and excitement around, *shūkatsu*.

Agreeing, the person who asked the second question saw the rupture in what greeted the dead until recently as directly responsible for the birth of new mortuary trends in Japan. As she put it, the shift has been sudden and sharp.

We all grew up emphasizing such a strong connection to our ancestors. Then we became adults and realized, I have nobody. Assuming someone will take care of me—that concept is gone. That's kind of shocking. And it's happened so fast—in thirty years, forty years? One generation.

That speed is really shocking. Suddenly no one is having a baby. Forty to fifty percent of Japanese women in their forties and fifties are not married. It's shocking. All these demographic, economic factors . . . makes us wonder. What's going on in Japan? Also, it's a challenge to what we used to do and can't do any more. Nor expect to do any more. It used to be: after I die, I could count on someone coming to the Obon festival in August just like I did for my grandparents. But nothing like that is going to happen anymore. Not for many people.

Seeing the situation around death as, indeed, a crisis, this woman recognized the dynamism with which new practices are quickly replacing the old. "Maybe this is why everyone is getting so hyper about all these new ending activities—it's a way of making oneself not so sad. Because people don't know what to do and are willing to try whatever makes them comfortable. Because they're not comfortable. They're not comfortable with what's going on. So they have to find something. You can't just sit there and wait for something to happen."

Discussion then turned to what a number of audience members were facing: trying to navigate, from a distance, attending to the ancestral graves of family members or ancestors in Japan. As my two hosts shared with everyone, they had recently arranged for the contents of their own family graves to be removed from the cemeteries they had been in for centuries and transported to Buddhist temples with which their families had long-standing ties. There, priests would perform Buddhist memorials (*eitaikuyō*) on the relevant anniversaries for a period of fifty years. In both cases, the male successors needed to caretake the ancestral graves were absent or living abroad. But the problem of abandonment had now been solved. With new homes and care providers for their ancestors, these diasporic descendants felt incredible relief. And, as one of the two further related, he was already on the case trying to make his own ending plans (green burial in the Smoky Mountains, perhaps) as creatively different from the in-ground grave he had recently moved his ancestors away from back home. Even for these expatriates, decades after having been transplanted to the United States, the pull of the dead in a land with traditions continued to call out to them. A call to which they are responding with new-style trends.

....

Crisis, as in the sensation of the loss of something one is much attached to, is part of what defines precarity—a concept that, adopted by autonomist

Marxists, among others, references shifts in capitalism in the 1970s toward more immaterial labor and the ensuing transformation to the temporality and sociality anchored to stable employment. As critics such as Brian Campbell and Christian Laheji (2021) have pointed out, however, precarity so defined skews to the privileges of the Global North. Most areas of the world and peoples in them have always been precarious, never secured by—or expecting—the stability of employment that Fordism accorded core workers in countries and time periods like postwar Japan. Leaving villages and traditions behind after the war to pursue middle-class aspirations, nuclear households, consumerist dreams, and respectability paid off during the period of high economic growth; but then success started to fracture, as did the bubble economy, in the early 1990s. But it is the sense of a loss of durable employment, and so much else coupled to it, that has spurred what I see as the seeds of a willingness, and urgency, to jump into a belonging otherwise, if only in death, in Japan today. The familiar and familial can no longer be counted on for the well-being it once afforded. For, as the person cited above put it so succinctly after my talk, what once grounded one within transgenerational ties looped through ancestors, routinized in the daily habit of tending to spirits at the household shrine, and promised oneself for the futurity of becoming an ancestor tended by kin at the family grave, is no longer viable. "Not for many people." For as radical and rapid as this loss feels to so many, I take it also to be both a desire and opportunity to replace the old form of death/place-making with something else. This is why necro-animism is such a vital and vibrant new life/death-style in Japan. Hovering above precarity, it crafts the potential for making do by alternative means.

Utopian hope is a concept feminist political theorist Kathi Weeks deploys in demanding the transformation of society by a policy of basic income that will make the sustainability of peoples' lives no longer dependent on the vagaries and inequities of wage-based work. Drawing on Ernst Bloch, Fredric Jameson, and Friedrich Nietzsche, among others, she envisions this, a cognitive practice beginning with the present, as something that must extend to, and radicalize, the future. That is, hope (which she prefers to call a demand), must be grounded in the "real-possible" of what is known from the past or the present, but also be willing, and able, to offer something "astonishingly new" for the future (Weeks 2011, 196–97). To overcome a system that plagues, excludes, and disadvantages the flourishing of so many demands entering into a different world, envisioning a different future, and becoming different subjects. But, to do so, one still needs

E.1 An overgrown plot next to a tidied one: the state of family graves in Japan. Tama Reian, Koganei, Tokyo.

strands of, or tetherings to, the familiar: "Affirmation in this sense requires that we not refuse what we have now become after measuring ourselves against the standard of what we once were or what we wish we had become, but affirm what we are and will be, because it is also the constitutive basis from which we can struggle to become otherwise" (Weeks 2011, 201).

While I am less eager than Weeks to deploy the rubric of either hope or utopia, I adopt the usage of "otherwise" to reference a struggle, a potential, a willingness, and a need to strike out in new directions for, in this case, managing the dead. Whether opting for an automated columbarium, a robot-priest to deliver mortuary sutras, or scattering ashes (retaining a few for portable memorial goods), contemporary Japanese have choices beyond the patrilineal national code of death making that has become even more hierarchical and exclusive in recent years. That the choice made by many, especially those with the financial and psychic wherewithal to do so, is to pursue alternative means for ritualizing the dead—even if this means doing so for and by oneself—bespeaks an attachment to sociological existence beyond the corporeal, temporal, and individual existence of the here and now self. Outlasting *this* for something or someone *else*. Ensconced in a fragment of the familiar—a grave that exists but rotates occupants in and out via a just-in-time system or emptying an ancestral grave and moving the contents to a temple or facility where memorial is performed in perpetuity—the activity of ritualization continues, albeit in the belly of a marketplace. Practicing a form of grievability in its refusal to let death making die out. Outside the governance of the nation-state, the normativity of the patriarchal family, or the "no future" of social reproduction dependent on children and ancestors.

Might this being dead contain the germ of being otherwise in life as well?

notes

ACKNOWLEDGMENTS

1   Following Japanese custom, I list Japanese names family name first throughout the book. If individual preference or convention is Western ordering, however (such as Marie Kondō, who is known that way throughout the world, and my friend Yoshiko Kuga), I use that order.

INTRODUCTION

1   The Meiji Constitution was instituted in 1885.
2   As in a front-page article in the *New York Times*, reporting on the skyrocketing rate of such deaths among homeless people in American cities: Thomas Fuller, "As Homeless Age, Cities See Surge in Lonely Deaths on the Street," *New York Times*, April 19, 2022, 1. https://www.nytimes.com/2022/04/18/us/homeless-deaths-los-angeles.html?searchResultPosition=1.
3   For more on the US policy of "prevention by deterrence," see De Léon 2015.
4   "Lonely death" (*kodukushi*) is also referred to as "solitary death" (*koritsushi*) or "death unrecognized by anyone else" (*kizuite moraenai shi*) (Yoshida 2010).
5   As dealt with by such scholars as Eric Klinenberg (2002) for the heat wave in Chicago in 1995 that killed 485, including 170 who died all alone; Jason De Léon (2015) for migrants who, trying to cross the Sonoran Desert into the United States, die in record numbers; and Sarah Wagner (2019) for the 4 percent of fatalities of US soldiers in the Vietnam War that remained unaccounted for, the condition of strandedness at death can take place either far from home or within a home shared by nobody else. More (scholarly, humanitarian, and political) attention has been paid to strandedness far from home: those whose bodies remain unretrieved or unidentified far from

home, leaving family members in an ambiguous state between mourning and hope. As Wagner notes, rituals are hard to perform when "there is nothing of the dead to bury or care for" (2019, 1): an absence that can incite incredible investments of money and labor to retrieve even a fragment of the deceased—which the American government has made to find, and repatriate, those MIA from the Vietnam War. To identify and possibly retrieve remains is the work of forensic science, done to provide closure for family members as well as to discover and document the circumstances leading to stranded death(s) in the first place.

A nascent body of critical scholarship on forensic science includes that by Jason De León (2015), Adam Rosenblatt (2015), and Sarah Wagner (2019); and by feminist scholars extending forensics into care like Elizabeth Davis (2017) and Amade M'charek and Sara Casartelli (2019). For the latter, the craft and attentiveness of forensic workers perform an act of humanization: a "becoming human of bones" as Davis puts it (2017, 229). Davis also points to the temporalization of remaking a different kind of relationality after death out of bone fragments. Working on exhumations undertaken to recover missing bodies from both sides of the civil war in Cyprus between Turkish and Greek Cypriots, she calls this a "time-machine" of ethico-politics that makes it "possible to think of a future not in teleological terms (of reconciliation, for example) but of becoming something different in the present which may also mean something different in the past" (2017, 237). Other forms of workers may also engage in reknitting bones into relational subjects of new sorts. Aslihan Sanal, for example, tracks anatomists in Turkey who, in using abandoned dead at mental institutions as medical cadavers, accord them a new social status (and "new time frame") in their position now serving humanity (2011, 137). Similarly, an Okinawan photographer tries to remake the relational order of the recently discovered bones of Japanese soldiers who died at the end of the war. As examined by Chris Nelson, Higa Toyomitsu was compelled to "listen to the bones" and make them beautiful and whole again by the "aesthetics of unity" performed by his art (2015, 155). But this is not to honor the imperial militarism by which they died, which he opposes. Rather it is to honor the dead in terms of a humanity that he (and other Okinawans) are much more able to share.

I have been influenced by all these scholarly strands in the work that follows, particularly chapters 6 and 7 on the stranded dead and those who work on their remains.

6   As they recognize, this requires building institutional infrastructure to support different and wider networks of care. For Weeks,

this would include a minimum guaranteed income, shorter working hours, universal health care, and more affordable housing (2021, 17).

7   Buddhist rites have long been facilitated by machines, as Fabio Rambelli has noted about the important role played by materiality throughout the history of Buddhism in Japan (2007). Machines to produce prayers—prayer wheels, early mechanical devices (*karakuri*), and *shakuhachi* flutes used to draw out and spread Dharma in a form different from the visual—were made and used by the beginning of the Tokugawa Era (Rambelli 2018).

8   In her book, *Animism in Contemporary Japan: Voices for the Anthropocene from Post-Fukushima Japan*, Shoko Yoneyama (2019) makes a similar argument. She traces efforts made to put "life" (*inochi*) at the center of modernity as a way of dealing with industrial disasters in Japan. Examining three key figures who have embraced different animist traditions in their environmental activism in postwar Japan, Yoneyama focuses on the concept of life they use to "repackage and reinterpret industrial problems in an attempt to produce something new" (2). This kineticism, where "super-modernity and intangible cultural heritage" meet, she calls the space of "grassroots Japan" (3).

CHAPTER 1. AMBIGUOUS BONES

Epigraph: Shinmon Aoki's *Coffinman* was originally published in Japan in as *Nōkanshi nikki* (Tokyo: Bungeishunju, 1991, 94, 95).

1   Kinki region, Kantō, Chūgoku.
2   Burakumin, the class assigned these professions, were legally emancipated from nonhuman status by the Meiji Constitution but are still discriminated against today (Hankins 2014).
3   Japanese native culture: *Kokugaku* (National Learning) or Yanagita's *Shin-Kokugaku* (New National Learning) are based less on doctrinaire Shintō scholarship than on the oral traditions and practices of rural Japanese.
4   The continuing relevance of the *obasuteyama* story has been related to me by many of my Japanese friends. Once, a friend and I encountered a roadside display featuring it as a landmark for the town we were driving through on the highway.
5   The six forms of existence are heavenly beings, humans, titans, animals, hungry ghosts, and hell dwellers.
6   "Reverse-style memorials" (*gyakushū kuyō*), done in advance of death and arranged by the person themself, were commonly practiced, at least by the elite, in the ninth century. Intended to accrue merit for

achieving rebirth in Pure Land (or other divine realms), efficacy was considered to be greater when conducted by the to-be-dead. When funeral rites were performed by the family after death, by contrast, living sponsors were thought to receive most of the benefit, with only one-seventh of the merit reaching the dead.

The first recorded case of a *gyakushū kuyō* was that of the wife of a Fujiwara clan courier who, with no children and parents deceased, performed it for herself in 883 CE to relieve her anxieties about dying. As Jacqueline Stone argues, death rituals during this period entailed multiple logics, not always consistent. But prominent here was "the logic of cultivation through personal effort" in which one's ability to achieve a "good death" was thought to rest (2018, 375). I thank Hank Glassman for alerting me to the practice of *gyakushū kuyō*—a precedent to the practice of self-death making today in Japan.

7   These Buddhist practices also intermingled with other customary behavior such as reversals done on the corpse to signal to the spirit that they are now somewhere other than earth. For example, the coffin is carried in a circle around the room so the dead can't find their way back home. The straw sandals of those who carry the coffin to the grave are left there for the same reason. The corpse is bathed in cold water to which hot water has been added—the opposite of the normal order. The body is placed with its head to the north, a position no one would sleep in when alive. The kimono worn by the corpse is folded in reverse fashion to those worn by the living. As described by anthropologist Hyunchul Kim (2012) based on fieldwork in a rural town in Ibaraki in 2005–2007, these are practices still upheld in the countryside.

8   As recorded in the *Nihongi* (History of Japan) in the eighth century. This was followed three years later when Empress Jitō was burned on a funeral pyre (Bernstein 2006).

9   As evidence of this, Bernstein cites what happened at the funeral of the founder of the Shinshū sect, Rennyo, when followers thrust their hands in the embers of his burning body to claim one of the remains as a sacred relic (2006).

10 Satō Hiroo writes that by the Tokugawa period, belief in a separate afterworld was no longer as widely upheld generally across the population. Instead of traveling far away to a separate realm (Pure Land), the dead were now thought to linger closer to where their bones and remains were buried. This meant a longer and more intense regimen of care on the part of humans tending to the dead, according to Satō. This also placed more weight—both symbolic and real—on the grave itself, treated now, as he puts it, as a portal between the living and the dead (2019).

11 Built in 1868 for the *shōkonsha*, it was renamed Yasukuni Shrine in 1879 (Takenaka 2015).

12 For more on this subject, see Bernstein (2000 and 2006). Both his book and his article on the Meiji cremation ban are excellent.

13 According to Hank Glassman (2009), significant changes in the kinship arrangements of burial practices occurred in Japan between the tenth and fourteenth centuries. Women were much more likely to be buried alongside their natal kin, separate from their husbands, in the tenth century. But this changed over time due primarily to the increasing influence of Confucianism, Glassman argues. By the fourteenth century, the patrilineal system came to dominate, and married women were commonly buried with their husbands and families in ancestral graves, where having a gravekeeper (*hakamori*) and visiting the grave (*hakamairi*) also assumed much more importance. In contrast, the latter barely existed prior to the eleventh century.

14 And yet this was also when the custom of mourners contributing funeral money (*kōden*) to help defray the family's expenses started. While *kōden* was mentioned in only 4 percent of obituaries in 1918, the figure had gone up to 61 percent by 1926 (Bernstein 2006, 152). When practiced today, the custom is to return half of what was contributed as a "return gift." Choosing an appropriate gift worth exactly half the money received also entails considerable work—one of the reasons, I have been told, that the trend today is toward paring down funerals to the immediate family.

15 Then considered the worst natural disaster in earthquake-prone regions, the fires following the quake were responsible for more deaths than the quake itself. This also triggered a massive scapegoating of residential Koreans (*zainichi*), six thousand of whom were massacred in a slaughter led mainly by groups of vigilantes.

16 In the wake of the Kantō earthquake, the city, trying to hold onto urban space, attempted to force the relocation of all cemeteries to the suburbs. Retreating in the face of opposition, it then gave permission for temples to construct walled-in sites one-third the size of their former cemeteries to hold remains. Called *nōkotsudō*, these became a popular space-saving addition to temple graveyards (Bernstein 2006).

17 I thank one of the anonymous reviewers of the book who pointed this out so eloquently.

18 By the 1899 Burial Law (墓埋法) and the Law Related to Travelers Who Die Away from Home (旅行病人及旅行者死亡取扱法) established in 1899, it is the city, neighborhood, or village (市町村) that bears responsibility for cremation and burial of the disconnected (Mori 2014).

19 This is similar to what anthropologist Josh Reno proposes in his ethnographic study of landfills in the United States—ecologically destructive and "cared for" by workers who are severely stigmatized for the "dirtiness" of the work. To make us more mindful of seeing the waste we produce and the damage wreaked on the earth by depositing it in landfills, Reno advocates burying our dead alongside our garbage—comingling human and nonhuman matter—in places to be treated with respect (Reno 2016).

20 This term is attributed to Tōjō Hideto who was a general of the Imperial Japanese Army during most of World War II and was subsequently tried and executed as a war criminal in 1948.

21 Emperor Hirohito's words upon ceding defeat in the Proclamation of Unconditional Surrender, issued on August 14, 1945, were reprinted in the newspapers. (This English translation ran in the *Nippon Times* on August 14, 1945; reproduced at http://ahoy.tk-jk.net/MoreImages/JapaneseSurrenderProclamation.jpg, accessed September 8, 2022.)

22 The Second Sino-Japanese War started July 7, 1937, but had been building since Japan invaded Manchuria on September 9, 1931. Japan entered the Pacific War after attacking the British colonies of Malaysia, Singapore, and Hong Kong; then the US Pacific Fleet in Pearl Harbor on December 7, 1941; then Wake Island, Guam, and the Philippines.

23 They have been variously called "comfort dolls" (*imonningyō*), "substitute dolls" (*migawari ningyō*), or "mascots" (*masukotto*) (Schattschneider 2005).

24 There are parallels here with what David Edwards has described of Afghan suicide bombers who, unmarried, design Facebook pages to resemble those of weddings (Edwards 2017, chapter 7, "Selfies.")

25 The depth of this commitment—to return the remains of fallen comrades to their families back in Japan—was such that, in one case, a soldier who was the sole survivor of his battalion during an attack along the Kokoda Trail in Port Moresby, Papua New Guinea, returned there in 1979, and spent twenty-five years trying to carry out this duty. A successful businessman, Nishimura Kokichi left all his assets to his wife and the business to his two sons (and never saw these three family members again as they opposed his decision) and moved to Papua New Guinea, where he recovered hundreds of remains of fallen Japanese soldiers. (See Happell 2008.)

26 Several hundred soldiers, mostly military officers, committed suicide as well (Dower 1999).

27 At the end of the war, at least 2.7 million people (military and civilian) or about 3–4 percent of Japan's total population had died.

In Tokyo, 5,000,000 of its once 7,000,000 residents had left the city. One-fourth of the country's wealth had been destroyed, as had four-fifths of all its ships and one-third of its industrial infrastructure. Sixty-six major cities had been bombed, 40 percent of its urban area destroyed (65 percent of residences in Tokyo were destroyed, 57 percent in Osaka, and 89 percent in Nagoya), and 30 percent of the population (almost 9,000,000 people) were now homeless (Dower 1999).

CHAPTER 2. THE POPULAR INDUSTRY OF DEATH

Epigraph: "Oh No, There Goes Tokyo: Recreational Apocalypse and the City in Postwar Japanese Popular Culture," in *Noir Urbanisms: Dystopic Images of the Modern City*, edited by Gyan Prakash, 96–115 (Princeton, NJ: Princeton University Press, 2010).

1 Starting in 1983, *U-Can* magazine has made annual "awards of new words and buzzwords." In 2010, *shūkatsu* was awarded 44th place. See U-Can, November 12, 2010, https://life.oricon.co.jp/news/81976/
2 Mikuni has written a book (2017) on this subject: *Ohitorisamade yukō: saigomade jibunrashiku* (Let's die alone: doing it one's own way until the end).
3 The first urban funeral parlor opened in 1887, in the Meiji era, with lavish death rituals. When, during the succeeding Taishō period, it was no longer mandated that citizens be members of Buddhist temples, expenditures decreased. But in the years immediately following the end of the war, the funeral industry began to flourish along with the formation of mutual-aid cooperatives (*gōjokai*), the first one of which was founded in 1948 as a means of helping local citizens assist one another in the labor and cost of funerals and burials (Suzuki 2000).
4 As seen today in the fashion of decluttering as advocated by Marie Kondō and in what is generically called *danshari*: making a conscious decision to reduce, and dispose of, material surfeit.
5 ¥1.830 million.
6 ¥1.542 million.
7 This includes the funeral, a meal for close attendees, and *henrinhin*: the custom of returning half of what is given as monetary offerings to the deceased in the way of a return gift by the family.
8 The mandate is actually that marital couples share the same family name but it is overwhelmingly the wife who changes her name rather than the husband. (See Linda White's *Gender and the Koseki in Contemporary Japan* [2018] for an anthropological study of the legality of the Family Registry and feminist challenges to it.)

9   Ending Center is more fully discussed in the next chapter.
10 Ogawa's successor wound up being his daughter, who became the fifty-fourth priest of Myōkōji in 2019 (and the first woman priest there). See the next chapter for a more detailed account.
11 For two excellent ethnographic studies on the subject, see Kawano (2010) on Sōsō no jiyū no susume kai and Boret (2014) on tree burials.
12 Originally published in 1993 as *Noanfu nikki*, it was released in English in 2002 as *Coffinman: The Journal of a Buddhist Mortician*. Richard Jaffe, a Buddhist scholar, told me it is the best book to read on Japanese Buddhism.
13 Shinmon Aoki considers his own work as a mortician to be part of his Buddhist practice—in a religion where practice is what matters, he joins the spiritual and everyday. "The Buddhist teachings Shakyamuni explained were invariably tied to practice, and it was in practice he found meaning" (Aoki 2002, 95). In his book, a diary of sorts, he tracks Buddhist philosophy through the physicality of touching dead bodies and his encounters with people accepting (or not) their own deaths. The notion of animism I am using here is Philippe Descola's: a continuity of souls over a discontinuity of bodies—a way of giving respect to the dead that otherwise would experience the fate of disregard, abandonment, the inanimate (Descola 2013).
14 Based on amazing fieldwork, Gould's book on the subject, *When Death Falls Apart*, is forthcoming from the University of Chicago Press.
15 This draws on a long history of performing *kuyō* on material objects that have lost their utility to humans: needles, scissors, dolls. The intention is to show gratitude for their service and to also extricate the spirit/human from the material thing.
16 Daniel White and Katsuno Hirofumi interviewed Ōi Bungen and Norimatsu Nobuyuki over a course of a year and attended one of the AIBO funeral services. In their article about this, they describe how they didn't at first "get" the sense of play stressed by both Ōi and Morimatsu in their crafting of the AIBO memorial service. Only over time did they come to appreciate the "pleasure derived from sensing the lifelike quality of objects like AIBO" that "sustains the affective intimacy of human-robot relations in entertainment robot culture" and also the Buddhist practice being implemented here (2021, 241).

CHAPTER 3. CARING (DIFFERENTLY) FOR THE DEAD

Epigraph: W. G. Sebald, *Campo Santo*, edited by Sven Meyer, translated by Anthea Bell (London: Hamish Hamilton, 2005), 31; Shinmon Aoki, *Coffinman* [*Nōkanshi nikki*] (Tokyo: Bungeishunju, 2002 [1991]), 48.

1. In *An Anthropology of the Machine: Tokyo's Commuter Train Network*, Michael Fish analyzes the phenomenon of commuter train suicides, called "accident resulting in bodily injury" (*jinshin jiko*), which have been a "facet of urban life" (2018, 167) ever since commuter trains became a mainstay of everyday city life in the early twentieth century in Japan. As he argues, commuter suicides are relatively common and create an "irremediable gap" (168) in the functioning of trains given their unpredictability—something the technography of the train systems attempts to incorporate, and thereby mediate, in its high-tech operations (169).
2. In his work on tree burials (*jūmokuso*), Sébastian Boret (2014) similarly finds that ancestral bonds are replaced with intentional bonds (*shien*/支援).
3. I am reminded of Angela Garcia's (2010) description of family members sharing heroin needles in the Española Valley of northern New Mexico as a method of life despite (and because of) its proximity to death.
4. Tony Walter, in *What Death Means Now: Thinking Critically about Dying and Grieving* (2017), also notes a sea change in the treatment given death in the United Kingdom and elsewhere today.
5. Anthropologist Shunsuke Nozawa describes various community-level and governmental initiatives launched to mitigate against the rise of lonely death across Japan, such as local post offices instituting "touching together postal services" (*fureai yūbin*). Youth will write notes and then, when delivered to the house of the elderly, the deliverer will make sure someone answers the door thereby establishing physical contact and also ensuring that the person is still alive. As Nozawa notes, it is less the semiotic content of the note that matters than the physical encounter itself—a staging of what he analyzes in his article as phaticity or the performance of sociality (Nozawa 2014).
6. As with all those I interviewed or conversed with about their mortuary plans, I have used pseudonyms. For those identifiable by position or work (such as Inoue Haruyo, the director of Ending Center), I use their real names.
7. When first dead, a spirit is commonly thought to become a Buddha (*hotoke*), and dying is sometimes referred to as *jōbutsu* (becoming a Buddha). When the spirit then transitions into an ancestor (*senzo*), it is thought to have joined all the other ancestors in the genealogical line, so the ancestors are a collective entity.
8. It should be noted that many Ending Center members have a Christian background, even if they not practicing Christians today.
9. Anthropologist Anna Tsing devotes a long section to *satoyama* in her 2015 book *The Mushroom at the End of the World* (151–52, 180–87).

10 The first plan is for simple burial in the communal grave, costing ¥280,000 ($2,700); the second plan includes seven steps along the way, including transportation of the body to a crematorium (costing ¥350,000, or $3,400).

11 As originally conceived by Russian literary theorist Mikhail Bakhtin, *chronotope* refers to the configurations of time and space, as taken up in language and discourse ([1981] 2020, 84–85).

12 See Edward Fowler's (1996) moving portrayal of the nexus of labor and life of workers here in the 1990s in *San'ya Blues: Laboring Life in Contemporary Japan*.

13 See Matthew Marr's (2019) excellent account of the Ohaka Grave Project, which is based on extensive ethnographic interviewing and analysis of its postsecular intervention into welfare and (necro)sociality. See also Hammerling 2022.

14 Onetime membership and entrance fee is ¥850,000 ($7,800). Engraving is ¥30,000–¥40,000 ($275–$365). Annual membership fee is ¥3,500 ($32). *Eitaikuyō* services are done four times per year (Obon, Higan in spring and fall, and at the collective memorial for a period of thirteen years). Succession is not based on kinship but on a contract (2019).

15 As religion retreats from the lives of Japanese, the economic decline of the 1990s has affected the willingness or ability of Japanese to pay the offerings and high fees expected of parishioners in long-standing relationships to temples.

CHAPTER 4. PREPAREDNESS

1 Both these presentations were held at Ending Center as part of their twice annual forum series. The first was conducted by Mikuni Hiroaki of Total Life Support and the second by Yagi Tomohiko, president of Relief Company.

2 The job market is called *shūshoku katsudō*/就職活動 or *shūkatsu*/就活 for short. Ending market uses the character for end (終) and couples this with activity (活) to come up with *shūkatsu*/終活.

3 In the end, the nationwide vaccination wasn't implemented, and the threatened pandemic didn't materialize.

4 Mikuni published a book in 2017 (available only in Japanese) with further details on his approach to death preparation based on his experience running Total Life Support.

5 おひとりさまとその予備軍のこの先の不安を丸ごとチームでさせます。

6 Matthew Marr describes the difficulties the Ohaka Project encountered when a few of the men who died without making their

desires to be buried there known ahead of time were deposited in the public cemetery for the disconnected. This included the case of someone who had had the funds and desire to be given a proper funeral, which didn't take place because he hadn't made his intentions officially known and no kin stepped forward to take responsibility themselves (Marr 2019, 17).

7 This figure excludes tax and health insurance. The municipality allows for a total monthly income of ¥180,000 ($1,732) plus less than ¥2,25 million ($21,648) total savings or less than ¥5 million ($48,106) in property. I call this constituency the "aging precariat."

8 The Life Care Law (*seikatsuhogohō*/生活保護法) will provide up to ¥206,000 ($1,982) for anyone who dies without anyone else to depend on and with insufficient savings to cover burial costs. But the law stipulates that there must be someone (a neighbor or acquaintance) who will "voluntarily" (*jihatsuteki*) do the burial in order to receive the support (*fujo*). According to one newspaper article reporting on this, up to 90 percent of local municipalities rely on a social worker (*minseiin*) to apply as the one "voluntarily" performing the funeral in order to receive this national support. But there are cities that allow funeral companies to do this, as Yokosuka City does (Fukusawa 2018–19).

9 Two of the cases were widows who, dying without other kin, had not recorded where their husbands' graves were. The third case was a single man whose desire and funds to pay for a funeral were only discovered six months after he died and had been buried in the public columbarium for the disconnected.

10 The eleven categories are (1) place where family records are kept (*honseki*), (2) whom to contact in an emergency, (3) support or end of life "circle," (4) doctor, allergies, and medical record, (5) location of living will, (6) location of ending notes, (7) display of will regarding organ donation, (8) living contracts for funeral, burial, clean-up, and medical donation of body, (9) location of will, (10) location of grave, and (11) other.

11 これはある一つの家族の物語。そして、誰にでも訪れる最期の物語。

12 The coordinator's business card reads, "Straightening up will put a smile on your face" and her profession is identified as *seizen seiri*. *Seirishūnō adobaiza*: advisor in lifetime ordering, ordering of receipts.

13 安置。ご面会。どこへでもお迎えにあがります 。

14 B1F -大ホール: big hall for accommodating funerals with over one hundred mourners.

    1F 葬送広場 (*sōso hiroba*): big open space where hearses load and unload caskets.

    3F 家族荘ホール (*kazokushō hōru*): hall for family-style funerals.

4F フアミリールーム（リビング家族葬）: family room (living family-style funeral), an apartment with bath, living room with big table and chairs, and sofa bed for the wake (*tsūya*) where a family can spend the night next to the casket.

6F ご面会室: visiting room (where family can view the body).

7F 個室面会室 (*koshitsu menkaishitsu*): for individual viewings of the body

15   This is part of the promotional campaign by SoftBank's Pepper humanoid robot (Nishimura 2021).

CHAPTER 5. THE SMELL OF LONELY DEATH AND THE WORK OF CLEANING IT UP

Epigraphs: Kimura Elji, *Ihinseirishi tolu shigoto* [The work of being a disposer] (Tokyo: Heibonsha, 2015), 16, 73. Translated by the author.

1   The term *ihinseirigaisha* derives from *ihinseiri* (ordering the belongings of the deceased) and *kaisha* (company).

2   みんなさん私の様にならないためにご近所とのおつきあいを大切にしてください。

3   My synopsis of the manga is based on my own translation of the original Japanese.

4   The book's title is *Koritsushi: anata ha daijōbu?* [Solitary death: Are you alright?].

5   A great deal of status and meaning are still pinned to jobs, endangering both those who work too hard, as in the phenomenon of death by overwork, and those who are beyond or without a job, who are stripped of the social ties, income, and identity employment brings.

6   All the quotes in this paragraph come from promotional material for Keepers.

7   人として生きて、人間らしく死ぬことの大切した。

8   He presented the story to a citizens' forum that was part of a public seminar in Yokohama City titled "How to Avoid Being Solitary until the End: From the Perspective of Ordering the Belongings of the Deceased" (遺品整理の現場から最期まで孤立しないために). A to fuo ramu azaminō newsletter, February 28, 2015.

9   Varying slightly by locale, cleanup costs are approximately ¥40,000 ($365) for a 1K (one room plus kitchen); ¥90,000 ($823) for a 1LDK (one room plus living room, dining room, kitchen); ¥140,000 ($1,280) for a 2LDK; and ¥180,000 ($1,646) for a 3LDK.

10   Across Japan, 18 percent of all residences qualify as abandoned; most but not all of these are in the countryside, where old family

residences may simply be left empty after the owner's death due to their having little personal or market value to those who inherit them. But, because taxes rise on properties without built structures on them, houses are often left as they are, to become what is considered a blight on the landscape.

11 The names of the crew heads and all clients are pseudonyms.

12 When I'm allowed to interview the workers during their half-hour lunch break, no one really wants to talk about how they feel about the work except for Hashimoto. Saying he really likes the job, he also tells me that, as the point person for many of the jobs, he enters a house first to case it. In doing so, he often—sometimes two or three times per week—encounters either a body still there or the immediate aftereffects of a lonely death. When I ask if he enters with protective gear on, he laughs and says, "Never." He admits that this part of the job can be rough.

13 As Kimura describes it, the job went extremely slowly and the worker wound up being underpaid given all the hours he put into the job. But the customer was exceedingly happy, which Kimura uses to showcase how much his company values caring work.

14 "You'll never lose touch with your memories" (あなたと思い出はけしてなくならない).

"We want to keep asking every day—what can we do while still living, what proof can we leave behind that we have lived?" (私たちが生きるこの時代に、私たちは何を出来るか、私たちは何を生きた証として残せるのかはわたしたちは毎日それを問い続けたい).

15 In the twenty-three districts of Tokyo, according to the chart Kone showed me, there were 3,000 disconnected deaths in 2004, 4,600 in 2010, and 4,500 in 2013.

16 Written by Kitagawa Shō in 2007, it was serialized in a youth (*seinen*) manga magazine, *Comic Charge* (now discontinued) and subsequently republished as a five-volume set by Kadokawa Charge Comics. Kitagawa also released a second version under the same name, published from 2017–18 in *Grand Jump Premium* (a *seinen* manga magazine from Shueisha that is already discontinued), with a target audience that would seem to be white-collar workers [*sararīman*]). The scenes I describe here come from no. 1, *Kotoshi no natsu ani ga jisatsushita* (Summer this year, my older brother committed suicide), 2007.

17 These descriptions are of the original exhibit at ENDEX in 2016 and also based on the textual accounts Kojima gave. Most of these scenes are also described in her book (Kojima 2019). All translations are my own.

18   I thank my colleague Harris Solomon for alerting me to the work of Frances Glessner Lee, and I thank Ruth Toulson for organizing a visit to view twenty of Lee's dioramas at Maryland's office of the chief medical examiner in Baltimore in 2021.

19   自分の家族の部屋のように感じて作業しています。

20   でも、それらは雄弁に故人の人生を語たってるようでもある。

CHAPTER 6. DE-PARTING

Epilogue: Hans Ruin, *Being with the Dead: Burial, Ancestral Politics, and the Roots of Historical Consciousness* (Stanford, CA: Stanford University Press, 2018), 61.

1   On the topic of the material disposal of sacred waste in contemporary Japan, see the important work of Hannah Gould (2019) and her forthcoming book (2023).

2   Some background: In a country where the law mandates cremation and compliance is virtually 100 percent, bodies tend to move quickly from corpse to cremains. By law, the process cannot be initiated any earlier than twenty-four hours after death and must be authorized by obtaining a death certificate from a doctor and taking it to the local municipality office for a certificate allowing for cremation and burial. Meanwhile, if the corpse is kept at home by the family, efforts will be made to stall decomposition by keeping it cold and to attend to the spirit, which is thought to hover for forty-nine days. Greeting the dead with water meant to signal life's end (*makki no mizu*), the family arranges the body to accord with the deceased's ontological shift: it is dressed in *haori* with the right side now overlapping the left, a white towel covering the face, palms pressed together as if in prayer (*gasshō*). The dead is also given protection for the spiritual journey ahead (a pair of scissors or knife placed over the chest to ward off evil ghosts) and accessories for the trip to the other world (*ano yo*)—straw sandals, wooden stick, white shoulder bag, paper money (Kim 2012). Incense and a candle will be kept burning and other arrangements made to signal the inversion of death: walls of the room covered in white, screens placed upside down, a bowl of sticky rice with chopsticks stuck in it vertically, the doors of the Shintō shrine kept closed to keep out evil spirits for forty-nine days.

If a mortician (*nōkanshi*) has been commissioned to handle the body, he may conduct a ceremony of bathing performed in front of immediate family: a ritual of both intimacy and respect movingly captured in the 2008 film *Departures*. Close family may also spend a night of mourning staying near, even sleeping next to, the body of the deceased. Then, if a wake and funeral are to be held, they are scheduled as soon as possible: the wake at dusk one night and the funeral (or farewell ceremony, *kokubetsukai*) the next morning around 9 o'clock. The corpse lies in a coffin during both of these and will be viewed by those present as they give an incense offering (*shōkō*) of farewell to the dead and condolences to the grieving family. While special clothing (*kyōkatabira*) is chosen and makeup (*shikeshō*) applied even to men, there seems to be little intent to preserve or recompose the corpse in lifelike form through embalming, which is little practiced in Japan. Rather, the emphasis seems to be on making the body tidy and neat and moving it quickly to a postbodily state. This has become ever more problematic due to the high death rate and shortage of crematoria; it may now take days to schedule an appointment. Responding to this need, new services have cropped up to hold corpses awaiting cremation: what the press has dubbed "corpse hotels" (*itai hoteru*).

3   Some instead take the *nodobotoke* and other bones from the head home with them in a small box (*kotsubako*; literally, bone box).

4   This is a temporary *ihai* that is normally kept, sometimes along with the urn, for forty-nine days at the home of the deceased. Then it will be replaced by the permanent *ihai* that will reside, along with the *iei* in the family's *butsudan*, at the temple they belong to, or at both.

5   Composing *kaimyō* is done carefully and can be exorbitantly expensive; characters are selected to match something in the life or personality of the deceased. There is also a prestige system: pricier *kaimyō* reflect a higher status (or quicker transition) for the spirit.

6   The food will typically be vegetarian and simple, nothing as enticing as what is served at a wedding to arouse the palate of the living. After seven days (at the time of the seventh-day celebration if carried out) a meat-based meal will be served, signaling the deceased's progress away from the carnal world and the mourners' transition back to it.

7   This is the landscape of social precarity I traced in *Precarious Japan* (2013). See it for more detail on case studies and the demographics, conditions, and activism surrounding socially precarious Japanese.

8   As police departments or other municipal buildings don't usually have the refrigerated units required for storing corpses, the task is outsourced to private facilities that charge around ¥10,000 ($90)—an increasingly big burden for cities where the rate of unclaimed deceased is rising rapidly (Fukusawa 2019).

9   New-style graves or repositories typically offer this as a service, calling it "eternal memorial" (*eitaikuyō*) and making it not dependent on having family members or successors. This is discussed in chapter 4.

10 In the case of Yokosuka City, the city columbarium has a capacity of four hundred urns. With fifty to sixty unclaimed corpses being deposited there every year, it fills within five or six years. But, in a practice I take to be relatively unusual, the city has been identifying all the urns of disconnected dead in the repository since 1995 by name instead of by number, as it used to do. This is not the case, however, when the ashes are moved to the collective grave and are identified as the disconnected of Yokosuka City.

11 Which isn't to say there are no prevention programs or initiatives. There are several at the municipal level; communities have patrols, for example, that walk neighborhoods looking for signs of distress or neglect (e.g., milk bottles or newspapers that remain unfetched outside) at residences of solitary dwellers. And a number of nonprofits have arisen to address this problem, awareness of which was triggered by the Hanshin earthquake in Kobe in 1995, when a number of deaths were of people living alone.

12 This collaboration and Kitami's involvement in Yokosuka City are more fully discussed in chapter 5.

13 Article 190 of the criminal code. See Tsuji (2002, 189) for a discussion of this.

14 By permission, I am using his real name.

15 *Kasōzankotsuhai no tekiseishori*/火葬残骨灰の適正処理

16 Though why smaller amounts of ash are not used instead of remaking the particles of ash, I am not sure.

17 In Japanese the company is called サライ, but they spell their transliterated English name as Serai, not Sarai.

18 一つの乳鉢から始まったサライ、今でも変わらぬ思いでご遺骨と向き合ってます。

19 In the article published in the magazine AERA where I first learned about Serai, the reporter put it this way: "The basic rule is to crush remains to the degree that they are no longer recognizable as 'human remains'" (遺骨とわからない程度に粉末化［一般的に2-3ミリ］することが基本ルールとなっている; Nomura 2016).

20 This practice is not necessarily observed these days, but when it is offered by a funeral company, it is promoted as a gift—of care and love—done by the bereaved for their beloved family member.

CHAPTER 7. AUTOMATED GRAVES

Epigraphs: Diego Semerene, "'Plan 75 Review': A Quietly Tragic Depiction of a World Where Empathy Is Scarce," *Slant*, May 22, 2022. Thomas W. Laqueur, *The Work of the Dead: A Cultural History of Mortal Remains*, 2015, 345.

1. Alex Blanchette makes a similar argument about the huge agricultural complexes producing pigs in the United States today. Designed to keep accelerating and expanding the (dis)assembly line—so as to maximize the size, utility, and profitability (of every particle) of the pig—this capitalistic system has now so exceeded its biological limits that sows are overproducing litters. The excess of runts get nurtured by (cheap) human labor: workers who serve as prostheses for the porcine mothers "overworked" beyond their natural capacity. "But the runt is a form of death in life that is not self-sufficient at even the biological-organismic level of forming its own muscle fibers. It requires human workers and working actions to become prostheses to its body" (Blanchette 2020, 160).
2. This chapter is based on two visits to automated graves in Tokyo and interviews with their staff as well as visits to a host of urban columbaria and cemeteries in Tokyo and elsewhere and multiple interviews with staff and priests there.
3. The warehouse is usually strictly out of bounds except for those who work here. I spent considerable energy arranging my access to it ahead of time, and was grateful that Ueno generously agreed.
4. Yet the machinery can have glitches, as I was told by Ueno at Sennichidani Jōen. As much as once a month the system fails to retrieve a container for a visitor who has come to pay their respects.
5. In response to the number of abandoned graves, an initiative arose to assemble all *muenbotoke* (disconnected souls) in Tokyo's administered cemeteries into one spot at Tama Reien (Bernstein 2006, 126).
6. Today, intermixing ashes with others' in collective graves or interring ashes directly in the earth (called *jumokusō*, or tree burial) is becoming more popular. (See Boret 2014).

bibliography

Adams, Vincanne, Michelle Murphy, and Adele E. Clarke. 2009. "Anticipation: Technoscience, Life, Affect, Temporality." *Subjectivity* 28: 246–65.

Agwunobi, John O. 2006. *Working through an Outbreak: Pandemic Flu Planning and Continuity of Operations: Hearing before the Committee on Government Reform.* 109th Congress, 2nd session, May 11, 2006. Serial 109–55. Washington, DC: US Government Printing Office.

Allison, Anne. 2006. *Millennial Monsters: Japanese Toys and the Global Imagination.* Berkeley: University of California Press.

Allison, Anne. 2013. *Precarious Japan.* Durham, NC: Duke University Press.

Amamiya Karin. 2007. *Ikisasero! Nanminkasuru wakamonotachi* [Survive! The refugeeization of young people]. Tokyo: Ōtashuppan.

Ambros, Barbara. 2012. *Bones of Contention: Animals and Religion in Contemporary Japan.* Honolulu: University of Hawai'i Press.

Amino Yoshihiko. 2012. *Rethinking Japanese History.* Translated by Alan S. Christy. Ann Arbor: University of Michigan.

Anderson, Ben. 2010. "Preemption, Precaution, Preparedness: Anticipatory Action and Future Geographies." *Progress in Human Geography* 34, no. 6: 777–98.

Anderson, Benedict. (1983) 2000. *Imagined Communities: Reflections on the Origin and Spread of Nationalism.* New York: Verso.

Antoon, Sinan. 2013. *The Corpse Washer.* New Haven, CT: Yale University Press.

Aradau, Claudia, and Rens van Munster. 2012. "The Time/Space of Preparedness: Anticipating the 'Next Terrorist Attack.'" *Space and Culture* 15, no. 2: 98–109.

Ariès, Philippe. (1977) 1981. *The Hour of Our Death.* Translated by Helen Weaver. New York: Knopf.

Asai, Atsushi, Miki Fukuyama, and Kobayashi Yasunori. 2010. "Contemporary Japanese View of Life and Death as Depicted in the Film *Departures* (*Okuribito*). *Medical Humanities* 36, no. 1 (June): 31–35.

Aslihan, Sanal. 2011. *New Organs within Us: Transplants and the Moral Economy*. Durham, NC: Duke University Press.

Ātofōramu azamino (アートフオーラムあざみ野). 2015. Yokohama shibūkōzarepo—to (横浜市部講座レポート). "遺品整理現場から最期まで孤立しないために (How to avoid being solitary until the end). February 28, 2015.

Bachelard, Gaston. (1958) 1994. *The Poetics of Space*. Translated by Maria Jolas. Boston, MA: Beacon Press.

Bakhtin, Mikhail Mikhailovich. [1981] (2020). "Forms of Time and of the Chronotope in the Novel: Notes toward a Historical Poetics." In *The Dialogic Imagination: Four Essays*, edited by Michael Holquist, and translated by Caryl Emerson, 84–258. Austin: University of Texas Press.

Banerjee, Dwaipayan. 2020. *Enduring Cancer: Life, Death, and Diagnosis in Delhi*. Durham, NC: Duke University Press.

Barthes, Roland. (1957) 1972. *Mythologies*. Translated by Annette Lavers. New York: Hill and Wang.

Barthes, Roland. 1982. *Empire of Signs*. Translated by Richard Howard. New York: Hill and Wang.

Bauman, Zygmunt. 1992. *Mortality, Immortality, and Other Life Struggles*. Stanford, CA: Stanford University Press.

Benjamin, Walter. 1969. "The Storyteller: Reflections on the Works of Nikolai Leskov." In *Illuminations*, edited by Hannah Arendt, and translated by Harry Zohn, 83–110. New York: Schocken Books.

Bernstein, Andrew. 2000. "Fire and Earth: The Forging of Modern Cremation in Meiji Japan." *Japanese Journal of Religious Studies* 27, nos. 3–4: 297–334.

Bernstein, Andrew. 2006. *Modern Passings: Death Rites, Politics, and Social Change in Imperial Japan*. Honolulu: University of Hawai'i Press.

Bird-David, Nurit. 1999. "'Animism' Revisited: Personhood, Environment, and Relational Epistemology." Supplement, *Current Anthropology* 40 (February): S67–S91.

Blanchette, Alex. 2020. *Porkopolis: American Animality, Standardized Life, and the Factory Farm*. Durham, NC: Duke University Press.

Bloch, Maurice, and Jonathan Parry, eds. 1982. *Death and the Regeneration of Life*. Cambridge: Cambridge University Press.

Boret, Sébastien Penmellen. 2014. *Japanese Tree Burial: Ecology, Kinship and the Culture of Death*. New York: Routledge.

Boss, Pauline. 2000. *Ambiguous Loss: Learning to Live with Unresolved Grief*. Cambridge, MA: Harvard University Press.

Boxall, Peter. 2020. *The Prosthetic Imagination: A History of the Novel as Artificial Intelligence*. Cambridge: Cambridge University Press.

Brennan, Teresa. 2004. *The Transmission of Affect*. Ithaca, NY: Cornell University Press.

Brown, Gabrielle. 2015. "Psychotherapy with People Who Smell." *Psychoanalysis, Culture and Society* 20: 29–48.

Buck-Morss, Susan. 1989. *The Dialectics of Seeing: Walter Benjamin and the Arcades Project*. Cambridge, MA: MIT Press.

Butler, Judith. 2009. *Frames of War: When Is Life Grievable?* New York: Verso.

The Care Collective (Andreas Chatzidakis, Jamie Hakim, Jo Littler, Catherine Tottenberg, and Lynn Segal). 2020. *The Care Manifesto: The Politics of Interdependence*. New York: Verso.

Carsten, Janet. 1995. "The Substance of Kinship and the Heat of the Hearth: Feeding, Personhood, and Relatedness among Malays in Pulau Langawi." *American Ethnologist* 22, no. 2: 223–41.

Caswell, Glenys, and Mórna O'Connor. 2015. "Agency in the Context of Social Death: Dying Alone at Home." *Contemporary Social Science* 10, no. 3: 249–61.

Coetzee, J. M. 1983. *Life and Times of Michael K*. New York: Viking.

Conklin, Beth. 1995. "Thus Our Bodies, Thus Was Our Custom: Mortuary Cannibalism in an Amazonian Society." *American Ethnologist* 22, no. 1: 75–101.

Conklin, Beth. 2001. *Consuming Grief: Compassionate Cannibalism in an Amazonian Society*. Austin: University of Texas Press.

Danely, Jason. 2014. *Aging and Loss: Mourning and Maturity in Contemporary Japan*. New Brunswick, NJ: Rutgers University Press.

Danely, Jason. 2019. "The Limits of Dwelling and the Unwitnessed Death." *Cultural Anthropology* 34, no. 2: 213–39.

Daniels, Inge. 2010. *The Japanese Home: Material Culture in the Modern Home*. New York: Berg.

Davis, Elizabeth. 2017. "Time Machines: The Matter of the Missing in Cyprus." In *Unfinished: The Anthropology of Becoming*, edited by João Biehl and Peter Locke, 217–42. Durham, NC: Duke University Press.

Dawdy, Shannon. 2016. *Patina: A Profane Archaeology*. Chicago: University of Chicago Press.

Dawdy, Shannon. 2019. "American Afterlives: Ghosts in the Commodity." *Journal of Contemporary Archaeology* 6, no. 2: 206–23.

De Boeck, Filip, dir. 2010. *Cemetery State*. Belgium: FilmNatie. 72 mins.

De Léon, Jason. 2015. *The Land of Open Graves: Living and Dying on the Migrant Trail*. Berkeley: University of California Press.

Descola, Philippe. 2013. "Beyond Nature and Culture." In *The Handbook of Contemporary Animism*, edited by Graham Harvey, 77–91. Durham, UK: Acumen.

Descola, Philippe. (2005) 2013. *Beyond Nature and Culture*. Translated by Janet Lloyd. Chicago: University of Chicago Press.

Desjarlais, Robert. 2016. *Subject to Death: Life and Loss in a Buddhist World*. Chicago: University of Chicago Press.

Douglas, Mary. (1966) 2003. *Mary Douglas Collected Works*. Vol. 2, *Purity and Danger: An Analysis of Concepts of Pollution and Taboo*. Abingdon, UK: Routledge.

Dower, John W. 1999. *Embracing Defeat: Japan in the Wake of World War II*. New York: W. W. Norton.

Dumit, Joseph. 2012. *Drugs for Life: How Pharmaceutical Companies Define Our Health*. Durham, NC: Duke University Press.

Durkheim, Émile. (1917) 1947. *Elementary Forms of the Religious Life*. Translated by A. M. Henderson and Talcott Parsons. New York: Free Press.

Duteil-Ogata, Fabienne. 2015. "New Technologies and New Funeral Practices in Contemporary Japan." In *Asian Religions, Technology and Science*, edited by István Keul, 227–44. New York: Routledge.

Edelman, Lee. 2004. *No Future: Queer Theory and the Death Drive*. Durham, NC: Duke University Press.

Edwards, David B. 2017. *Caravan of Martyrs: Sacrifice and Suicide Bombing in Afghanistan*. Oakland: University of California Press.

Escobar, Arturo. 2018. *Designs for the Pluriverse: Radical Interdependence, Autonomy, and the Making of Worlds*. Durham, NC: Duke University Press.

Endingu sangyōten (ENDEX). 2017. *Daisankai endingusangyōten shiryōshu* (Materials for the Third Annual Ending Industrial Exhibit). Tokyo: Endingu sangyōten.

Fassin, Didier. 2009. "Another Politics of Life Is Possible." *Theory, Culture and Society* 26, no. 5: 44–60.

Fisch, Michael. 2018. *An Anthropology of the Machine: Tokyo's Commuter Train System*. Chicago: University of Chicago Press.

Fisch, Michael, and Erez Glani Solomon. 2018. "Resituating the Place of Living and Non-living in Contemporary Urban Japan." *Scapegoat* 11: 130–48.

Fisher, Berenice, and Joan C. Tronto. 1991. "Toward a Feminist Theory of Care." In *Circles of Care: Work and Identity in Women's Lives*, edited by Emily Abel and Margaret Nelson, 36–54. Albany: State University of New York Press.

Floyd-Davis, Robbie. 2003. "Windows in Space and Time: A Personal Perspective on Birth and Death." BIRTH 30, no. 4 (December): 272–77.

Foucault, Michel. (1977) 1979. *Discipline and Punish: The Birth of the Prison*. Translated by Alan Sheridan. New York: Vintage.

Foucault, Michel. (1997) 2003. *"Society Must Be Defended": Lectures at the Collège de France: 1975–1976*. New York: Picador.

Fowler, Edward. 1996. *San'ya Blues: Laboring Life in Contemporary Tokyo*. Ithaca, NY: Cornell University Press.

Freud, Sigmund. (1917) 1953–1974. "Mourning and Melancholia." In *The Standard Edition of the Complete Psychological Works of Sigmund Freud*. Vol. 14, *On the History of the Psycho-Analytic Movement, Papers on Metapsychology and Other Works*, translated by James Strachey, in collaboration with Anna Freud, assisted by Alix Strachey, 237–58. London: Hogarth Press.

Fukusawa Yuki. 2018–19. "Ohitorisama no shigo no tezukishien" (Postmortem procedure support for singles). *AERA* magazine (*Asahi Shimbun* weekly) December 31, 2018–January 7, 2019: 24–25.

Fuller, Thomas. 2022. "As Homeless Age, Cities See Surge in Lonely Deaths on the Street." *New York Times*. April 19, 2022.

Fry, Tony. 2015. *City Futures in an Age of Changing Climate*. New York: Routledge.

Garcia, Angela. 2010. *The Pastoral Clinic: Addiction and Dispossession along the Rio Grande*. Berkeley: University of California Press.

Garcia, Angela. 2016. "The Blue Years: An Ethnography of a Prison." *Cultural Anthropology* 31, no. 4: 571–94.

Genda Yūji. 2013. 孤立無職 スネップ (SNEP) [Solitary non-employed: SNEP]. Tokyo: Nihon Keizaishinbun Shuppansha.

Giddens, Anthony. 1991. *Modernity and Self-Identity: Self and Society in the Late Modern Age*. Cambridge: Polity.

Glassman, Hank. 2009. "Chinese Buddhist Death Ritual and Transformation of Japanese Kinship." In *The Buddhist Dead: Practices, Discourse, Representations*, edited by Bryan J. Cuevas and Jacqueline I. Stone, 378–404. Honolulu: University of Hawai'i Press/Kuroda Institute.

Glassman, Hank. 2012. *The Face of Jizō: Image and Cult in Medieval Japanese Buddhism*. Honolulu: University of Hawai'i Press.

Goldberg, David Theo. 2021. *Dread: Facing Futureless Futures*. Cambridge: Polity.

Gould, Hannah. 2019. "Caring for Sacred Waste: The Disposal of Butsudan (Buddhist Altars) in Contemporary Japan." *Japanese Religions* 43, nos. 1–2): 197–220.

Gould, Hannah. 2023. *When Death Falls Apart: Making and Unmaking the Necromaterial Traditions of Contemporary Japan*. Chicago: University of Chicago Press.

Green, James W. 2008. *Beyond the Good Death: The Anthropology of Modern Dying*. Philadelphia: University of Pennsylvania Press.

Gygi, Fabio R. 2018a. "Things That Believe." *Japanese Journal of Religious Studies* 45, no. 2: 423–52.

Gygi, Fabio. 2018b. "The Metamorphosis of Excess: 'Rubbish Houses' and the Imagined Trajectory of Things in Post-Bubble Japan." In *Consuming Life in Post-Bubble Japan: A Transdisciplinary Perspective*, edited by Katarzyna J. Cwiertka and Ewa Machotka, 129–51. Amsterdam: Amsterdam University Press.

Hallam, Elizabeth. 2010. "Articulating Bones: An Epilogue." *Journal of Material Culture* 15, no. 4 (December): 465–92.

Hallam, Elizabeth, Jenny Hockey, and Glennys Howarth. 1999. *Beyond the Body: Death and Social Identity*. New York: Routledge.

Hanam, Shira. 2020. "Jewish Burial Societies Face Difficult Choices as Deaths from Coronavirus Mount." *Jewish Telegraphic Service*, April 21, 2020.

Hankins, Joseph. 2014. *Working Skin: Making Leather, Making a Multicultural Japan*. Berkeley: University of California Press.

Happell, Charles. 2008. *The Bone Man of Kokoda*. Sydney: Pan MacMillan.

Hara Katsufumi. 1992. *Gendai muenbotoke to muenbaka* [Modern disconnected souls and disconnected graves]. Tokyo: Kokusho Kankōkai.

Haraway, Donna. 1991. "A Cyborg Manifesto: Science, Technology, and Socialist-Feminism in the Late Twentieth Century." In *Simians, Cyborgs, and Women: The Reinvention of Nature*, 149–81. New York: Routledge.

Hardt, Michael. 1999. "Affective Labor." *boundary 2* 26, no. 2 (Summer): 89–100.

Harootunian, H. D. 1970. *Toward Restoration: The Growth of Political Consciousness in Tokugawa Japan*. Berkeley: University of California Press.

Harootunian, H. D. 1988. *Things Seen and Unseen: Discourse and Ideology in Tokugawa Nativism*. Chicago: University of Chicago Press.

Harootunian, H. D. 2019. *Uneven Moments: Reflections on Japan's Modern History*. New York: Columbia University Press.

Harrison, Paul. 2008. "Corporeal Remains: Vulnerability, Proximity, and Living On after the End of the World." *Environment and Planning A: Economy and Space* 40: 423–45.

Heath-Kelly, Charlotte. 2018. "Sacred Rituals of the Security State: Reclaiming Bodies and Making Relics from Ground Zero." In *The Materiality of Mourning: Cross-Disciplinary Perspectives*, edited by Zahra Newby and Ruth E. Toulson, 205–21. New York: Routledge.

Hertz, Robert. (1907) 1960. *Death and the Right Hand*. Translated by Rodney Needham and Claudia Needham. Glencoe, IL: Free Press.

Hetherington, Kevin. 2004. "Secondhandedness: Consumption, Disposal, and Absent Presence." *Environment and Planning D: Society and Space* 22: 157–73.

Holden, Samuel. 2017. "The Vacant City: An Ethnography of Alternative Spatial Cultures in Post-growth Tokyo." Master's thesis, University of Tokyo.

Ingold, Tim. 2006. "Rethinking the Animate, Re-animating Thought." *Ethnos* 71, no. 1 (March): 9–20.

Ingold, Tim. 2007. "Materials against Materiality." *Archaeological Dialogues* 14, no. 1: 1–16.

Inoue Haruyo. 2012. *Sakurasō: sakura no shita de nemuritai* [Cherry blossom departures: I want to sleep under a cherry tree]. Tokyo: Sanseido.

Inoue Ritsuko. 2018. *Imadoki no nōkotsudō: Kawariyuku kuyō to ohaka no katachi* [Columbaria today: the shape of changing memorial and graves]. Tokyo: Shogakkan.

Irizarry, Joshua A. 2014. "Signs of Life: Grounding the Transcendent in Japanese Memorial Objects." *Signs and Society* 2, no. S1. https://www.journals.uchicago.edu/doi/full/10.1086/674538.

Jensen, Casper Bruun, and Anders Blok. 2013. "Techno-Animism in Japan: Shinto Cosmograms, Actor-Network Theory, and the Enabling Powers of Non-human Agencies." *Theory, Culture and Society* 30, no. 2: 84–115.

Kakudasan Myōkōji Temple. 2019. *Kakudasan Myōkōji Anniversary Document of Succession, Myōkōji—Until Now and After Now*. Niigata City, Japan: Kakudasan Myōkōji.

Kanagawa Shinbun. 2016. 身寄りなし献体可能性 [Possibility of body donation for those without anyone to depend on: first in country: big agreement between Yokosuka City and Dental Department]. November 16, 2016.

Kawano, Satsuki. 2010. *Nature's Embrace: Japan's Aging Urbanites and New Death Rites*. Honolulu: University of Hawai'i Press.

Kawano, Satsuki. 2011. "Who Will Care for Me When I Am Dead? Ancestors, Homeless Spirits, and New Afterlives in Low-Fertility Japan." *Journal of the German Institute of Japanese Studies* 26, no. 1: 49–69.

Kelly, William K. 1993. "Finding a Place in Metropolitan Japan: Ideologies, Institutions, and Everyday Life." In *Postwar Japan as History*, edited by Andrew Gordon. Berkeley: University of California Press.

Kennedy, Dana. 2020. "Coronavirus in Italy: The Elderly Are Being Left to Die Alone during Crisis." *New York Post*, March 21, 2021.

Kidder, J. Edward, Jr. 2007. *Himiko and Japan's Elusive Chiefdom of Yamatai: Archaeology, History, and Mythology*. Honolulu: University of Hawai'i Press.

Kim, J. 2016. "Necrosociality: Isolated Death and Unclaimed Cremains in Japan." *Journal of the Royal Anthropological Institute* 22: 843–63.

Kim, Hyunchul. 2012. "The Purification Process of Death: Mortuary Rites in a Japanese Rural Town." *Asian Ethnology* 71, no. 2: 225–57.

Kimura Eiji. 2015. *Ihinseirishi toiu shigoto* [The work of a disposer]. Tokyo: Heibonsha.

Kimura Eiji. 2016. *Ihinseirishi ga oshieru [nokosu gijutsu] yutakani ikirutameno "sonoe to katazuke"* [Instructions from a cleanup worker on techniques of leaving: how to prepare and tidy up to live affluently]. Tokyo: Meitsu (メイツ) Publishing.

Kitagawa Shō. 2007. *Death Sweeper* (デス・スウイーパー). No. 1, *Kotoshi no natsu ani ga jisastushita* [This summer my older brother committed suicide]. Tokyo: Kadokawa Charge Comics.

Klinenberg, Eric. 2002. *Heat Wave: A Social Autopsy of Disaster in Chicago.* Chicago: University of Chicago Press.

Kojima Miyu. 2019. *Toki ga tomatta heya: ihinseirinin ga minichua de tsutaeru kodokushi no hanashi* [Rooms where time has stopped: stories of lonely deaths as conveyed by miniatures]. Tokyo: Hara Shobo.

Koff, Clea. 2004. *The Bone Woman: A Forensic Anthropologist's Search for Truth in the Mass Graves of Rwanda, Bosnia, Croatia, and Kosovo.* New York: Random House.

Kondō, Marie. 2015. *The Life-Changing Magic of Tidying Up: The Japanese Art of Decluttering and Organizing.* Old Saybrook, CT: Tantor.

Kotani Midori. 2010. "家墓"の終焉 人口減や都会へ流出で"無縁墓"が増えている."エコノミスト [The economist]. September 21, 2010 (21日号).

Kotani Midori. 2018. "*Dare ga shisha wo tomurai, haka wo mamoru no ka?*" [Who is going to bury the dead, who tend to the grave?]. In *Gendai nihon no sōso to hakasei* [Japan's contemporary grave and funeral system], edited by Suzuki Iwayumi and Mori Kenji, 115–30. Tokyo: Yoshikawa Kobunkan.

Krasnostein, Sarah. 2017. *The Trauma Cleaner: One Woman's Extraordinary Life in Death, Decay, and Disaster.* New York: St. Martin's.

Kretschmer, Angelika. 2000. "Mortuary Rites for Inanimate Objects: The Case of Hari Kuyō." *Japanese Journal of Religious Studies* 27, nos. 3–4: 379–404.

Kyodo. 2018. "Going It Alone: Solo Dwellers Will Account for 40% of Japan's Households by 2040, Forecast Says." *Japan Times*, January 13, 2018. https://www.japantimes.co.jp/news/2018/01/13/national/social-issues/going-alone-solo-dwellers-will-account-40-japans-households-2040-forecast-says/.

Lakoff, Andrew. 2008. "The Generic Biothreat, or, How We Became Unprepared." *Cultural Anthropology* 23, no. 3: 399–428.

Lamarre, Thomas. 2018. *The Anime Ecology: A Genealogy of Television, Animation, and Game Media.* Minneapolis: University of Minnesota Press.

Laqueur, Thomas W. 2015. *The Work of the Dead: A Cultural History of Mortal Remains.* Princeton, NJ: Princeton University Press.

Latour, Bruno. 2004. *Politics of Nature: How to Bring the Sciences into Democracy.* Cambridge, MA: Harvard University Press.

Lévinas, Emmanuel. 1974. *Otherwise Than Being or Beyond Essence*. Translated by Alphonso Lingis. Dordrecht: Kluwer Academic.

Livingston, Julie. 2012. *Improvising Medicine: An African Oncology Ward in an Emerging Cancer Epidemic*. Durham, NC: Duke University Press.

Lofland, Lyn H. 1978. *The Craft of Dying: The Modern Face of Death*. Beverly Hills, CA: Sage.

Long, Susan. 2001. "Negotiating the 'Good Death': Japanese Ambivalence about New Ways to Die." *Ethnology* 40, no. 4: 271–89.

Luo, Ye, and Linda J. Waite. 2014. "Loneliness and Mortality among Older Adults in China." *Journals of Gerontology Series B: Psychological Sciences and Social Sciences* 69, no. 4 (July): 633–45.

Marr, Matthew D. 2021. "The *Ohaka* (Grave) Project: Post-secular Social Service Delivery and Resistant Necropolitics in San'ya Tokyo." *Ethnography* 22, no. 1: 1–23.

Mbembe, Achille. 2003. "Necropolitics." *Public Culture* 15, no. 1: 11–40.

Mbembe, Achille. 2004. "Aesthetics of Superfluity." *Public Culture* 16, no. 3: 373–405.

M'charek, Amade, and Sara Casartelli. 2019. "Identifying Dead Migrants: Forensic Care Work and Relational Citizenship." *Citizenship Studies* 23, no. 7: 738–57.

Mikuni Hiroaki. 2017. *Ohitorisamade yukō: Saigomade jibunrashiku* [Let's die alone: doing it one's own way until the end]. Tokyo: Yudachisha.

Millar, Kathleen. 2018. *Reclaiming the Discarded: Life and Labor on Rio's Garbage Dump*. Durham, NC: Duke University Press.

Miller, Laura J. 2001. "Francis Glesser Lee: Brief Life of a Forensic Miniaturist: 1878–1962." *Harvard Magazine*. September–October 2005. https://www.harvardmagazine.com/2005/09/frances-glessner-lee -html.

Mitsui, Tōru, and Shūhei Hosokawa, eds. 1988. *Karaoke around the World: Global Technology, Local Singing*. New York: Routledge.

Monden, Yasuhiro. 2012. *Toyota Production System: An Integrated Approach to Just-in-Time*. 4th ed. New York: Productivity Press.

Mori Kenji. 2014. *Haka to sōsō no yukue* [The whereabouts of graves and funerals]. Tokyo: Yoshikawa Kobunkan.

Morris-Suzuki, Tessa. 1994. *The Technological Transformation of Japan: From the Seventeenth to the Twenty-First Century*. Cambridge: Cambridge University Press.

Morris-Suzuki, Tessa. 2007. *Exodus to North Korea: Shadows from Japan's Cold War*. Lanham, MD: Rowman and Littlefield.

Muehlebach, Andrea. 2012. *The Moral Neoliberal: Welfare and Citizenship in Italy*. Chicago: University of Chicago Press.

Murakami Kōkyō. 2018. "葬送研究から見た弔いの意味づけの変化" [Changes of meaning in mourning seen from the perspective of research on funerals]. In 現代日本の葬送とは墓制：イエ亡き時代の死者 [Contemporary Japan's grave and funeral system: the whereabouts of the dead in an era without family], edited by Suzuki Iwayumi and Mori Kenji, 131–48. Tokyo: Yoshikawa Kobunkan.

Murakoshi Kotoyo. 1981. *Tama Reien* [Tama spirit park]. Tokyo: Tokyo kōen bunko.

Myōkōji. 2019. *Kakudasan Myōkōji kinen denshō bunsho Myōkōji no kore made to korekara* (Kakudasan Myōkōji Anniversary Document of Succession, Myōkōji—Until Now and After Now). Tokyo: Myōkōji.

Nakazawa Shinichi. 1997. *Poketto no naka no yasei* [Wildness inside a pocket]. Tokyo: Iwanami Shoten.

Nancy, Jean-Luc. 2000. *Being Singular Plural*. Translated by Robert D. Richardson and Anne E. O'Byrne. Stanford, CA: Stanford University Press.

Nelson, Christopher T. 2015. "Listening to the Bones: The Rhythms of Sacrifice in Contemporary Japan." *Boundary 2* 42, no. 3: 143–55.

Nelson-Becker, Holly, and Christina Victor. 2020. "Dying Alone and Lonely Dying: Media Discourse and Pandemic Conditions." *Journal of Aging Studies* 55 (December): 1–9.

Newell, Sasha. 2014. "The Matter of the Unfetish: Hoarding and the Spirit of Possessions." *HAU Journal of Ethnographic Theory* 4, no. 3 (December): 185–213.

Nishimura, Keiko. 2021. "Communication Robot: Animating a Technological Solution in Twenty-First Century Japan." PhD diss., University of North Carolina, Chapel Hill.

Nomura Shōji. 2016. "散骨のため遺骨を粉末に、下町の粉骨時工場を見学した" [Touring a bone powdering factory downtown that powders ash for scattering]. *AERA* magazine (*Asahi Shimbun* weekly). August 12, 2016.

Nomura Shōji, Ono Hideko, Nagakura Katsue, and Yamagichi Ryoko. 2017. "Furui sōshikiyo sayōnara: Bukkyō bigguban" [Good-bye to old-style funerals: Buddhist Big Bang]. *AERA* magazine (*Asahi Shimbun* weekly), August 7, 2017.

Norbert, Elias. 2009. *The Loneliness of the Dying*. Translated by Edmund Jephcott. Oxford: Blackwell.

Ooms, Herman. 1967. "The Religion of the Household: A Case Study of Ancestor Worship in Japan." *Contemporary Religions in Japan* 8, nos. 3–4 (September–December): 201–333.

Osawa, Machiko, and Jeff Kingston. 2015. "The Future of Gender in Japan: Work/Life Balance and Relations between the Sexes." In *Japan: The Precarious Future*, edited by Frank Baldwin and Anne Allison, 58–86. New York: New York University Press.

Otsuki, Grant Jun. 2019. "Frame, Game, and Circuity: Truth and the Human in Japanese Human-Machine Interface Research." *Ethnos: Journal of Anthropology* 86: 712–29. https://doi.org/10.1080/00141844.2019.1686047.

Ozawa de Silva, Chikako. 2021. *The Anatomy of Loneliness: Suicide, Social Connection, and the Search for Relational Meaning in Contemporary Japan*. Berkeley: University of California Press.

Pachirat, Timothy. 2011. *Every Twelve Seconds: Industrialized Slaughter and the Politics of Sight*. New Haven, CT: Yale University Press.

Parry, Richard Lloyd. 2017. *The Ghosts of the Tsunami: Death and Life in Japan's Disaster Zone*. New York: Farrar, Strauss and Giroux.

Povinelli, Elizabeth. 2011. *Economies of Abandonment: Social Belonging and Endurance in Late Liberalism*. Durham, NC: Duke University Press.

Puig de la Bellacasa, María. 2017. *Matters of Care: Speculative Ethics in More Than Human Worlds*. Minneapolis: University of Minnesota Press.

Rambelli, Fabio. 2007. *Buddhist Materiality: A Cultural History of Objects in Japanese Buddhism*. Stanford, CA: Stanford University Press.

Rambelli, Fabio. 2018. "Dharma Devices, Non-hermeneutical Libraries, and Robot-Monks: Prayer Machines in Japanese Buddhism." *Journal of Asian Humanities at Kyushu University* 3: 47–75.

Reader, Ian. 1991. *Religion in Contemporary Japan*. Honolulu: University of Hawai'i Press.

Redfield, Peter. 2013. *Life in Crisis: The Ethical Journey of Doctors Without Borders*. Berkeley: University of California Press.

Reiter, Rayna. 1975. *Toward an Anthropology of Women*. New York: Monthly Review Press.

Reno, Joshua O. 2015. *Waste Away: Working and Living with a North American Landfill*. Oakland: University of California Press.

Roach, Joseph. 1996. *Cities of the Dead: Circum-Atlantic Performance*. New York: Columbia University Press.

Rosaldo, Michelle Z., and Louise Lamphere, eds. 1974. *Women, Culture, and Society*. Stanford, CA: Stanford University Press.

Rosenblatt, Adam. 2015. *Digging for the Disappeared: Forensic Science after Atrocity*. Stanford, CA: Stanford University Press.

Rose, Nikolas S. 2007. *The Politics of Life Itself: Biomedicine, Power, and Subjectivity in the Twenty-First Century*. Princeton, NJ: Princeton University Press.

Ross, Fiona. 2010. *Raw Life, New Hope: Decency, Housing and Everyday Life in a Post-Apartheid Community*. Cape Town: University of Cape Town Press.

Rowe, Mark M. 2011. *Bonds of the Dead: Temples, Burial, and the Transformation of Contemporary Japanese Buddhism*. Chicago: University of Chicago Press.

Ruin, Hans. 2018. *Being with the Dead: Burial, Ancestral Politics, and the Roots of Historical Consciousness*. Stanford, CA: Stanford University Press.

Sanal, Aslihan. 2011. *New Organs within Us: Transplants and the Moral Economy*. Durham, NC: Duke University Press.

Sasaki Fumio. 2015. *Bokutachini, mō mono ha hitsuyōnai* [We no longer need things]. Tokyo: Wani Books.

Satō, Hiroo. 2019. "The Dead Who Remain: Spirits and Changing Views of the Afterlife." Translated by Emily B. Simpson. In *Spirits and Animism in Contemporary Japan: The Invisible Empire*, edited by Fabio Rambelli, 17–28. London: Bloomsbury.

Schattschneider, Ellen. 2005. "The Bloodstained Doll: Violence and the Gift in Wartime Japan." *Journal of Japanese Studies* 31, no. 2: 329–456.

Sebald, W. G. 2005. *Campo Santo*. Edited by Sven Meyer. Translated by Anthea Bell. London: Hamish Hamilton.

Seidensticker, Edward. 1983. *Low City, High City: Tokyo from Edo to the Earthquake*. New York: Knopf.

Semerene, Diego. "'*Plan 75* Review': A Quietly Tragic Depiction of a World Where Empathy Is Scarce." *Slant*, May 22, 2022. https://www.slantmagazine.com/film/plan-75-review-hayakawa-chie/.

Seremetakis, C. Nadia. 1991. *The Last Word: Women, Death, and Divination in Inner Mani*. Chicago: University of Chicago Press.

Shimada Hiroshi. 2014. *0 (zero) sō: Assari Shinu* [Zero funerals: dying easily]. Tokyo: Gentōsha Shinsho.

Shinmon Aoki. (1993) 2002. *Coffinman: The Journal of a Buddhist Mortician*. Anaheim, CA: Buddhist Education Center. First published as *Nōkanfu nikki* (Tokyo: Bungeishunju, 1991).

Shirahase, Sawako. 2015. "Demography as Destiny: Falling Birthrates and the Allure of a Blended Society." In *Japan: The Precarious Future*, edited by Frank Baldwin and Anne Allison, 11–35. New York: New York University Press.

Shunsuke Nozawa. 2015. "Phatic Traces: Sociality in Contemporary Japan." *Anthropological Quarterly* 88, no. 2 (Spring): 373–400.

Siegel, James. 1983. "Images and Odors in Javanese Practices Surrounding Death." *Indonesia*, no. 36 (October): 1–14.

Smith, Robert J. 1974. *Ancestor Worship in Contemporary Japan*. Stanford, CA: Stanford University Press.

Stack, Carol. 2003. *All Our Kin: Strategies for Survival in a Black Community*. New York: Harper and Row.

Standing, Guy. 2011. *The Precariat: The New Dangerous Class*. London: Bloomsbury.

Stevenson, Lisa. 2014. *Life beside Itself: Imagining Care in the Canadian Artic*. Oakland: University of California Press.

Stevenson, Lisa. 2020. "Looking Away." *Cultural Anthropology* 35, no. 1: 6–13.
Stewart, Kathleen. 2007. *Ordinary Affects*. Durham, NC: Duke University Press.
Stone, Allucquére [Sandy]. 1984. "Split Subjects, Not Atoms: Or, How I Fell in Love with My Prosthesis." *Configurations* 2, no. 1: 173–89.
Stone, Jacqueline I. 2018. *Right Thoughts at the Last Moment: Buddhism and Deathbed Practices in Early Medieval Japan*. Honolulu: University of Hawai'i Press/Kuroda Institute.
Stonington, Scott. 2020. *The Spirit Ambulance: Choreographing the End of Life in Thailand*. Berkeley: University of California Press.
Strathern, Marilyn. 1992. *The Gender of the Gift: Problems with Women and Problems with Society in Melanesia*. Berkeley: University of California Press.
Strathern, Marilyn. 2000. *Audit Cultures: Anthropological Studies in Accountability, Ethics, and the Academy*. New York: Routledge.
Sunday Mainichi. 2018. おひとりさまの在宅大往生 [A peaceful death at home for singles]. December 2, 2018.
Suzuki, Hikaru. 2000. *The Price of Death: The Funeral Industry in Contemporary Japan*. Stanford, CA: Stanford University Press.
Suzuki Iwayumi, and Mori Kenji, eds. 2018. *Gendainihon no sōso toha hakasei: Ienakijidai no shisha* (現代日本の葬送とは墓制：イエ亡き時代の死者). [Contemporary Japan's grave and funeral system: the whereabouts of the dead in an era without family.] Tokyo: Yoshikawa Kobunkan.
Takenaka, Akiko. 2015. *Yasukuni Shrine: History, Memory, and Japan's Unending Postwar*. Honolulu: University of Hawai'i Press.
Tanaka Satoko. 2017. "一人の最期　自治体サッポト" [Local municipality support: a single person's last moments]. *Asahi Shinbun*, September 5, 2017.
Traphagan, John W. 2004. *Practice of Concern: Ritual, Well-Being, and Aging in Rural Japan*. Durham, NC: Carolina Academic Press.
Traphagan, John, and Blair Connor. 2014. "Negotiating the Afterlife: Emplacement as Ongoing Concern in Contemporary Japan." *Asian Anthropologist* 13, no. 1 (January): 3–19.
Tsing, Anna Lowenhaupt. 2015. *Mushroom at the End of the World: On the Possibility of Life in Capitalist Ruins*. Princeton, NJ: Princeton University Press.
Tsuji, Yohko. 2002. "Death Policies in Japan: The State, the Family, and the Individual." In *Family and Social Policy in Japan: Anthropological Approaches*, edited by Roger Goodman, 177–99. Cambridge: Cambridge University Press.
Tsuji, Yohko. 2021. *Through Japanese Eyes: Thirty Years of Studying Aging in America*. New Brunswick, NJ: Rutgers University Press.

Tsukamoto Yu. 2019. "Sōsō jyu-narisuto Tsukamoto Yu no shūkatsu tanbōki" [Expedition into ending business with funeral journalist, Tsukamoto Yu]. *Shinia gaido*, January 10, 2019.

Tsutsui, William M. 2010. "Oh No, There Goes Tokyo: Recreational Apocalypse and the City in Postwar Japanese Popular Culture." In *Noir Urbanisms: Dystopic Images of the Modern City*, edited by Gyan Prakash, 96–115. Princeton NJ: Princeton University Press.

Ueno Chizuko. (1994) 2009. *The Modern Family in Japan: Its Rise and Fall*. Melbourne: Trans Pacific Press.

Ueno Chizuko. 2012. "Otoko yo, sotsujiki ni yowasa wo mitomeryō" [Men, let's recognize their weakness at graduation]. In *Kozoku no kuni: Hitoriga tsunagaru jidai he* [Solitary tribe country: Toward single people making relationships], 115–18. Tokyo: Asahi Shinbun Shuppan.

Ueno Chizuko. 2015. *Kea no karisumatachi: mitori wo sasaeru purofuesshyonaru* [Care charismatics: professionals who support nursing]. Tokyo: Akishobo.

Ukai Hidenori. 2016. *Musōshakai: hōkō itai kawaru bukkyō* [Society without burial: Buddhism that is changing the wandering of corpses]. Tokyo: NikkeiBPsha.

Uriu Daisuke, and Naohito Okude. 2010. "Thanato-Fenestra: Photographic Family Altar Supporting a Ritual to Pray for the Deceased." *Proceedings of DIS* (August): 422–25.

Uriu, Daisuke, William Odom, and Hannah Gould. 2018. "Understanding Automatic Conveyor-Belt Columbaria: Emerging Sites of Interactive Memorialization in Japan. *Proceedings of DIS* (June): 727–52.

Verdery, Katherine. 1999. *The Political Lives of Dead Bodies: Reburial and Postsocialist Change*. New York: Columbia University Press.

Wagner, Sarah E. 2019. *What Remains: Bringing America's Missing Home from the Vietnam War*. Cambridge, MA: Harvard University Press.

Walter, Tony. 2003. "Historical and Cultural Variants on the Good Death." *BMJ* 327 (July): 218–20.

Walter, Tony. 2017. *What Death Means Now: Thinking Critically about Dying and Grieving*. Cambridge: Polity.

Wang, Min'an. 2011. "On Rubbish." *Theory, Culture and Society* 28, nos. 7–8: 340–53.

Weeks, Kathi. 2011. *The Problem with Work: Feminism, Marxism, Antiwork Politics, and Postwork Imaginaries*. Durham, NC: Duke University Press.

Weeks, Kathi. Forthcoming. "Abolition of the Family: The Most Infamous Feminist Proposal." *Feminist Theory*, 1–21. Published online, ahead of print, May 18, 2021. https://doi.org/10.1177/14647001211015841.

Weston, Kath. 1991. *Families We Choose: Lesbian, Gays, Kinship*. New York: Columbia University Press.

White, Daniel, and Hirofumi Katsuno. 2021. "Toward an Affective Sense of Life: Artificial Intelligence, Animacy, and Amusement at a Robot Pet Memorial Service in Japan." *Cultural Anthropology* 36, no. 2: 222–52.

White, Linda. 2018. *Gender and the Koseki in Contemporary Japan: Surname, Power, and Privilege*. New York: Routledge.

Willerslev, Rane, Dorthe R. Christensen, and Lotte Meinert. 2013. "Introduction." In *Taming Time, Timing Death: Social Technologies and Ritual*, edited by Rane Willerslev and Dorthe R. Christensen, 1–16. Farnham: Ashgate.

Yamada Masahiro. 2014. *Kazoku nanmin* [Refugees from the family]. Tokyo: Asahi Shinbun Shuppan.

Yamada Shinya. 2018. "納骨堂の成立とその集合的性格" [The establishment of columbaria and their collective nature]. In 現代日本の葬送とは墓制：イエ亡き時代の死者 [Contemporary Japan's grave and funeral system: the whereabouts of the dead in an era without family], edited by Suzuki Iwayumi and Mori Kenji, 63–86. Tokyo: Yoshikawa Kobunkan.

Yanagita, Kunio. (1946) 1970. *About Our Ancestors: The Japanese Family System* [*Senzo no hanashi*]. Translated by Fanny Hagin Mayer and Ishiwara Yasuyo. Tokyo: Ministry of Education (Japan Society for the Promotion of Science).

Yanagita, Kunio. (1910) 1975. *The Legends of Tōno*. Collected by Yanagita and Sasaki Kizen. Translated and edited by Ronald A. Morse. Tokyo: Japan Foundation.

Yoneyama, Shoko. *Animism in Contemporary Japan: Voices for the Anthropocene from Post-Fukushima Japan*. New York: Routledge.

Yoshida Taichi. 2006. *Ihinseirishi ha mita! Koritshushi or kodokushi* [What a disposer saw! Solitary death or lonely death]. Tokyo: Fusosha.

Yoshida Taichi. 2010. *Koritsushi: Anata ha daijōbu?* [Solitary death: Are you alright?] Tokyo: Fusosha.

Yoshida Taichi. 2015a. *Anata no fudōsan ga "fudōsan" ni naru* [Your property can become negative property]. Tokyo: Poplar Shincho.

Yoshida Taichi. 2015b. *Sōgi. Sōzoku. Yuigon no manzen gaido* [The complete guide for funerals, inheritance, and wills]. Tokyo: Futabasha.

Yoshimi, Shunya. 2000. "Consuming 'America': From Symbol to System." In *Consumption in Asia: Lifestyle and Identities*, edited by Chua Beng-Huat, 202–24. New York: Routledge.

Yuasa Makoto. 2008. *Hanhinkon: "Suberidai shakai" kara no dasshutsu* [Reverse poverty: Escape from a "sliding down society"]. Tokyo: Iwanami shinsho.

Zhang, Sarah. 2017. "How a Gilded-Age Heiress Became the 'Mother of Forensic Science.'" *Atlantic*, October 4, 2017.

Index

abandonment, 94–95, 192–93. *See also under* graves
abduction, 102–3, 113, 120. *See also* anticipation
Adams, Vincanne, 102, 113, 120, 175–76
affect: affective labor, 68, 87–88; of anticipation, 102, 105–7, 116–17, 175–76; and attachment, 9, 66–68; of death work, 38–39, 165–69; of ending activity (*shūkatsu*), 102–3, 107–8, 115; and imaginative enactments, 105–6; and *imonningyō* dolls, 42–43; of lonely deaths, 144, 146–47; and ordering one's feelings (*kimochi no seiri*), 129–30; of smell, 124
aging, ix–x, 31, 86, 99, 103–10, 115–18, 183; and abandonment of elderly (*obasuteyama*), 31; and lonely deaths, 139–40; and loss, 138–39; negotiating, 55; and precarity, 207n7. *See also* death, dying; dementia; population
AIBO robotic dogs, 66–68, 204n16. *See also* robots; technology
Aladdin (nonprofit), 117
altar (*butsudan*), 32, 34, 38–39, 54, 58, 63–65, 73–75, 78–82, 86–87, 119, 134, 149, 154–55
Alzheimer's, 106, 117–18. *See also* aging; dementia
Amamiya, Karin, 9, 52–53
ambiguity, 25–27, 33–34, 42–45, 87–88, 113, 125, 152, 169–70, 197n5. *See also* loss
ambivalence, 31, 36–37, 43–44, 48–49, 146

amulets, 42–43, 151–52, 169. *See also* graves; memorials
ancestors (*senzo*): altars to, 79–81; caring for, 6–7, 12; communicating with, 81–82; gifts for, 79–81; and line of succession, 39–40, 56–57; worship of, 29–32, 35–36. *See also* death, dying; patrilineal system
Anderson, Ben, 11–12, 15–16
animism, 28, 63, 199n8, 204n13; of material objects, 129–30; necro-animism, 11–12, 15–16, 19–20, 55, 108–9, 112–13, 130, 192–94; techno-animism, 8–9
Annonbyō (collective memorial mound), 60–61, 95–98
Ano toki no inochi (dir. Zeze), 131–32
anticipation, 100–106, 113–17, 120, 175–76. *See also under* affect; time, temporality
Antigone, 4
anxiety, 9–12, 14–15, 54–55, 87–88, 94–96, 102–7, 113, 115, 125, 148, 174–78
Ariès, Philippe, 86
ashes: and cremation, 151–52; pulverizing (*funmatsuka*), 165–69; scattering (*sankotsu*), 89–90, 115–16, 159–60, 163–64. *See also* cremation
Association for Certified Disposers, 138–39
Association for Making Connections in Housing and Living for Old Age, 117
Association to Think about the Relationality of Graves in the Twenty-First Century, 83–84
Atoms for Peace initiative, 48–49

Bachelard, Gaston, 174
Ballad of Narayama, The (dir. Imamura), 31
Barthes, Roland, 185
Bauman, Zygmunt, 14–15, 25–26
belonging: alternative forms of, 61, 89–92, 95–96; and care, 148; and disconnected (*muenbo*), 40–41, 93–94; failures of, 13; and family, 56, 73, 91–92; and handling of dead, 38–39; national, 158; and patrilineal system, 56; and ritual, 73; of socially single, 110–11; sociology of, 49–50. *See also* relationality; social, sociality
Benjamin, Walter, 146, 181
Berger, John, 77
Berman, Michael, 78–79
Bernstein, Andrew, 32–33, 36–37, 40–41, 200n9, 201n12
biolegitimacy, 159–60
biopolitics, 34–35, 56, 100–102, 137; as ethopolitics, 108; of postproductivity, 130–31; of well-being, 108
Bloch, Ernst, 194–96
body: in death, ix–x, 137–38; disposal of, 40–41; of fallen soldiers, 44–45; and identity, 138; management of, 30; materiality of, 17, 151–52; parts, 17, 153–54; and relationality, 150, 170; and self, 150; as site for regulation, 123; and smell, 123–24; and social, 150; and solitary deaths, 130–31, 137; and soul, 40–41; and well-being, 108. *See also* corpses; remains
bone business (*hone ya san*), ix, 164–65
Boret, Sébastien, 89–90, 205n2
Boxall, Peter, 177–78
Brown, Gabrielle, 123, 148
Buddhism, 199n7, 200n7; and alternative forms of belonging, 59–61, 95–96; and ancestor worship, 29, 35–36; and care for dead, 63, 78–79, 204nn12–13; changing practices of, 59–61, 70, 178–79; and cremation, 32–33; economics of, 79–81; mercantilism of, 35–36; mortuary rites, 19–20, 32, 34–35, 56; and mourning, 1–2; necro-topography of, 31–32; as religion of death, 35, 78–79. *See also* patrilineal system; ritual
burials, 3, 159–60, 201n18; collective, 2, 13–14, 110–11; commodification of, 38–39; direct burial (*chokusō*), 156; for disconnected (*muenbo*), 2–3, 33–34, 110–13, 149–50; documentation of, 39–40; and "eternal tomb" (*fumetsu no funbo*), 13; history of, 27–29; and inequality, 76–77, 94, 188–89; innovation in, 183–84, 188–89; natural burial (*shizensō*), 159–60; and "no place to go" (*ikiba ga nai*), 10–11; and patrilineal system (*ie*), 1–2, 37–40, 56–57, 84, 201n13; and "picking of the bones" (*kotsuage*), 1, 149; and preparedness, 110–11; and relationality, 84; of remains, 159–60; for robotic dogs, 66–68; and separation of dead from living, 28–29; tree burial (*jumokusō*), 61, 89–90, 205n2; wind burial, 27–28. *See also* cremation; death, dying; graves, graveyards; ritual
Butler, Judith, 150
butsudan. *See* altar

Campbell, Brian, 193–94
capitalism, 49–50, 57, 102, 108, 193–94. *See also* neoliberalism; precarity, precariat
care, 9, 11, 88–89, 198n6; absence or refusal of, 12–14, 83–84, 184, 189–90; and accompaniment, 89; and belonging, 148; as commercial contract, 184–85; and continuous regeneration, 6–7; for dead, 3–4, 11–12, 26–27, 42, 63, 74–77, 185; ethics of, 18–19; forensics of, 138; and gender, 117; and Japan's aging population, 53; and kin relations, 13–14, 18–19; and marketplace, 18–19; narrow circumscription of, 76–78; phenomenology of, 137–38; and precarity, 94; and preparedness, 117–18; promiscuity of, 13–14, 18–19, 148; refugees, 83–84; relationality of, 77–78; for remains, 197n5; self-care (*kokoro no seiri*), 19, 84–86, 116–20; by supplemental or "parafami-

lies" (*giji kazoku*), 117; and technology, 176–77, 189–90; of waste removal, 125, 128–29, 148; work of, 87–88, 137–38, 146–47, 165–68, 184–85. *See also* death, dying; relationality; social, sociality

Care Collective, 13–14, 18–19

Casartelli, Sara, 94, 138, 197n5

citizenship, 6–7, 12–13, 37–38, 41–42. *See also* nation-state

Clammer, John, 19–20

Clarke, Adele E., 102, 113, 120, 175–76

climate change, 191–92

coffins, 19, 38–39, 87–88, 191–92

collective, collectivity, 11–12, 14–15, 27, 40–41, 74–75, 88–95, 110–11, 116–17, 149–50, 157–58, 174–76, 181–82, 184–85, 189. *See also under* graves

columbaria (*nōkotsudō, nōkotsudan*), 78–79, 110–11, 158–60, 163–64, 183–84; automated delivery system, 176–90, 213n4; as commercial contract, 184–85, 188–89; spatiality of, 184–85; temporality of, 184–85

commodity, commodification, 38–39, 58–59, 66; of human remains, 150, 163; of ending business (*shūkatsu*), 102–3; and memorializing death, 152; and waste removal, 128–29

communication, 81, 92, 97–98, 111, 146–47, 155

community, 3–5, 14–15, 79, 117, 177–78. *See also* relationality; social, sociality

Conklin, Beth, 154, 168–69

consumerism, 7, 18–19, 38–39, 49–50, 54, 57, 115–20, 127–28, 188–89, 193–94

consumption, 57–58, 182

contingency, 9, 102, 111–13

corpse, 3–4; abandoned (*shitaiikizai*), 156, 159–60; and bones of deceased (*ikotsu*), 153–55; and identity, 138; materiality of, 26–30, 128–29, 137–41, 146–47, 151–55; and pollution, 28–29; and remains, 159–60; smell of, 124; sociality of, 150–52; storage of (*hokan*), 157–58; substitution for, 44–45; work on, 26–27. *See also* body; remains

COVID-19 pandemic, 101, 191–92

cremation, ix, 1–3, 32–33, 37, 118–19, 159–62; and cremains (*shūkotsu*), 33, 64, 151–52, 162–64, 168–69, 176–77, 183–84, 188; and disposal (*shorigyōsha*), 33, 163; of fallen soldiers, 44–45; and "picking of the bones" (*kotsuage*), 1, 149, 153–55; process of, 161–62, 210n2; public, 160–62; and remainder (*zanhai*), 162–63; of unclaimed deceased, 157–58. *See also* ashes

crisis, 12–14, 18–19, 50, 192–94

cyborg, 62

Daifuku (company), 183–84

Daiichi nuclear power plant, 48–51

Danely, Jason, 31, 138–39

Davis, Elizabeth, 138, 197n5

Dawdy, Shannon, 152, 158–59

de Boeck, Filip, 140–41

death, dying, ix–x, 1–2, 18–19, 25–27, 52, 56, 86, 161, 205n7; abandoned corpses, 156; and afterworld, 200n10; ambiguity of, 42–45, 129–30; "bad death," 4, 130–31; bare, 137; and belongings, 129–30; and caring for dead, 3–7, 10–11, 42, 74, 77, 149, 181–82, 188–89; commodification of, 58–59, 119, 152; and dignity, 106, 112–13; disconnected (*muenbotoke*), 16–19, 75–76, 197n5; and everyday, 73; "good death," 3–4, 16–17; and grievability, 4, 77–78; and habitation, 88–89; and human rights, 83–84; and humanity, 3, 70, 146–47, 159–60, 189–90; and inequality, 12–13, 188–89; and insecurity, 104; lonely or solitary (*kodokushi*), ix–x, 2–3, 17–18, 75, 91–94, 100–103, 124–31, 135–37, 139–48, 156, 197n2, 197n4, 205n5; management of, 54–55; materiality of, 124–25, 129–30, 138–41, 144–48, 163, 176–77; and mattering, 25, 76, 108–9, 140, 147–48; and playfulness, 66–70; politics of, 36; precariousness of, 25–26, 40; preparing for, 18–19, 54–55, 84–86, 100–116, 119–20, 130–31; as productive,

death (continued)
11–12; relationality of, x, 3–4, 11, 20, 42–43, 53, 84–86, 170; and respect (*songen*), 112–13; ritualized, 31–32; scenes of, 144; smell of, 124, 147–48; sociality of, 4, 17, 20, 34–35, 150, 190; and spirituality, 154–55; and subjectivity, 89; and sustainability, 181–82; and temporality, 12–16; and unclaimed remains, 109–13, 149–50, 156–58; unnoticed by others (*kizuite moraenai shi*), 124–27; and vitalism, 112. *See also* burial; care; corpses; ending activity (*shūkatsu*)

death midwife, 84–85

Death of a Japanese Salesman: Ending Note (dir. Sunada), 113–14

Death Sweeper (manga), 131–32, 140–41

decluttering (*danshari*), 115, 131–32, 203n4. *See also* Kondō, Marie; Sasaki Fumio; waste removal

dementia, 103–5, 115–16

Descola, Philippe, 9, 204n13

design, 87–89, 181–82

Desjarlais, Robert, 26–27, 129–30

detachment, 26–27, 31, 115, 129–30, 139

dignity, 83–84, 93–94, 106, 112–13

disconnected (*muenbotoke*), 5–6, 33–34, 37–38, 40–41, 75, 93–94, 110–13, 116–17, 120, 125, 149–50, 156–58, 213n5. *See also under* belonging; death, dying; grief, grievability

dolls (*imonningyō*), 42–43, 202n23

Douglas, Mary, 26, 123

Dower, John W., 44–45

Durkheim, Émile, 40, 192

economy, economics: and insecurity, 9, 127–28, 157; of Japan, 7–8, 31, 48–52, 57–58, 75, 92–93, 157, 176, 182–83, 193–94; moral, 176; of vitality, 102. *See also* biopolitics; Japan; precarity, precariat

Edelman, Lee, 13

elderly. *See* aging

empathy, 137–38, 144, 146

employment, ix–x; irregular or flexible, 9, 50, 52–53; job-seeking practice (*shūkatsu*), 52–53, 206n2; and security, 193–96; solitary nonemployed persons (SNEP), 9–10; and status, 52–53, 208n5

emptiness, 8–9, 11

ENDEX (ending exhibit), 51–55, 58, 63–70, 142

ending activities (*shūkatsu*), ix–x, 52–55, 85–86, 100–103, 206n2; and capitalism, 108; and everyday, 113–14; and governance, 110–13; and individualism, 107–9; mass marketing of, 118–20, 191–92; as moral endeavor, 106–7, 112; ordering (*seiri*) while still alive (*seizen*), 115, 119–20, 129–31, 140–41, 175–76, 191–92; as self-care, 116–18; and special cleanup companies (*ihinseirigaisha*), 125. *See also* death, dying; individualism

Ending Center (nonprofit), 60, 83–87, 89–91, 96, 103, 174–75, 205n8, 206n1; "cherry blossom departures" (*sakurasō*), 84; One More Home, 83–87

ending notes, 19, 111, 113–16, 120, 191–92

enjoyment, 8–9, 86–87, 119, 130–31

Escobar, Arturo, 181–82

estrangement. *See* isolation; loneliness

ethics: of ending activity (*shūkatsu*), 107–8; fading of, 27; of promiscuous care, 13–14, 18–19; of self-management, 130–31; of sustainability, 88–89; of technological innovation, 189

ethopolitics. *See under* biopolitics

everyday, 9, 14–15, 19–20, 29–30; of ancestor worship, 6–7, 39, 57, 73–76; and design, 181–82; and ending activities (*shūkatsu*), 106–7, 113–14; objects of, 129–30; of present, 85–86; and sacred, 82; and technology, 181–82; and uncertainty, 49–50

family: abolition of, 18–19; alternatives to, 151–52, 188–89; and caring for dead, 1–3, 13–14, 18–19, 30–31, 117, 149; and gendered divisions, 183; and industrialization, 183; and inequality, 12–13; and mortuary system, 5–6; and municipality, 111; nuclear, 7, 49–50, 57, 133, 182; patrilineal system (*ie*), 6–7, 37–40, 56–57, 89; and sociality, 73, 91–92; and unclaimed remains, 109–10. *See also* patrilineal system

Fassin, Didier, 159

feminism, 13–14, 60; and care ethics, 18–19, 77, 88–89, 181–82; and forensics, 197n5; and interdependence, 76; and single people, 108–9; and utopian hope, 194–96. *See also* care

Fisch, Michael, 186–88, 204n1

Fischer, Berenice, 77, 88–89, 181–82

Ford, Henry, 182–83

forensic science, 17, 94, 138, 145–46, 197n5

Foucault, Michel, 27

Freud, Sigmund, 43

friendship, 86–87, 138–39; "grave friends" (*haka tomo*), 2, 84–88, 107, 174–75, 191–92

Fry, Tony, 88–89

Fujimi Shikiten (funeral hall), 58–59

funerals, funeral companies (*sōgisha, sōsaigyō*), 1–2, 56–59, 203n3; collective ceremonies, 2; commercialization of, 119; "direct ceremony" (*chokusō* or *jikisō*), 2, 58–59, 156; family (*kazokusō*), 58–59, 156; farewell ceremonies (*kokubetsu-shiki*), 153–56; farewell incense (*shōkō*), 153; funeral money (*kōden*), 153, 201n14; general (*ippansō*), 58–59. *See also* burials

future, futurity: catastrophic, 15–16; and disconnected (*muenbotoke*), 93–94; and ending business (*shūkatsu*), 101–3, 106–7; and hope, 194–96; and modernity, 113; and reproductive futurism, 13, 50–51; and preparation, 15–16, 106–7, 120; as uncertain, 14–15, 115, 175–76. *See also* time, temporality

Garcia, Angela, 106–7, 205n3

Genda Yūji, 9–10

gender: and care, 13–14, 117; collective graves for women, 90–91; and death work, 68; and ending activities (*shūkatsu*), 86–87; and *imonningyō* dolls, 42–43; and industrialization, 183; and nuclear family, 183; and patrilineal system, 37–38, 59–60, 83–84; and single women, 90–91

genealogical system (*kokka*), ix–x, 13–16, 37–38, 40, 56, 76–77, 130–31, 165, 205n7. *See also* patrilineal system

Géricault, Théodore, 77

Giddens, Anthony, 86

gifts, 43; for ancestors, 79–81; exchanges, 76; and funeral money (*kōden*), 153, 201n14

Gojira, 48–50

Gould, Hannah, 63–64, 176–77, 210n2

governance: of corporate patrilineage, 34–35; of death, 11–12, 36–37, 56; of parishioner membership at temples, 34–35; and security, 14–16; of unclaimed deceased, 157–58

grave, graveyards: abandoned (*muenka*), 164–65, 213n5; ancestral (*funbo*), ix–x, 5–7, 10–14, 19–20, 30–33, 37–40, 44–45, 54–60, 149, 163–65, 173–81, 185–90, 192–93, 201n13; and automated columbaria, 176–81, 187–90; as data, 187; care for, 74–75, 94–95, 185; closing (*hakajimai*), 57, 164–65; collective (*gōdōbo*), 27, 40–41, 90–95, 157–58; for disconnected (*muenbotoke*), 75, 156–58; double-grave system, 28–29; flexibilizing, 60–61; "grave friends" (*haka tomo*), 2, 107; municipal, 188–89; sacredness of, 6–7; legal meaning of, 57; and sociality, 88–89, 93–94; and spatial efficiency, 183–84; topography of, 39; visiting, 188. *See also* burials; death, dying; funerals, funeral companies

Grave Project, 93–94, 206n13

Grave-Free Promotion Society of Japan, 89

INDEX 235

grief, grievability, 140, 151–52, 156, 169–70; of aging, 138–39; and communal graves, 40–41; and cremation, 163–64; management of, 5; and mattering, 4, 77–78; and ordering one's feelings (*kimochi no seiri*), 129–30; performing, 48–49; and pulverizing ashes, 165; and state, 12–13; transformation of, 77. *See also* affect; death, dying

habitation, 88–89
Hallam, Elizabeth, 150–51
Hanshin Material Corporation, 162–63
Haraway, Donna, 62
Harootunian, Harry, 69–70
Heath-Kelly, Charlotte, 14–15
Hertz, Robert, 3–4, 28–29, 40
Hirata Atsutane, 36
Hirohito, Emperor, 48, 202n21
hoarding, 15–16, 100, 128–29, 139–40, 147. *See also* waste removal
home: and belongings, 138–39; homelessness, 174; sociomaterial complex of, 125; uncanniness of, 144–46
hope, xi–xii, 19–20, 93–94, 102–3, 194–96; hopelessness, 8–11. *See also* future, futurity
Hosono Ungai, 40–41, 188–89
hospice, 106
human, humanity, 3–4, 88–89, 137–38, 144, 147–48, 150, 181–82, 197n5; and animism, 8–9, 19–20, 108; and artificial, 67–70, 176–77, 189–90, 204n16; and care, 13–14, 200n10; categorizing, 159–60, 163–64, 169–70; and nonhuman, 19–20, 36–37, 41–42, 199n2, 202n19; and objects, 129–30, 204n15

identity, 30, 75, 112, 120, 154–55, 158–59; and body, 138; group, 91–92
imaginary, imagination, 14–16, 50, 70, 73, 100–101, 105–6, 125, 146
Imamura Shōhei, 31
imperial system, ix–x, 29, 37–38. *See also* genealogical system

individualism, 7, 18–19, 49–50, 54, 57, 96, 102, 107–9, 156–59, 182, 185
Inoshita Kiyoshi, 39–40
Inoue Haruyo, 59–60, 83–87, 96, 103
intimacy: and care work, 1, 7, 12, 16–17, 61–62, 74, 87–88, 189–90; with death, 30–31, 78, 86, 140–41, 149–54; of material, 168–69; necrointimacy, 78
Irizarry, Joshua, 154–55
isolation, 8–10, 93, 124–28, 147, 156. *See also* death; loneliness
Itami Jūzō, 57–58, 63

Jacobsen, Roman, 92
Jameson, Fredric, 194–96
Japan Environment Management Association (JEMA), 162–63, 170
Japan External Trade Organization (JETRO), 54
Japan: abandoned residences, 208n10; and ancestors, 6–7, 12, 29; and animism, 19–20; burial rituals, 27–28; and changing attitudes toward death, ix–x, 5–6, 16–17, 151–52, 184, 192–93; and death workers, 36–37, 199n2; democratic constitution of 1946, 7; demographic and social shifts, 139–40, 183, 192, 205n5; economic crash of 1991 and post-bubble economy, 8–10, 50, 52–53, 156–57, 183, 193–94, 206n15; and economic (post) industrialization, 7, 48–50; and foreign immigration, 50, 53; and futurity, 9–13, 50; imperial system, 6–7, 29–30, 41–43, 76–77; and inequality, 12–13; and "Japaneseness," 19, 29–31, 73, 100–101; and "just-in-time" automation, 176, 182–83; laws related to death and burial, 34–35, 109–10, 201n18, 207n8; "lost generation," 50, 52–53; as "mass death society" (*kasha shakai*), 53, 112, 160–61; Meiji period, 36–41; modernization of, 39, 47–48; native culture of, 28–30, 35–36, 199n3; and religious identity, 29–30, 74; and single-person households, 109–10; and social bonds, 11, 31, 75–77, 158;

236 INDEX

Taishō period, 38–39; and technological innovation, 182–83; Tokugawa Era, 34–36; and World War II, 6–7, 48–49, 202n22, 202n25, 203n27. *See also* Buddhism; death, dying; rituals

JEMA. *See* Japan Environment Management Association

JETRO. *See* Japan External Trade Organization

Kai Koji, 164–69
Kaibara Ekken, 35–36
Kakudasan Myōkōji temple, 61, 83–84, 95–98, 112, 204n10, 206n14
Kantō earthquake (1923), 39, 201nn15–16
Katsuno Shubin, 78–82
Kawano, Satsuki, 89
Keepers (キーパーズ), 128–37
Kimura Eiji, 129, 138–40
Kitami Takayuki, 109–13, 156–59
Kobayashi Tsuyoshi, 109, 162–63
Koff, Clea, 17
Kojiki, 28, 36
Kojima Miyu, 17–18, 142–48
Kondō, Marie, 115, 139, 203n4
Kone Hideto, 138–39
Kuma Kengo, 178–80
Kumazawa Banzan, 35–36
kuyō. See rituals, of separation

Laheji, Christian, 193–94
Lakoff, Andrew, 101, 105–6
Laqueuer, Thomas, 3, 25, 76–77
Lastel ("last hotel," funeral hall), 58–59, 118–20
leave-taking (*kokubetsushiki*), 2, 153
Lee, Frances Glessner, and Nutshell Studies of Unexplained Death, 144–46
life, 9, 66–68; aesthetics of, 115; "good life," 49–50; and managing death, 100–101, 106–7; and modernity, 199n8; and optimization, 175–76; sustenance of, 76; and well-being, 107–8. *See also* death, dying
Livingston, Julie, 137–38

loneliness, 8–9, 86, 93, 125. *See also* isolation; *under* death, dying
loss, 17, 26, 31, 63, 138–39, 193–94. *See also* grief, grievability

M'charek, Amade, 94, 138, 197n5
MacArthur, Douglas, 48
March 11, 2011, 45, 158
market, marketplace: of endingness (*shūkatsu*), 11–14, 18–19, 27, 51–53, 59, 64–65, 68, 100–101, 118, 130–31, 190, 206n2; job, 50, 52–53, 86–87, 206n2; for "leftover ash," 162–63; for ritual, 196
Marr, Matthew, 93, 206n6, 206n13
marriage, ix–x, 6–9, 16, 29, 39–40, 49–55, 117, 192
Marxism, 188–89, 193–94
materiality: of belongings, 100, 115–17, 128–32, 138–40, 146–47, 151–52; in Buddhist rites, 199n7; and commodity relics, 152; of corpses, 151–55; of cremains (*shūkotsu*), 162–64; of death, 17–18, 26–29, 124–31, 135–48; and disorder, 127–28, 135–37; of human remains, 159–60, 163–65, 168–70; and intimacy, 168–69; and memory, 138–39; of social bonds, 125, 149–50, 154–55; and touch, 17; vital materialism, 138
Meiji Civil Code of 1898, 37–38, 40
Meiji Constitution, 6–7, 41–42, 197n1, 199n2
memorial, memorialization, 11–14, 32–35, 42, 45, 56–57, 64–70, 95, 110–11, 129–30, 146–47; just-in-time, 186; on-hand (*temoto kuyō*), 169; reverse-style (*gyakushū kuyō*), 199n6
memory, 26, 76, 138–40
Mikuni Hiroaki, 55, 103–6, 108–9, 206n1
miniatures/dioramas, 142–48. *See also* Kojima Miyu
minimalism, 58, 115
morality: and anticipation, 175–76; of care for dead, 140–41; of ending activities (*shūkatsu*), 106–7, 112
Mori Kenji, 12, 33, 156

INDEX 237

mortuary system: alternative forms of (necro-animism), 17, 19–20, 175–78, 183–84, 189–90, 196; and care, 26–27, 189–90; family-based, ix–x, 5, 35, 51, 54, 57–59, 64–65, 75, 94–95, 151–52, 183–84; planning (self-death making), 10–11, 14–19, 54–55, 87–90, 110–15, 118, 120, 140–41, 158–59; practices, 3–4, 35, 57–59, 63, 75, 129–30, 159–60; shifts in, 57–60, 64–65, 151–52; and sociality, 11–13, 94–95, 156, 170. *See also* burials; ending activities (*shūkatsu*); funerals; funeral companies

Motoori Norinaga, 36

mourning, 1–2, 17–18, 32, 86, 129, 149, 153–55, 197n5, 201n14, 210n2, 211n6. *See also* grief, grievability

Moyai no Hi (collective grave for women who never married), 90–91

Moyai no Kai (nonprofit), 61

Muehlebach, Andrea, 106–7

Murphy, Michelle, 102, 113, 120, 175–76

mutuality, 30–31

Nagai Yoko, 184

Nakazawa Shinichi, 8–9

name, posthumous (*kaimyō*), 32, 75–77, 95–96, 154–55, 211n5

nation-state: and ancestor worship, 39; and belonging, 6–7, 158; and biopolitics, 102; and death, 14–16, 36–37; desacralization of, 29–30; and disposal of bodies, 40–41; and "good death," 100–101; and nativism, 35–36; and patrilineal system (*ie*), 37–38, 40; and politics of life itself, 107–8; and reproductive futurism, 13–16, 50; and ritual gatherings of family, 73; and security policies, 14–15. *See also* biopolitics; Japan

necro-animism. *See under* animism

necro-utopia. *See under* utopia

necrointimacy. *See under* intimacy

necronominalism. *See* name, posthumous

necropolitics, 100–101. *See also* biopolitics

Nenge-san Ryōshinji, 78–79

neoliberalism, 19, 156–57, 193–94

New Year (Oshōgatsu), 74

Newell, Sasha, 128–29

Nietzsche, Friedrich, 194–96

Nihongi (History of Japan), 200n8

Nishimura, Keiko 69–70

Norbert, Elias, 86

Norimatsu Nobuyuki, 66–68, 204n16

Nozawa Shin, 95

Nozawa Shunsuke, 91–92, 205n5

objects: belongings, 100, 115–17, 128–32, 138–40, 146–47, 151–52; commodity relics, 152; and death, 19–20, 31–32, 85–86; and *kuyō* (ritual of separation), 66–68, 119, 129–34, 169, 204n15; ritual, 38–39, 42; "unfetish" of, 128–29, 140; and techno-animism, 9

Obon, 28–29, 33–35, 51, 56, 61, 73–76, 78–82, 96–98, 181, 187, 206n14. *See also* ancestors; care

Odom, William, 176–77

Ogawa Eiji, 60–61, 83–84, 95–96, 112

Ogawa Ryōkei, 95–98

Ōhasama, 89–91

Ōi Bungen, 66–68, 204n16

Okuribito (*Departures*), 61–63, 65–66

Okuribito Academy (training school for morticians), 65–66, 68

Onna no Hi no Kai (collective grave association for single women), 90–91

Onna no Ishibumi (burial ground), 61

Ooms, Herman, 30–31

Osōshiki (*The Funeral*, dir. Itami), 57–58, 63

otherwise, 3, 77, 196

Parry, Richard Lloyd, 45

pastoralism, 107–8

patrilineal system (*ie*), ix–x, 6–7, 12–13, 34–40, 49–50, 56–60, 185–86, 196, 201n13. *See also* family

Pepper (robot), 68–70

performance, performativity, 7, 26, 87–88, 91–92, 125, 137–38, 197n5, 199n6, 205n5

Perry, Matthew, 47–48

phaticity, 91–92, 205n5
poiesis, 26–27, 129–30, 134–35
Pokémon, 7–12
politics: of abduction, 102; of care, 181–82; of dead, x, 36; of life itself, 107–8, 175–76; of technological innovation, 189. *See also* biopolitics
population: aging, ix–x, 53, 109, 183–84, 192; and changing mortuary practices, 5–6, 11–14, 100–102, 109, 151–52, 183–84, 192; declining, 50, 53, 175–76, 192
Povinelli, Elizabeth, 94–95
precarity, precariat, 9–10, 150, 193–94; and aging, 207n7; and care for dead, 19–20, 26–27, 186, 189–90, 192; and disconnected, 12–13, 127–28; of familial model, 59–60, 94; and gender, 59–60; and national crises, 50; and sociality, 99; and unclaimed remains, 109–13; and un-/underemployment, 52–53
preparedness, 100–107, 110–11, 115–16, 119–20; and care, 117–18; and daily life, 113–14; and duty, 112; and imaginative enactments, 105–6; and individualism, 107–8; sociality of, 130–31
primogeniture. *See* family; patrilineal system
productivity, 7, 11–12, 49–50, 57–58, 100–102, 130–31
prosthesis, prosthetics, 19–20, 68–69, 177–78, 190, 212n1
public health, 101, 105–8, 123
Puig de la Bellacasa, María, 181–82

Reader, Ian, 56
recognition, 76–78, 93–94, 112–13, 137, 140, 147–48, 189–90
Recruit (company), 100
Redfield, Peter, 137
relationality: alternative forms of, 84, 89–94; and body, 150, 170; and caring for dead, 17, 63, 76–78, 82; of corpse, 150–51; and death, x, 3–4, 42–43, 53, 170; degeneration of, 11–12, 158; flexible, 89; and graves, 88–89, 93–94; and lack, 5–6; and pastoralism, 107–8; of patrilineal familial system, 6–7, 59–60, 83–84; of preparedness, 113–14; and self, 86; of smell, 124; and temporality, 95–96. *See also* social, sociality
remains: bones, 164–68; disposal of, 163–64; and human, 159; legal treatment of, 159–60, 165; materiality of, 159–65, 168–70; relationality of, 197n5; sociality of, 159–60, 165, 169–70; temporality of, 197n5; touching, 168–69. *See also* ashes; cremation
remediation, 186–88
Reno, Josh, 125, 202n19
reproduction, social, 6–7, 50–51, 186
respect (*songen*), 87–88, 112–13
rights, of dead, 83–84
ritual, 26–28; and ancestors, 35–36; and burials, 27–29, 38–39, 61, 89–90, 149–50, 156, 159–60, 205n2; commodification of, 38–39, 196; and death, 31–32, 96–98, 129–30, 170, 210nn2–5; history of, 27–29; and kinship, 30–31, 73; materiality of, 199n7; memorial ritual (*kuyō*), 11, 13–14, 32–34, 57, 61, 64, 66–68, 78–79, 110–11, 119, 129–34, 151–52, 157–58, 162–63, 169, 181, 193, 199n6, 204n15, 206n14, 211n9; "picking of the bones" (*kotsuage*), 1, 149, 153–55; of purification, 29; and repetition, 74; sociality of, 64–65, 154–55, 192; work of, 154. *See also* burials; funerals, funeral companies
Roach, Joseph, 26
robots, 68–70, 204n16. *See also* technology
Rose, Nikolas, 107–8, 175–76
Rubeau, Jean, 93–94
Ruin, Hans, 170
Rurikō-in (Buddhist burial ground), 186–88

sacred, 6–7, 29–31, 39–40, 43, 74, 82, 155, 185–87, 190, 200n9. *See also* spirit, spirituality; Sanya (Tokyo), 92–93
Sanyūkai Ohaka Project (nonprofit), 93–94, 110–11

smell, scent: and body, 124; and care, 148; of lonely death, 124–27, 135–41, 147–48; and modernization, 123; relationality of, 148. *See also* senses and sensation

Schattschneider, Ellen, 42–43

self: and belongings, 129–31; and body, 150; and care, 77, 84–86, 116–17; and performativity, 7; and presentism, 115; and responsibility, 108–9; self-death making, 18–19, 120, 192, 199n6; and smell, 124; and well-being, 107–8

Sennichidani Jōen (automated columbarium), 178–81, 185–86

Senses and sensation, 124, 148. *See also* affect; smell, scent; touch, tactility

Serai Remains (bone business), 164–69

Shimada Hiroshi, 12–13, 76–77

Shin Gojira (New Godzilla), 50–51

Shinmon Aoki, 62

Shintō, 19–20, 28, 31–32; and cremation, 37; and nation-state, 29–30, 36–37; and purification, 29, 32, 36–37

Siegel, James, 124

singleness (*miyori ga nai; ohitori-san*), 40, 55, 60–61, 90–91, 99, 104, 108–11, 127–28. *See also* aging

Single Smile Senior Life (SSS), 91

Smith, Robert, 35–36

social, sociality: anticipatory, 107, 115, 130–31; of body, 150–52; and burial, 89–94; of caregiving, 77; collective, 89; and death, 4–5, 16–17, 34–35, 38–39, 53, 75–76, 140–41, 150–52; dissolution of, 40, 75–76; of ending notes, 113–14; of human remains, 159–60, 165, 169–70; imaginary, 14–15; and imperial system, 41–42; and materiality, 125, 149–50; of national belonging, 158; ontological grounding of, 76, 88–89, 181–82; and patrilineal system, 13, 37–38, 57, 91–92, 158–59; and phaticity, 91–92; and precarity, 99, 109–13; and prosthesis, 43, 177–78; reproduction of, 6–7, 50–51, 186; and ritual, 64–65, 154–55, 192; and sacred, 74, 186; and singleness, 99, 108–11; of smell, 123–24; and solitude, 68–69, 140–41, 158–59; of technological innovation, 189–90; of waste removal, 125, 137–38

SoftBank, 68–69

Solomon, Erez Golani, 186–88

Son Masayoshi, 68–69

Sōsō No Jiyū No Susume Kai (Association Advocating Freedom of Send-offs), 61

space: of anticipation, 116–17; and caring for dead, 184–85; and disconnection, 174; and modern ossuaries, 183–84; scarcity of, 176; and structure, 69–70

spirit, spirituality, 1–6, 11, 19–20, 28–39, 45, 62, 73–74, 78–79, 89–90, 154–55, 204n13, 205n7

Stevenson, Lisa, 77

Stewart, Susan, 144

Stone, Sandy, 177–78

Strathern, Marilyn, 116–17, 175–76

substitution, 42–45, 87–88

succession principle (*keishō seido*), 39–40, 56–60, 75, 83–84, 89, 149, 184–85, 206n14. *See also* family; patrilineal system

suicide, 43, 75, 83, 144–46, 204n1

Sunada Mami, 113–14

survival, 69–70

sustainability, 88–89, 181–82, 189, 194–96

Suzuki Shunichi, 90–91

Tajiri Satoshi, 8–9

Takeya Kiyoshi, 186–87

Tama Cemetery, 39

Tamagotchi, 7–12, 43, 189

Taylorism, 182–83

technology, 181: and commercialization of death, 38–39, 64–65, 184–85; and cremation, 37; and death care, 176–77, 189–90; and everyday, 181–82; and innovation, 182–83, 187; and prosthesis, 177–78; of substitutes, 42

time, temporality: and abduction, 102–3, 120; anticipatory, 14–16, 95–96, 100–103, 113–15, 120, 158–59, 175–76;

and becoming familiar but new, 177–78; of burial rites, 13–15; of caring for dead, 184–85; compression of, 38–39; and continuity, 34–35, 56, 149; and durability, 183–84; and ending market, 53; and eternity, 6–7, 13–14, 37, 56, 95–96, 184–85, 187–89; and everyday, 69–70, 82, 175–76; and future, 9–13, 94–95, 100–103, 113, 120, 175–76; and human remains, 197n5; and irregularity, 9; management of, 175–76; movement between, 134–35; of postmodernity, 14–15; and present, 86–87, 175–76; and relationality, 89–90, 95–96; and repetition, 147–48; and uncertainty, 175–76; and utopia, 194–96. *See also* future, futurity

To-Do Company (*ihinseirigaisha*), 142

Tokyo People, Action Volunteer Center, 117

Tokyo Professional Union of Morticians and Goods (Tōkyō Sōsaigu Eigyōkumiai), 38–39

Total Life Support, 55, 99, 103–8, 206n1

touch, tactility, 17, 86, 154, 168–70, 204n13. *See also* senses, sensation

Toyota, Toyotism Toyota Production System (TPS), 182–83, 186

transhuman. *See* human, humanity

Traphagan, John, 74, 78

Tronto, Joan, 77, 88–89, 181–82

Ueno, Chizuko, 60, 83–84, 108–9

ungrievable. *See* death; grief, grievability

urban, urbanization, ix–x, 49–50, 56–57, 182; deathscapes, 39, 163–65, 169–70, 176–77, 183–90, 201n16, 203n3; and suicide, 204n1

Uriu Daisuke, 64–65, 176–77

utopia, 194–96; necro-utopia, 188–89

value, 13–14, 108, 128–29, 134–35, 208n10

Verdery, Katherine, 151

vitalism, 74 108, 112, 138

Wang, Min'an, 128–29

waste, waste removal, 125, 202n19; disposal (*shori*), 128–29, 163; and human, 163–64; and remainder from cremation (*zanhai*), 162–63; special cleanup companies (*ihinseirigaisha*), 126–44, 147–48, 208n1. *See also* decluttering; objects

Weeks, Kathi, 18–19, 194–96

witnessing, 2–4, 137, 148–49

work: affective, 38–39; of anticipation, 113; of care, 120, 137–38; death work, 26–27, 61–63, 68–70, 199n2; embodied, 137–38; by living, 26–27; performativity of, 87–88; of ritual, 154; and stigmatization, 202n19; of waste removal (*ihinseirigaisha*), 129–30, 132–38

Yamaguchi Masao, 43

Yamato Saijō (public crematorium), 160–62

Yanagita Kunio, 28–29

Yokosuka City, 108–11, 207n8, 210n9; "ending registration card" (*shūkatsu tōrokusho*), 111–12, 115, 158–59; Ending Support Plan, 110–11, 115; rates of citizens who die at home, 112; and unclaimed remains, 149–50, 156–59

Yoshida Taichi, 126, 128–37

Yoshimi Shunya, 52